Early Praise for *Hands-on Rust*

One of the first books about Rust gamedev! Great at filling the gap between learning the language itself and actually writing complex applications in it. Definitely recommended for anyone interested in either game development or Rust.

➤ **Andrey Lesnikov**
   Editor, Rust GameDev Newsletter

I absolutely loved this book! *Hands-on Rust* is accessible, easy to read and Herbert does a great job distilling a wealth of knowledge and experience for making games in Rust.

➤ **Olivia Ifrim**
   Senior Software Engineer

Hands-on Rust marks a new level of maturity for the Rust game development ecosystem. And while the primary selling point of the book is to learn Rust and game programming in one go, there's also an immensely important lesson of creative constraints to be learned from the plain-text ASCII tooling used throughout; bracket-lib.

When the only visuals you have to play with are letters and symbols, you've no choice but to delve deep into the mechanics of your game. Herbert's bracket-lib teaches a form of minimalist game design that is perfect for rapid prototyping or complex world-building, without the distraction of HD aesthetics.

➤ **Erlend Sogge Heggen**
   Lead Member, Rust GameDev Working Group

Hands-on Rust

Effective Learning through 2D Game Development and Play

Herbert Wolverson

The Pragmatic Bookshelf

Raleigh, North Carolina

Many of the designations used by manufacturers and sellers to distinguish their products are claimed as trademarks. Where those designations appear in this book, and The Pragmatic Programmers, LLC was aware of a trademark claim, the designations have been printed in initial capital letters or in all capitals. The Pragmatic Starter Kit, The Pragmatic Programmer, Pragmatic Programming, Pragmatic Bookshelf, PragProg and the linking *g* device are trademarks of The Pragmatic Programmers, LLC.

Every precaution was taken in the preparation of this book. However, the publisher assumes no responsibility for errors or omissions, or for damages that may result from the use of information (including program listings) contained herein.

For our complete catalog of hands-on, practical, and Pragmatic content for software developers, please visit *https://pragprog.com*.

The team that produced this book includes:

CEO: Dave Rankin
COO: Janet Furlow
Managing Editor: Tammy Coron
Development Editor: Tammy Coron
Copy Editor: Vanya Wong
Indexing: Potomac Indexing, LLC
Layout: Gilson Graphics
Founders: Andy Hunt and Dave Thomas

For sales, volume licensing, and support, please contact *support@pragprog.com*.

For international rights, please contact *rights@pragprog.com*.

ISBN-13: 978-1-68050-816-1
Book version: P1.0—July 2021

Contents

Part II — Building a Dungeon Crawler

Acknowledgments

This book would not have been possible without the patience, support, and love of my wife, -Mel Wolverson.

A huge "thank you" is owed to my parents—Robert Wolverson and Dawn McLaren. They introduced me to computers at a tender age, taught me basic programming, and put up with years of "look what I made." They instilled in me a life-long love of learning and teaching.

I would also like to thank Erlend Sogge Heggen of the *Amethyst Foundation* for introducing me to *The Pragmatic Bookshelf*. The wonderful community in *r/roguelikedev* on Reddit persuaded me to return to game development many years ago, and continued to provide support throughout the development of this book. Special thanks are due to Josh Ge—author of *Cogmind*, and Brian Bucklew—of *Caves of Qud* fame—for encouraging the whole Roguelike development community. Thanks to Steve Cotterill for writing tips and being a great sounding board while I structured the book. Finally, Walter Pearce deserves special thanks for all of the Rust help they provided.

Kent Froeschle and Stephen Turner at *iZones* deserve acknowledgment for their continual encouragement and work schedule flexibility, patiently dealing with both a global pandemic and my writing schedule.

This book would not be what it is without the patient and thorough help of the tech reviewers: Bas Zalmstra, Josh Snaith, Vladyslav Batyrenko, Thomas Gillen, Remco Kuijper, Forest Anderson, Olivia Ifrim, and Jurgis Balciunas.

Finally, thank you to Tammy Coron—the editor—for her help and enthusiasm on this project, keeping me focused and shepherding me through the publishing process.

Preface

Rust is an exciting programming language that combines the power of C with memory safety, fearless concurrency, and productivity boosters. It offers close-to-the-metal power and performance, while also providing a safety net to avoid many of the more common bugs found in low-level languages. Because of its features, Rust is a very competitive systems and game development language and is currently enjoying rapid growth amongst industry giants, including Amazon, Google, Microsoft, and many game development houses.

A great way to learn and study Rust is through game development. Don't be discouraged by the scale and polish of AAA titles. Small indie games are fun, and hobby game development can kickstart careers in professional game dev or unrelated development fields. Every successful game developer started small, gradually gaining skills until they could work on the game of their dreams.

In this book, you'll learn Rust by walking through game development examples. You'll gain knowledge and confidence in both Rust and game development as you work through a series of practical examples, building increasingly complicated games. The text emphasizes a pragmatic "learn by doing" approach. Theory sections are short and are followed by concrete examples for you to try. By the end of the book, you'll have mastered the basics of the Rust language and be well-equipped for tackling more complicated game development problems.

Who Should Read This Book

This book assumes that you have some prior programming experience. It gently introduces you to Rust and game development concepts. If you've written anything more complicated than a "Hello, World" program in another programming language, you should feel comfortable working through this book's examples.

This book is ideal for anyone who wants to give Rust a try—it does not assume that you know the Rust language. It's also well suited for Rust developers who want to try their hand at game development. Alongside an introductory programming tutorial, it could also be helpful to new developers.

What's in This Book

This book walks you through a typical game developer's journey while also teaching Rust's key concepts. Each chapter adds to your knowledge and skillset as you build playable games:

Chapter 1, Rust and Your Development Environment, on page 3, begins your Rust journey. In this chapter, you'll install the language toolchain and work with Rust source code in a text editor. You'll step through creating a "Hello, World" program and learn to use Rust tools like *Cargo* and *Clippy* to improve your productivity.

Chapter 2, First Steps with Rust, on page 19, walks you through the basics of Rust development. You'll hone your skills by building a treehouse guest manager. The chapter covers text input and output, grouping data in structures, and core Rust concepts such as iterators, pattern matching, if statements, functions, and loops.

The first two chapters teach you everything you need to know to make simple games. Chapter 3, Build Your First Game with Rust, on page 45, puts this knowledge to use as you create your first game—*Flappy Dragon*.

Chapter 4, Design a Dungeon Crawler, on page 71, helps you plan your game design. You'll learn to make a game design document, and you'll use it to transform an idea into a playable game. You'll design a roguelike dungeon crawler game and whittle your ideas down to a *Minimum Viable Product (MVP)*.

In Chapter 5, Build a Dungeon Crawler, on page 75, you'll begin building the dungeon crawler you designed. You'll learn about random numbers, map structure, and handling an interactive player. You'll also add the beginnings of monsters to your map, and you'll discover how to make tile-based graphics.

Games become increasingly complex as they grow. In Chapter 6, Compose Dungeon Denizens, on page 103, you'll use *Entity Component Systems (ECS)* to tame complexity, reuse code, and manage interactions between game entities. You'll implement the player and monsters with the ECS, reusing systems to cut down on the code that you have to write. You'll finish the chapter with a multi-threaded, concurrent game.

In Chapter 7, Take Turns with the Monsters, on page 127, you'll add a turn-based structure to your game where the player moves, and then the monsters move. You'll learn how to structure games to implement game rules and schedule different ECS systems based upon the game phase. You'll also learn to make your monsters wander randomly.

Chapter 8, Health and Melee Combat, on page 141, gives game entities hit points. You'll also make a Heads-Up Display to show the player's current status. You'll learn to make monsters search for the player, and you'll implement a combat system to slay—and be slain by—your player's enemies.

In Chapter 9, Victory and Defeat, on page 161, you'll add a game over screen, indicating that the player has lost the game. You'll also add a winning condition to the game and a second screen to congratulate the player on their victory.

Before Chapter 10, Fields of View, on page 185, your character is omniscient—they can see the entire map. This chapter introduces vision and a way to increase the player's knowledge of the map as they explore more of it. Using ECS systems, you'll give the same restriction to monsters—if they don't know where you are, they can't chase you.

Chapter 11, More Interesting Dungeons, on page 203, introduces new map generation techniques. This chapter also teaches you the more advanced Rust topic of *traits*, and how they can provide interchangeable functionality with a common code interface—particularly useful when working in teams.

Chapter 12, Map Themes, on page 231, adds new ways to render your maps, building upon the trait knowledge from the previous chapter. You can turn your dungeon into a forest or any other setting by changing the map's tile-set.

Chapter 13, Inventory and Power-Ups, on page 241, adds items, backpack management, and power-ups to your game.

Chapter 14, Deeper Dungeons, on page 257, replaces your single-level dungeon with a sprawling, deep dungeon. It walks you through using tables to provide increasing difficulty as the player progresses.

Chapter 15, Combat Systems and Loot, on page 269, adds "loot tables" and better items as you progress through the dungeon. You'll find more interesting swords and adjust combat to reflect their powers. You'll also balance increasing difficulty with better loot, and learn about the risk/reward curve.

Finally, in Chapter 16, Final Steps and Finishing Touches, on page 287, you'll learn to package your game for distribution. You'll also find suggestions for making the game your own, and taking your next steps in game development.

What's Not in This Book

This book emphasizes learning theory by following practical examples and explaining the theory behind the technique you learned. This book isn't an in-depth guide to every facet of the Rust language; instead, this book guides you to sources for this information when it introduces a concept.

Likely, this book doesn't describe the game idea you've always wanted to make. That's OK. This book teaches *concepts* that are useful whether you want to make the next great online board game or a shooter. These concepts are readily transferable to other engines, including *Unity*, *Godot*, *Unreal*, and *Amethyst*. By the end of the book, you'll be much better equipped to start work on the game you've always wanted to make.

How to Read This Book

If you're new to Rust development, you'll want to work through the book and associated examples in order. If you're experienced with Rust, you may want to skim over the introductory sections and dive straight into game development. If you're already a skilled game developer, you can still learn a lot about Rust and data-oriented design from this book.

Tutorials are as much about the journey as they are the destination. Working through tutorials should give you ideas for what *you* want to make next. Start keeping notes about what you'd like to create and how the game development concepts in this book can help you. When you finish the book, you'll be ready to start making your own games.

Conventions Used in This Book

The code accompanying this book is provided as a Rust *Workspace*. This combines several projects into one. The code is divided into directories as follows:

```
root
   /chapter_name
      /example_name
         /src --- the source code for this example
         /resources --- files that accompany this example
         Cargo.toml --- a file telling Rust's Cargo system how to build/run
            the example.
```

```
/src --- a simple program source reminding you that you probably meant to
         navigate to an example and run that---not the workspace.
Cargo.toml --- a file telling Rust's Cargo system that the other
         projects are part of the workspace.
```

You can run code examples by navigating to the chapter_name/example_name directory and typing cargo run.

As you progress through chapters, the example code is referenced with the location in the book's source code. The linked code sometimes refers to a different project within the chapter's code directory. It's designed to provide you with working examples for each stage of incremental development and to help you follow along. For example, you might see file snippets referencing code/FirstStepsWithRust/hello_yourname. Later in the same chapter, you might see code in code/FirstStepsWithRust/treehouse_guestlist_trim/.

Online Resources

Here are some online resources that can help you:

- *Rust by Example* provides a good, example-driven introduction to the Rust Language.[1]

- *The Rust Programming Language [KN19]* supplies in-depth concepts and tutorials to learn the finer details of Rust. It is also available online.[2]

- *The Rust Standard Library* documentation provides detailed descriptions of everything found in Rust's std library. It is a great reference when you can't remember how something works.[3]

- Reddit hosts several useful communities. /r/rust and /r/rust_gamedev are excellent resources. /r/roguelikedev is very helpful for games similar to the dungeon crawler in this book. These subreddits also include links to Discord forums full of people eager to help you.

Wrap-Up

Whether you're focused on learning Rust or want to dabble in game development, this book can help. It's exciting to finish a new game—or section of a game, run it, and enjoy the rush of seeing your creation in action. Let's start by setting up your Rust development environment and jumping straight into your first Rust code.

---

1. https://doc.rust-lang.org/rust-by-example/
2. https://doc.rust-lang.org/book/
3. https://doc.rust-lang.org/std/index.html

Herbert says:
My Game Development Journey

I was very lucky growing up. My father was teaching computing skills and introduced me to many of the computers of the day. One fateful day he brought home a BBC Micro, Model B. It featured 32k of RAM, color graphics, and programs that loaded from audio cassettes—it felt like an incredible machine. My parents provided an ever-expanding library of games to play, from puzzle games like *Repton* to clones of arcade machine games. It didn't take long for me to want to make my own games, and my father patiently walked me through learning *BASIC*. My early games were objectively terrible —and that didn't matter at all. I'd made something and discovered the thrill of showing it to my friends.

My early BASIC games set me on a fun path. I learned *Pascal* and later *C* and *C++*. I learned to make games for Windows and later Linux. I collaborated on a few group projects, and eventually found work writing business and networking software—much of which benefits from my experience creating games. When I first tried Rust, it felt like the perfect fit—and I haven't looked back.

This book teaches Rust and game development. More than anything, I hope that it inspires you to go forth and make something fun.

Part I

Getting Started with Rust

In this part of the book, you'll learn the basics of Rust and you'll build your first game, Flappy Dragon.

CHAPTER 1

Rust and Your Development Environment

In this chapter, you'll download and install Rust and the essential tools that go with it. You'll get comfortable with your development environment, using it to create and run your first Rust program.

You'll also learn about Cargo, Rust's Swiss Army knife build tool. Cargo incorporates rustfmt to help you format your code and Clippy to help avoid common code issues. Cargo can also help you find and install dependencies and keep your programs up-to-date.

As you work through this chapter, you'll gain familiarity with Rust and the tools you can use to improve your Rust development experience. By the end of the chapter, you will be ready to forge ahead into the world of Rust development.

Installing Rust

Rust requires that you install a *toolchain* on your computer. The toolchain includes the Rust compiler and various tools to make working with the language easier. The easiest way to install the toolchain is to visit the RustUp website.[1] *RustUp* detects the operating system you're running and displays instructions for your platform. Launch a web browser and open *rustup.rs*. You'll be greeted with a page similar to the image shown on page 4.

The next step varies by operating system. The *RustUp* site will direct you with step-by-step instructions.

---

1. https://rustup.rs/

RustUp on Microsoft Windows   **RustUp on Linux, OS X and UNIX-based Systems**

Opening a Command Prompt/Terminal

 On Windows, press ⊞ + R, type cmd in the Run box and press ENTER.
On Mac OS, search for Terminal in Finder and run it.

Starting the Install on Microsoft Windows

If you're a Microsoft Windows user, download and run the linked rustup-init.exe file.[2] RustUp might ask you to install the C++ build tools before proceeding. Microsoft Windows doesn't ship with development tools and the Windows platform tools aren't open source—so RustUp cannot legally give them to you. If you see this message:

1. Go to the Visual Studio download page.[3]

2. In the *Tools for Visual Studio 2019* section, download *Build Tools for Visual Studio 2019* and run the installer.

3. Follow onscreen instructions, and install the C++ build tools.

Starting the Install on Other Operating Systems

If you're using a UNIX-derived operating system such as Mac OS X or Linux, RustUp presents you with a command line and a copy button. Copy the command to your clipboard, open your terminal program, and paste the command into your terminal. Press ENTER and the install will begin.

Finishing the Installation

The RustUp installer is verbose, telling you *exactly* what it intends to do:

---

2.   https://win.rustup.rs/x86_64
3.   https://visualstudio.microsoft.com/downloads/

```
Welcome to Rust!

This will download and install the official compiler for the Rust
programming language, and its package manager, Cargo.

RustUp metadata and toolchains will be installed into the RustUp
home directory, located at:

    C:\Users\herbe\.rustup

This can be modified with the RUSTUP_HOME environment variable.

The Cargo home directory located at:

    C:\Users\herbe\.cargo

This can be modified with the CARGO_HOME environment variable.

The cargo, rustc, rustup and other commands will be added to
Cargo's bin directory, located at:

    C:\Users\herbe\.cargo\bin

This path will then be added to your PATH environment variable by
modifying the HKEY_CURRENT_USER/Environment/PATH registry key.

You can uninstall at any time with rustup self uninstall and
these changes will be reverted.
```

You are then presented with installation options:

```
Current installation options:

   default host triple: x86_64-pc-windows-msvc
     default toolchain: stable (default)
               profile: default
  modify PATH variable: yes

1) Proceed with installation (default)
2) Customize installation
3) Cancel installation
```

In most cases you can type 1 followed by ENTER. If you need to change the location into which Rust will be installed, select option 2 and follow the on-screen instructions. Note that you don't need administrative privileges to install Rust inside your account.

Once you proceed with the installation, RustUp will download several Rust packages and install them on your computer. RustUp adjusts your path, so it's a good idea to restart your terminal if you want to keep using it. Congratulations! Rust is installed and ready to use.

Now that you have Rust installed, let's take a moment to ensure that it works.

Verifying Your Rust Installation

When you finish the installation process, open a new terminal/command prompt. At the command prompt, type rustup -V and press ENTER:

```
⇒ rustup -V
❮ rustup 1.22.1 (b01adbbc3 2020-07-08)
```

The version numbers, git build hashes, and dates will vary. If you see the package installed, then the installation was successful.

Now that you know Rust works on your computer, let's prove it by running "Hello, World."

Testing Rust with "Hello, World"

Rust can build a program that prints "Hello, World!" with a simple command. You'll learn about the details of the program in Creating Your First Rust Program, on page 10. For now, whet your appetite and test that Rust works on your computer:

1. Create a new directory in which to place your Rust projects.
2. Open a command prompt or terminal.
3. Navigate to the Rust project directory you created with cd. For example, cd Rust.
4. Type cargo new testrust ENTER .
5. Change to the new testrust directory by typing cd testrust ENTER .
6. Run your new program by typing cargo run ENTER .

You'll see the following:

```
⇒ cargo run
❮    Compiling hello v0.1.0
     Finished dev [unoptimized + debuginfo] target(s) in 0.85s
       Running `C:\Pragmatic\Book\code\target\debug\hello.exe`
Hello, world!
```

Now that you have a working Rust toolchain, you need to know how to keep it updated.

Updating Rust

Rust releases minor updates every six weeks. Minor releases include bug-fixes and enhancements that won't break your code. Major Rust releases occur every two to three years and may make larger-scale changes to the Rust language. The Rust developers are very careful to maintain compatibility. If something is going to change substantially, you will start seeing "deprecation warnings" when you compile your code long before the feature is removed.

You can check if a new release is available at any time using rustup check:

```
C:\WINDOWS\system32\cmd.exe                                    —    □    ×
C:\Users\herbe>rustup check
stable-x86_64-pc-windows-msvc - Up to date : 1.47.0 (18bf6b4f0 2020-10-07)
nightly-x86_64-pc-windows-msvc - Update available : 1.49.0-nightly (91a79fb29 2020-10-07)
 -> 1.49.0-nightly (c71248b70 2020-10-11)

C:\Users\herbe>_
```

The displayed versions will vary and there may not be any updates available. If new versions are available, you can install them by typing rustup update in your command prompt or terminal.

Congratulations! Rust is installed and working, and you now know how to keep it up-to-date. The next step is to set up your development environment.

Installing and Configuring Your Development Environment

Much of your time writing Rust will be spent in a text editor. Text editors are like clothes. Most people need them, and nobody agrees on what type is best. Also, like clothes, you spend enough time in your text editor that you want to find one that's a good fit for you—and update it if it starts to fall apart. If you've written code before, you probably already have a favorite text editor or IDE.

It's a good idea to find an editor that supports Rust. At the least, syntax highlighting can make reading code a lot easier. Autocompletion and debugger integration can also be very helpful. There are *many* choices, including:

- On the low end, *Kate*, *Notepad++*, and *GEdit* are all quite usable with Rust. You don't get much language integration beyond syntax highlighting.

- *EMACS* and *Vim/Neovim* can both integrate with *Rust Analyser*, the *Rust Language Server*, and debugging tools.

- JetBrains makes *CLion* and *IntelliJ*, both of which integrate well with Rust.

- Microsoft's *Visual Studio Code*, used alongside the Rust Analyzer, CodeLLDB plugins, works very well for Rust.

- *Sublime Text* has Rust integration available.

Find an editor or IDE that works for you. Once you've selected a development environment, it's time to learn about how Rust arranges and manages your projects.

Managing Projects with Cargo

Rust ships with a tool named Cargo that assists with your day-to-day interactions with the language. Cargo handles everything from making projects to fetching packages of pre-made code. It can run your programs and call other tools to fix your code formatting and find common errors. Cargo is a Swiss Army knife—it has a tool for everything.

Cargo derives its name from Rust's structure. Rust programs are called *crates*. Collections of crates are managed by Cargo. This section walks you through creating your first Rust project and explores what Cargo can do for you.[4]

The first decision you need to make is, "Where do I put my Rust projects?"

Selecting a "Home" Directory for Your Code

You need to decide where you want to store your Rust projects. I use c:\users\herbert\rust when I'm running Windows—and /home/herbert/rust when running Linux. You may place your projects anywhere you like. I recommend a location that's easy to find, remember, and type.

If your project directory doesn't already exist, create it using your regular operating environment tools. Now that you have a home directory selected, let's add a project to it.

Starting a New Project with Cargo

Every new project begins as an empty crate. To create a new project:

1. Open a terminal/command prompt.
2. Navigate to the home directory you selected for your Rust code (using cd).
3. Don't create a new subdirectory for your project—Cargo will do that for you.
4. Type cargo new [project name].
5. Rust has created a subdirectory named [project name]. Enter it with cd [project name].

For example, to make a project named "Hello" in my preferred rust directory, I'll use:

```
cd c:\users\herbert\rust
cargo new hello
Created binary (application) `hello` package
```

---

4.   https://doc.rust-lang.org/cargo/

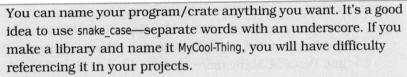

Use snake_case for Crate Names

You can name your program/crate anything you want. It's a good idea to use snake_case—separate words with an underscore. If you make a library and name it MyCool-Thing, you will have difficulty referencing it in your projects.

Choosing a good name is hard. Don't worry, you can change it later by editing Cargo.toml. A common quip is that "only two things are hard in Computer Science: naming, cache-invalidation, and off-by-one errors."

Launch your text editor/IDE and open the project directory you just created. Cargo has created the following directories and files:

- Cargo.toml: Project "meta-data", describing your project.
- A src directory (containing your source code).
- src/main.rs: A minimal source code file containing the code required to print "Hello, World!" to your terminal.

cargo new has created a "Hello, World" program—just like when you were testing Rust. Let's take a closer look at what's happening in the sample program.

Run Hello, World

Open a terminal and navigate to your project directory. Run your new program by typing cargo run:

```
⇒ cargo run
‹    Compiling hello v0.1.0 (C:\Pragmatic\Book\code\InstallingRust)
     Finished dev [unoptimized + debuginfo] target(s) in 1.18s
      Running `target\debug\hello.exe`
Hello, world!
```

If you look closely at your created project, you may notice a new .git directory has appeared. Cargo can help you integrate with git and other version control systems.

Version Control System Integration

Version Control Systems (VCS)

Version Control is a very useful category of software. It tracks your changes when you "commit" files to it. Every version of every file in your project is stored. You can then browse the history, look for what changes broke something, or revert to a previous version if you went down a blind alleyway.

Version Control Systems (VCS)

It is a great idea to learn to use a source control program. *git* is the most popular, developed by Linus Torvalds for use in Linux development. Other popular options include *Subversion, Mercurial,* and *Perforce.* Many more exist.

Git also integrates with GitHub. Much of the Rust ecosystem may be found on GitHub, and resumes commonly include a GitHub link to your profile.

Initializing your project with cargo new created a git repository for your program. Teaching the full range of git options is beyond the scope of this book (it could be—and is—the topic of entire tomes).

If you would like to *not* use git, your cargo new command expands slightly:

```
cargo new --vcs=none [project name]
```

Let's take a deep dive into "Hello, World" and learn some Rust basics.

Creating Your First Rust Program

Creating a program that greets the user with "Hello, World" is a very popular way to kick the tires of a new programming language. Comparing "Hello, World" programs in different languages is a great way to get a feel for the syntax of a language without diving too deeply into specifics. The *Hello World Collection* provides "Hello, World" in 578 different programming languages.[5]

When you start a project with cargo new, Rust creates "Hello, World" for you. It also creates the necessary metadata for Cargo to be able to run your program.

Cargo Metadata

Open the Cargo.toml file created in your "Hello" project:

```
InstallingRust/HelloWorld/Cargo.toml
[package]
name = "hello"
version = "0.1.0"
authors = ["Your Name"]
edition = "2018"

# See more keys and their definitions at
# https://doc.rust-lang.org/cargo/reference/manifest.html

[dependencies]
```

---

5.   http://helloworldcollection.de/

This file describes your program and how to build it. It uses the TOML format (Tom's Obvious, Minimal Language), and divides information about your crate into sections.[6] The [package] section describes your crate—if you publish your crate, this information will be used to describe it to potential users. It can be extended to include a lot of information about your project.[7]

Cargo has created everything you need to run "Hello, World"—so you don't have to edit the Cargo.toml file if you don't want to. The default entries are:

- name: the name of your program—in this case "Hello". It defaults to the project name you provided when you called cargo new. When you compile your program, the name will be used as the name of your program. On Windows, hello becomes hello.exe. On UNIX-derived systems, it will be named hello.

- version: the version of your project. Cargo will start you at 0.1.0. You only *need* to update the version number when you publish a new version of your crate. Otherwise, you may update the version number when you feel it helpful to indicate that significant progress has been made. You'll learn about Rust semantic versioning in Package Management with Cargo, on page 17. For now, stick to version 0.x.y. You can go above 10 on each number—0.10.0 is fine.

- authors is a list, denoted by the square braces. It may contain a comma-separated list of author names in quotation marks. If you have git setup, it automatically pulls your name and email address from there.

- edition: the *major edition* of Rust used by the project. It will always default to the current edition—2018—at the time of writing. Editions are allowed to make substantial changes to Rust syntax and may break older programs. Specifying the edition tells the Rust compiler which set of syntax rules it may use.[8]

With the metadata in place, it's time to look at the main program source code.

Hello, World

Open the src/main.rs file from your "Hello" project. Cargo has written just enough source code to display "Hello, World" on the terminal.

Let's work through the program, one line at a time:

---

6. https://github.com/toml-lang/toml
7. https://doc.rust-lang.org/cargo/reference/manifest.html
8. https://doc.rust-lang.org/edition-guide/editions/index.html

InstallingRust/HelloWorld/src/main.rs

```
❶ fn main() {
❷     println!("Hello, world!");
  }
```

❶ The main function. Main is a special function, marked as the *entry point* of your program.

The syntax of the 'main' function is defined as follows:

```
fn main() {
```
Begin the function's scope block.
Function parameters - none.
The function name ("main").
Declare a new function.

❷ The println! macro and string literal, see Printing Text, on page 12.

Rust uses a lot of curly brackets ({..}). These denote *scopes*. A scope represents a block of code that runs together. Variables created inside a scope remain inside the scope—they don't leak out, and are cleaned up automatically when the scope exits. In this case, printing "Hello, World" happens inside the main function's scope.

The main function is special. It acts as the *entry point* for your Rust program. It doesn't matter what order you put your functions in—main *always* runs first.

Printing Text

The body of the main function contains the line:

```
println!("Hello, world!");
```

The exclamation mark marks a *macro*. Rust's macro system is very powerful—and allows for syntax that wouldn't work with regular functions. That can make macros surprising—so Rust warns you that a call is a macro by using an exclamation mark in the macro's name. println! is a very flexible macro, offering *many* formatting features.[9] In this case, you don't need the extended syntax options; you just want to print some text.

"Hello, World!" is a *string literal*. It's a "literal" because it is *literally* the text you typed into the quotation marks, stored in the program. You can put any text into the string, instead of the default "Hello, World!" It supports Unicode. "Привет, мир" or " こんにちは世界" are valid string literals that you can print. It even works with emojis.

---

9.   https://doc.rust-lang.org/std/fmt/

Use Hard-to-Type Symbols Sparingly

 Being able to use symbols is great, but be careful not to overdo it. I once worked on a project that used beautiful math symbols for everything. It was lovely to read, let θ = π * Δ is a natural expression of the underlying math. When it came time to *edit* the code, changes to it became really tricky because my keyboard didn't have buttons for most of the symbols. Rust limits your use of symbols for variable and function names for this reason.

Using Cargo to Build, Check, or Run Your Project

You've already used Cargo to run your project, in Run Hello, World, on page 9. Cargo offers a few other ways to interact with your program. You can type cargo help for a full list, or cargo [command] --help for detailed help about a command's options. You can:

- Quickly check to see if a project is valid by typing cargo check. This checks your project and its dependencies for basic structural errors. This is typically a lot faster than a full build.

- Compile—but do not run—your project with cargo build.

- Remove the entire target directory (into which compiled code is placed) with cargo clean.

Cargo provides a few options to customize your build setup.

Debug and Release Builds

When you execute cargo run or cargo build, your project is built in *debug* mode. It contains very few optimizations, making it run a lot more slowly than it should. This makes it easier to debug and for Rust to tell you exactly what went wrong—but your program may run slowly. It also emits "debug information" —data your debugging tool can read to associate errors with lines of code. This makes for a much larger compiled program.

You can compile/run your program in *release* mode with the command cargo run --release. The compiler applies optimizations and doesn't use extra space to provide debugger support. You get a much faster and smaller program—but it's much harder to fix. When it comes time to *release* your program, compile it in release mode.

Formatting Your Code

When you're sharing your code with others, it's helpful to have a standardized layout for your code. Rust provides a style guide, but it can be difficult to remember.[10] Rust includes a formatter that can help you adhere to the standard. The command `cargo fmt` will reformat your code to follow the Rust style guide.

Suppose you were in a hurry and wrote "Hello, World!" as a one-line program:

```
fn main() { println!("Hello, world!"); }
```

This program will compile and run, but it's very different from the recommended style guide. If you were to share it with your coworkers or as part of an open-source project, you would likely receive comments on the formatting. You can run `cargo fmt` to transform the terse code back into the recommended format.

When you run `cargo fmt`, it formats your *entire* project. I recommend running it regularly while you work, keeping your project's formatting consistent. If you dislike its formatting, it has a lot of options for configuring it.[11]

The formatted result looks much better:

```
fn main() {
    println!("Hello, world!");
}
```

Rust also includes tools to help you find issues with the *content* of your code.

Finding Common Mistakes with Clippy

Rust ships with a tool called *Clippy*. Clippy provides hints and guidance while you code. You can type `cargo clippy` at any time to get a list of suggestions for your project. Many clippy warnings will also appear when you compile your programs. Most development environments that support Rust integrate with Clippy and will show you warnings and hints as you work.

Let's use Clippy to fix a simple project. Create a new project by navigating to your source code folder and typing `cargo new clippy` (see Starting a New Project with Cargo, on page 8). Edit your src/main.rs file to contain the following:

---

10. https://doc.rust-lang.org/1.0.0/style/README.html
11. https://github.com/rust-lang/rustfmt

InstallingRust/Clippy/src/main.rs
```
fn main() {
    let MYLIST = [ "One", "Two", "Three" ];
    for i in 0..3 {
        println!("{}", MYLIST[i]);
    }
}
```

Run the program by typing cargo run into your terminal. You will see the following (as well as several warnings about the code):

```
⇒  cargo run
❮  One
   Two
   Three
```

The program works but has room for improvement. It's ignoring some of Rust's better features and naming conventions. These are common issues and Clippy can help. Type cargo clippy into your terminal, and you'll receive a list of suggestions. The first warning is:

```
Checking clippy v0.1.0 (C:\Pragmatic\Book\code\InstallingRust\Clippy)
warning: the loop variable `i` is only used to index `MYLIST`.
 --> src\main.rs:3:14
  |
3 |      for i in 0..3 {
  |               ^^^^
  |
  = note: `#[warn(clippy::needless_range_loop)]` on by default
```

It also suggests a webpage that explains the warning in more detail.[12]

The second warning is:

```
warning: variable `MYLIST` should have a snake case name
 --> src\main.rs:2:9
  |
2 |      let MYLIST = [ "One", "Two", "Three" ];
  |          ^^^^^^ help: convert the identifier to snake case: `mylist`
  = note: `#[warn(non_snake_case)]` on by default
```

Clippy found two issues with the code:

- A *stylistic* error: Rust convention is to use snake_case names for variables. Instead of MYLIST, the code should contain my_list.

- A *poor choice of code.* You don't need to iterate by index on the list. Rust has an iterator system to avoid indexing mistakes (it would be easy to

---

12. https://rust-lang.github.io/rust-clippy/master/index.html#needless_range_loop.

change the list and forget to update the index numbers). Clippy has both identified this common issue for newcomers to Rust and suggested code to replace it.

Let's fix these two errors:

1. Replace the for loop with a ranged-for loop. The Clippy hint indicates how to do this; you will cover this issue in detail in Storing Strings in an Array, on page 26.

2. Use your text editor's find/replace feature to replace MYLIST with my_list.

The fixed code looks like this, and produces the same output—but without Clippy complaints:

```
InstallingRust/ClippyFixed/src/main.rs
fn main() {
    let my_list = [ "One", "Two", "Three" ];
    for num in &my_list {
        println!("{}", num);
    }
}
```

Making Clippy Pedantic

If you don't feel that Clippy is complaining enough, you can configure Clippy to be even more strict in its analysis. As the first line of your main.rs file, add:

```
#![warn(clippy::all, clippy::pedantic)]
```

Increased pedantry can be helpful when writing code—especially if you plan to share it. Clippy has even more pedantic options available, but they aren't recommended for common use.[13] Sometimes, in-development Clippy rules contradict one another or are unreliable. Normal and pedantic Clippy levels have been vetted for correctness and are usually all you need.

Trust Clippy

 Clippy is a busy body—a bossy little mascot who criticizes all of your code. When I started using Clippy, I found myself cursing its advice—especially the sheer volume of changes it suggested. After working with Rust for a while and following Clippy's advice, I rarely write code it complains about. Clippy is a learning tool and can help you avoid mistakes.

---

13. https://github.com/rust-lang/rust-clippy

> **Trust Clippy**
>
> Turning Clippy up to *pedantic* can feel like an exercise in masochism, but it's a great way to improve your code.

Package Management with Cargo

Cargo can install dependencies for you. There's an ever-growing number of "crates" (Rust's name for packages) available for free on the crates.io system.[14] Cargo makes it easy to install and use these crates, as well as to publish your own.

You can search available crates by typing `cargo search [search term]` or visiting the crates website. For example, searching for `bracket-terminal` produces the following:

```
⇒ cargo search bracket-terminal
❮ bracket-terminal = "0.7.0"    # ASCII/Codepage 437 terminal emulator with a
                                  game loop. Defaults to OpenGL, also support
                                  Amethyst,…
```

Searching also searches crates' descriptions. For example, if you find yourself needing a "slot map"—a few crates appear to offer one:

```
⇒ cargo search slotmap
❮ slotmap = "0.4.0"                    # Slotmap data structure
  beach_map = "0.1.2"                  # Implementation of a slotmap
```

Once you've found a crate you wish to use, add it to Cargo.toml. In the [dependencies] section, add a line for the dependency and version:

```
[dependencies]
bracket-lib = "0.8.0"
```

Version numbers use semantic versioning, just like your project's version number.[15]. Semantic versioning states that:

- The first digit is the "major" version. Once released, crates try not to break compatibility without increasing the major version number. Version zero is special. Crates with a major version of 0 are pre-release—and are allowed to break things.

- The second digit is the "minor" version. Changes that add functionality but don't break compatibility generally increment the minor version number.

---

14. https://crates.io/
15. https://semver.org/

- The third digit is the "patch" version. A quick fix to a bug generally increments the "patch" version.

You can add a few qualifiers to provide fine-grained control over what crate version you use:

- =0.8.0 will *only* use version 0.8.0 - nothing lower or higher.

- ^0.8.0 will use any version equal to or greater than 0.8.0, but *only* within the 0.x version range.

- ~0.8.0 will use any minor version greater than 0.8.0. Updates will automatically be applied, even if they break the crate's API.

A few different options are available; you can specify a version to download from crates.io, a Git repository address, or even a local path for a crate stored on your computer.[16] For example, if you wanted to use the GitHub version of bracket-lib, you could specify it as follows:

```
[dependencies]
bracket-lib = { git = "https://github.com/thebracket/bracket-lib" }
```

Crates can also provide *feature flags*. This allows a crate to offer *optional* functionality. For example, bracket-lib can be configured to use *Amethyst* as its back end, rather than OpenGL. You would specify this as follows:

```
[dependencies]
bracket-lib = {
    git = "https://github.com/thebracket/bracket-lib",
    default-features = false,
    features = [ "amethyst_engine_vulkan" ]
}
```

You can remove dependencies from your project by deleting them from your Cargo.toml file. Run a cargo clean, and they are gone from your computer. You'll begin using Cargo dependencies in Create a New Project that Uses Bracket-Lib, on page 48.

Wrap-Up

You now have Rust installed and a degree of familiarity with the tools it provides. You edited your first Rust program and you have a comfortable text editing environment. In the next chapter, you'll put this knowledge to use and start writing Rust programs.

---

16. https://doc.rust-lang.org/cargo/reference/specifying-dependencies.html

CHAPTER 2

First Steps with Rust

In the previous chapter, you installed Rust, set up a comfortable development environment, and examined the "Hello, World" program. This chapter pushes you further into Rust development as you build a program designed to assist your security team at a swanky new treehouse. In building this program, you'll learn to accept input from the keyboard, store data in variables, store collections of variables in arrays and vectors, and begin to learn the power of Rust iterators and enumerations.

It's going to be a whirlwind tour as this chapter introduces a lot of *concepts*, but hang in there—you're in for a real treat. (And don't worry if you don't remember everything you read here; the more you use Rust, the more you'll remember how it works.)

You'll get started by creating a new project, which you'll use throughout this chapter, gradually adding functionality as you learn more Rust.

Creating a New Project

You created your first project in Starting a New Project with Cargo, on page 8; however, as a refresher, here are the steps to follow:

1. Open a terminal/command prompt.
2. Change the directory to your "Learn Rust" directory. e.g., cd /home/bert/learnrust).
3. Use Cargo to make a new "treehouse" project: type cargo new treehouse.
4. Launch your favorite text editor/IDE, and load your new project.

You now have a new "Hello, World" program ready for editing. Let's add some functionality to make it interactive.

Capturing User Input

Most computer programs operate in a cycle of accepting input from the user and transforming that into some form of—hopefully useful—output. A calculator without buttons is useless, and a computer program without input is equally limited to always doing the same thing. You used println! in "Hello, World" to output text; you can use read_line() to accept data from the terminal.

In this section, you'll use the terminal to ask the visitor to type their name and receive the result. Finally, you'll make use of Rust's formatting system to print a personalized greeting to the terminal.

Prompting for the Visitor's Name

When a visitor arrives at your swanky new treehouse, you need to ask them for their name. In Printing Text, on page 12, you used println! to print text to the screen. You'll do the same thing here, too.

Replace println!("Hello, World") with:

FirstStepsWithRust/hello_yourname/src/main.rs
```
println!("Hello, what's your name?");
```

Why Did the Project Name Change?

 Don't worry, you're still working on the treehouse project. The source code examples in this book are provided in chunks, representing each stage of development within the chapter. When you see the source file name change, it means that the code is referring to the next example along the way—you don't need to change anything.

You replaced the output string asking for the visitor's name. Now you're ready to receive and store the answer.

Storing the Name in a Variable

You'll store the visitor's name in a variable. Rust variables default to being *immutable*. Once an immutable variable is assigned, you cannot change the value stored in the variable. You can make more variables, reference, or copy a previously assigned variable, but you can't change the immutable variable once it is assigned. You can explicitly mark a variable as *mutable* with the mut keyword. Once marked as mutable, a variable may be changed as needed.

Add a second line of code to your program:

FirstStepsWithRust/hello_yourname/src/main.rs
```
let mut your_name = String::new();
```

Be Wary of Mutation

Mutants are scary and mutable variables can be too. It's tempting to mark everything as mutable so you don't need to remember to add mut when you need it. Rust/Clippy will warn you when a variable doesn't need to be marked as mut. It's a good idea to heed the warnings, because it's much easier to think about what a program does if you can be sure that a variable still means what you think it means.

This code creates a mutable variable named your_name, and sets it to be an empty text string. The syntax for the variable declaration looks like this:[1]

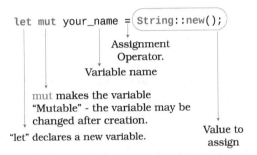

String is a *type*, built into Rust.[2] Types can have functions associated with them; you'll learn how to do this for your types in Grouping Data with Structs, on page 29.

Use snake_case for Variable Names

Rust encourages you to use snake_case for variable names. Use lowercase and replace spaces with _. Clippy will remind you if you forget.

Let's obtain the user's name from the keyboard and store it in a string.

Receiving Keyboard Input

Rust's standard input system provides an easy way to receive keyboard input. Rust provides terminal input functions in std::io::stdin.[3] You can find read_line as std::io::stdin::read_line. That's a lot of typing just to read a line of text from the keyboard. Let's import the name with Rust's use keyword so that you don't have to type out the full version every time.

---

1. https://doc.rust-lang.org/book/ch03-01-variables-and-mutability.html.
2. https://doc.rust-lang.org/1.7.0/book/strings.html.
3. https://doc.rust-lang.org/std/io/struct.Stdin.html.

Add the following line to the top of main.rs:

FirstStepsWithRust/hello_yourname/src/main.rs
```
use std::io::stdin;
```

This line imports std::io::stdin into your project. Now you can just type stdin instead of remembering all of the namespace prefix.

Reading User Input

Now that you have access to stdin, and a variable in which to store the user's name, you're ready to read that name from the console input. Add the following code to your main function, immediately after the variable declaration:

FirstStepsWithRust/hello_yourname/src/main.rs
```
stdin()
    .read_line(&mut your_name)
    .expect("Failed to read line");
```

Combining functions like this is called *function chaining*. Starting from the top, each function passes its results to the next function. It's common to format a function chain with each step on its line, indented to indicate that the block belongs together. The cargo fmt command (see Formatting Your Code, on page 14) will automatically apply this formatting standard for you.

Why Create the Variable First?

 read_line() wants to write its results into an existing string, rather than returning to a new one. You have to create the empty String first so that it has somewhere to store the function's results.

Here are the sections of the read_line call explained:

```
stdin()  ⟶  stdin() returns an object granting access to the Standard Input.
   ↓
   .read_line(&mut  your_name)
                ↓            ↓
                &mut : "Borrow" the variable, allowing changes to be made
                       to your variable by the called function.
            read_line() is a method, from the Stdin object.
            It receives keyboard input until you press ENTER.
   .expect("Failed to read line");
       ↓
   .expect(...) : "Unwrap" a Result object, and terminate the program
                  with the specified message if an error has occurred.
```

You can learn two important concepts from this code:

• Prefixing a variable with an ampersand (&) creates a *reference* to the variable. A reference passes access to the variable itself, not a copy of the variable. This is also called *borrowing*—you're *lending* the variable to the function you are calling. Lending with &mut permits the borrowing function to mutate your variable. Any changes it makes to the variable are written directly into the variable you lent. Passing &mut your_name to read_line allows the read_line function to write directly into your_name.

- You expect the read_line function to work correctly. If it doesn't, your program will crash. Rust is returning a Result object, and you are checking that the function worked by calling expect. Don't worry about the details of this yet. You'll learn about error handling in Handling Errors in the Main Function, on page 51.

Printing with Placeholders

Now that the your_name variable contains the visitor's name, you can greet them properly. Greeting the user requires another println! call:

FirstStepsWithRust/hello_yourname/src/main.rs
```
println!("Hello, {}", your_name)
```

The println macro is almost the same as before, but it has gained a *placeholder*. Including {} in your println! string indicates that a variable's value goes here. You then provide the variable as a second parameter to the macro call. Rust includes a very powerful formatting system and can take care of most of your string formatting needs out of the box.[4]

The Completed Greeter Program

Your treehouse admission program now looks like this:

FirstStepsWithRust/hello_yourname/src/main.rs
```
use std::io::stdin;

fn main() {
    println!("Hello, what's your name?");
    let mut your_name = String::new();
    stdin()
        .read_line(&mut your_name)
        .expect("Failed to read line");
    println!("Hello, {}", your_name)
}
```

Run the program with cargo run (see Run Hello, World, on page 9 if you need a refresher on running programs), and you'll see the following:

```
⇒ cargo run
❮ Hello, what's your name?
```

---

4. https://doc.rust-lang.org/std/fmt/

⇒ `Herbert`
‹ `Hello, Herbert`

Congratulations, you now have working input and output. Let's learn about *functions* by moving your input code into a reusable block of code.

Moving Input to a Function

You're frequently going to be asking the user for their name in this chapter. Whenever you have commonly used code, it's a good idea to move it into a function. This has two advantages: you don't keep typing the same code, and a single call to what_is_your_name() is less disruptive of the overall flow of your function, which lets you concentrate on the important parts. This is a form of *abstraction*: you replace detailed code with a function call and move the detail into a function.

When Should I Use a Function?

Try to use a function when you are typing the same code repeatedly. This is called the DRY principle: *Do not Repeat Yourself. Code Complete [McC04]* provides an excellent overview of the DRY Principle and its practical application.

You should also consider breaking code up into functions if it becomes very large. It's much easier to read a shorter function that calls other functions, especially when you come back to a piece of code after a break.

In Hello, World, on page 11, you declared the main function; making your own functions is similar:

FirstStepsWithRust/hello_yourname_function/src/main.rs
```
use std::io::stdin;

❶ fn what_is_your_name() -> String {
❷     let mut your_name = String::new();
    stdin()
        .read_line(&mut your_name)
        .expect("Failed to read line");
❸     your_name
}

fn main() {
    println!("Hello, what's your name?");
❹     let name = what_is_your_name();
    println!("Hello, {}", name);
}
```

❶ The function signature is very similar to the main function. The function name is different, and -> String denotes that it *returns* a String.

❷ The read_line code is the same, moved into your function.

❸ This line doesn't end with a semicolon. This is Rust shorthand for return. Any expression may return this way. It's the same as typing return your_name;. Clippy will complain if you type return when you don't need it.

❹ Instead of calling read_line directly, call your function and store the result in name.

Now that you have your input function, you're ready to move on.

Trimming Input

The program's output looks good on screen, but it contains a subtle bug. The string contains some extra characters representing the ENTER key. You can see this by replacing your last println! call with the following:

FirstStepsWithRust/treehouse_guestlist_problem/src/main.rs
```
println!("{:?}", name);
```

Replacing the {} placeholder with {:?} uses the *debug* placeholder. Any type that supports debug printing will print a detailed debugging dump of its contents, rather than just the value. If you run the program now, you can see the problem:

```
❮ Hello, what's your name?
⇒ Herbert
❮ "Herbert\r\n" (or "Herbert\n" on UNIX-based systems)
```

\r is a special character that means carriage return. On old printers, it returned the printhead to the left of the page. \n means a new line. Windows generates these two characters for an ENTER keypress. UNIX-derived systems just append \n.

Rust's strings include a trim() function to remove these extra characters. If you don't remove these characters, you'll be surprised when you type "Bert" but Bert in your code doesn't match, because the string contains Bert\r\n.

It's also a good idea to convert the input to lowercase. This allows "Bert," "bert," and even "bErt" to correctly match a name. Rust's strings provide the to_lowercase() function to do this for you.

Amend your function to use both trim and to_lowercase:

FirstStepsWithRust/treehouse_guestlist_trim/src/main.rs
```rust
fn what_is_your_name() -> String {
    let mut your_name = String::new();
    stdin()
        .read_line(&mut your_name)
        .expect("Failed to read line");

    your_name
        .trim()
        .to_lowercase()
}
```

That's much better. Your input is now always lowercase, and it doesn't include non-printing characters. A treehouse with only one visitor isn't much of a party. Let's add support for more of your friends.

Storing Strings in an Array

The treehouse is an exclusive club. Only individuals on the approved list of friends are allowed inside. You could accomplish this with if statements. If you only want to admit your friend "Bert," you could use the following code:

```rust
if your_name == "bert" {
  println!("Welcome.");
} else {
  println!("Sorry, you are not on the list.")
}
```

The if/else control flow system works much like it does in other programming languages: if the *condition* is true, then it executes the code in the first block. Otherwise, it runs the code in the else block.

When you do your comparison, make sure that you compare your string with "bert" in lowercase. You need to use lowercase because the input function converts the user's input to lowercase, so you need to *compare* with lowercase strings for there to be a match.

If you have a second friend named "Steve," you could also allow them inside by using an or expression. Or in Rust is expressed with ||:

```rust
if your_name == "bert" || your_name == "steve" {
```

Booleans

 Combining comparisons is called *Boolean logic*. || means "or." && means "and." ! means "not." You'll use these throughout the book. But don't worry, they'll be explained when you need them.

Now, both Steve and Bert are allowed inside. Once you start inviting more friends, repeatedly adding or statements becomes unwieldy. Rather than making a huge list of or statements, let's use a *data structure* designed to help with lists of data.

Declaring an Array

Rust's simplest list type is the *array*. An array holds a list of values with two rules: the values must be of the same type, and the array *cannot change size*. Once you've decided whom to admit, you can't change the list size without recompiling your program.

To declare an array of string literals (&str types), you can do this:

FirstStepsWithRust/treehouse_guestlist/src/main.rs
```
let visitor_list = ["bert", "steve", "fred"];
```

Rust once again *infers* the type of the array. All of the entries are string literals, so Rust assumes that you want an array of the same type. The array creation contains three entries, so Rust deduces that you want an array of size 3. If you wanted to declare the type, the full syntax is let visitor_list : [&str;3] = ...

You can access the contents of an array by index. visitor_list[0] contains "bert." visitor_list[2] contains "fred." If you aren't used to C-like languages, index numbering can trip you up. Rust arrays start counting at zero, not one. This ensures that you can check if index < my_array.len() to determine if an index falls within the array.

Two Types of Strings

Rust has two types of strings, which can be a source of confusion for new Rust programmers. The first type is str. These types are generally used as string *literals*, which are strings entered in the source code and generally unchanging. The second type is the String. Strings are *dynamic* because they store a location, length, and capacity. You can append Strings and edit them.

Searching an Array

To determine if a visitor is on the approved treehouse patrons list, you need to search the visitor list for the new visitor's name. Rust provides a few ways to do this.

You can run an operation repeatedly with the for loop.[5] Rust for loops operate on *ranges* rather than an explicit set of numbers and a step. Rust numerical ranges do not include the last number in the range. 0..10 includes 0 through 9. You can make them inclusive by using 0..=10 instead of 0..10. For example, this code prints the numbers zero to nine:

```
for i in 0..10 {
  println!("{}", i)
}
```

You can visit every element in an array by index, iterating a variable—known as an *enumerator*—from zero to the array's length. Arrays provide a len() function to determine their length. This also demonstrates why Rust chose to use exclusive ranges: len() returns the number of entries in the array. Arrays are zero-based, so valid entries range from zero to the array's length minus one. The following code iterates the array by index:

```
for i in 0..visitor_list.len() {
  if visitor_list[i] == your_name { ... }
}
```

This works, but Clippy (the linter) will complain about it. In Finding Common Mistakes with Clippy, on page 14, this was an example of what *not* to do. Rust can directly access the contents of an array or other container, without needing to use index numbers. This is shorter and safer. You can't mess up your index numbers and crash your program by accessing an element that doesn't exist.

The following code uses the entire visitor_list as the range:

```
for visitor in &visitor_list {
  if visitor == your_name { ... }
}
```

To iterate the array with a for loop, and flag if a visitor's name is included in the list, you need to:

1. Create a new, mutable variable named allow_them_in. It stores whether the name has been found on the list. Initialize it to false.

2. Use for visitor in &visitor_list to compare every name on the list with your_name. The & means "borrow a reference." The loop looks at the original data and does not copy it.

3. If the names match, set allow_them_in to true.

---

5. https://doc.rust-lang.org/1.2.0/book/for-loops.html

4.   After the for list, if allow_them_in is true, then greet the visitor. Otherwise, reject them.

You've already encountered the building blocks you need. Here's the relevant code in Rust:

FirstStepsWithRust/treehouse_guestlist/src/main.rs

```
let mut allow_them_in = false;
for visitor in &visitor_list {
    if visitor == &name {
        allow_them_in = true;
    }
}

if allow_them_in {
    println!("Welcome to the Treehouse, {}", name);
} else {
    println!("Sorry, you aren't on the list.");
}
```

Run the program now and try different names. You'll see something similar to the following output:

```
⇒ cargo run
❮ Hello, what's your name?
⇒ Bert
❮ Welcome to the Treehouse, Bert
⇒ cargo run
❮ Hello, what's your name?
⇒ bob
❮ Sorry, you aren't on the list.
```

Sometimes you want to remember more about your visitors than just their name. Rust makes it easy to group more information about a visitor in a single variable, which you can then store in an array.

Grouping Data with Structs

The treehouse bouncer would like both a name and a customized greeting for every visitor. You *could* create a new array for greetings, and be careful to add every visitor and their greeting in the same order. That would quickly become tricky to maintain. A better approach is to store all the information about a guest together, in a *struct*.

A *struct* is a type that groups data together. Structs contain *member fields*—variables of (almost) any type. Grouping data together makes it easier to access complicated information—once you're looking in the right struct, individual pieces of data are available by name.

Structures are ubiquitous in Rust: String and StdIn are both struct types. Rust's struct types combine related data, and can implement functionality for that type. They are similar to class types in other languages.

You can define your structures.[6] Structures are a *type*, just like i32, String, and enumerations. A type isn't a variable—it's a description of what variables of that type can contain. You can make one Visitor type, and then use it over and over again for different visitors (known as an *instance*). This is another form of abstraction. In main.rs, above your functions, add:

FirstStepsWithRust/treehouse_guestlist_struct/src/main.rs
```
struct Visitor {
    name: String,
    greeting: String,
}
```

This defines a struct type named *Visitor*. The structure contains a name and greeting field, each of type String.

Structures can also have associated functions and methods. String::new and StdIn::read_line are both methods associated with a structure.

Making a visitor should be easy, so you need to create a *constructor*. Constructors are functions associated with a type that provides a quick way to create an instance of that type. The bouncer needs a way to greet the visitor, so you also want to implement a function to do that. Associated functions that operate on an instance of the struct are sometimes called *methods*. In Rust, &self as a parameter denotes a method that has access to the instance contents:

FirstStepsWithRust/treehouse_guestlist_struct/src/main.rs
```
❶ impl Visitor {
❷     fn new(name: &str, greeting: &str) -> Self {
❸         Self {
               name: name.to_lowercase(),
               greeting: greeting.to_string(),
           }
       }

❹     fn greet_visitor(&self) {
           println!("{}", self.greeting);
       }
   }
```

---

6. https://doc.rust-lang.org/book/ch05-01-defining-structs.html

❶ You *implement* functions for a structure with impl and the struct name.

❷ This is an *associated function*. The parameter list does not include self. You can't access new with name.new(); instead, it's available in the structure's namespace. You can call it with Visitor::new().

The constructor returns the type Self. This is Rust shorthand. Clippy will suggest using the shorthand if you use the longform. You could equally write "Visitor" in its place, but if you were to change the struct name, you would have to remember to go back and change every implementation. Use Self to save yourself that pain.

❸ The lack of a semicolon denotes "implicit return" syntax. It creates a new instance of the structure, again using Self instead of Visitor. Every field *must* be listed, in the format field_name : value,.

The function accepts parameters of type &str, but stores values of type String. The to_lowercase and to_string functions perform the conversion. By taking &str, the function accepts string literals without conversion. This saves us from typing String::from("bert") when calling the constructor.

Title case Self refers to the struct type itself. Lowercase self refers to the *instance* of the structure.

❹ This function is a *member function* or *method*. It accepts self as a parameter, which is automatically passed into the function when you reference an instance of the struct (e.g. my_visitor.greet_visitor()) with the contents of that specific structure instance.

Now that your Visitor is defined, you can create a new and improved visitor list. Replace your visitor_list creation with:

FirstStepsWithRust/treehouse_guestlist_struct/src/main.rs
```
let visitor_list = [
    Visitor::new("bert", "Hello Bert, enjoy your treehouse."),
    Visitor::new("steve","Hi Steve. Your milk is in the fridge."),
    Visitor::new("fred", "Wow, who invited Fred?"),
];
```

This is still an array, but it now contains Visitor structures rather than strings, created with the constructor you wrote. You can still access individual members by index; visitor_list[0].name now contains "bert." The period (.) denotes "member access," visitor_list[0] refers to a single instance of Visitor. The period grants you access to its fields and functions.

Trailing Commas

When you are building a big list, it's easy to miss a comma or add an extra one. This is especially true when you are using cut and paste to rearrange your list. Rust helps with this by ignoring any trailing commas at the end of a list. If you *always* add a comma after each list item, you can't forget that you need one when you rearrange the list.

As you gain more visitors, it's helpful to have more efficient ways to manipulate your visitor list.

Searching with Iterators

With visitors now represented as structures, you still need to be able to search them. You could use the same search code as before, comparing your_name with visitor.name and call the greeting method directly. This gets unwieldy as your visitors become more complicated and you add more visitors to the list.

Rust provides a powerful feature known as *iterators* for manipulating data.[7] Iterators are a bit of a catch-all feature—they can do a *lot*. When you are working with lists of data, iterators are the first place to look for the functionality you need. Iterators are designed around function chaining—each iterator step works as a building block to massage the data from the previous step into what you need.

Iterators include a find() function to locate data within a collection—whether it's an array, a vector, or something else. Replace your for loop with the following:

FirstStepsWithRust/treehouse_guestlist_struct/src/main.rs
```
❶ let known_visitor = visitor_list
❷     .iter()
❸     .find(|visitor| visitor.name == name);
```

❶ Assign the result of the iterator function chain to the variable known_visitor.

❷ Create an iterator with iter() that contains all of the data from the visitor_list.

❸ find() runs a *closure*. If the closure returns true, find() returns the matching value. The semicolon finishes the statement.

---

7.   https://doc.rust-lang.org/std/iter/trait.Iterator.html

Closures

Closures are used a lot in Rust.[a] You don't need to worry about the finer details of closures at this point—they will be introduced gradually as you need them. For now, think of a closure as a function you define in place. The inline closure |visitor| visitor.name == name is the same as defining a function:

```
FirstStepsWithRust/inline_closure_include.rs
fn check_visitor_name(visitor: &Visitor, name: &String) -> bool {
    return visitor.name == name;
}
```

Closures can also *capture* data from the scope from which they are called. You didn't pass 'name' to the closure; however, you were still able to use it anyway.

_____

a.   https://doc.rust-lang.org/1.18.0/book/first-edition/closures.html

This function chain creates an iterator and stores the results of the find function in known_visitor. You can't be sure that the name you searched for is on the visitor list. Find() returns a Rust type called an Option. Options either contain a value or they don't. Some languages use null or nullptr to represent the absence of a value but weak rules for handling null values have resulted in countless bugs.[8]

Rust options are an enumeration (you'll make your own in Categorizing with Enumerations, on page 38). Options have two possible values: Some(x) and None. There are a lot of different ways to interact with—and extract data from—an option. For now, you'll use match. Add the following code immediately after the known_visitor assignment:

```
FirstStepsWithRust/treehouse_guestlist_struct/src/main.rs
❶ match known_visitor {
❷     Some(visitor) => visitor.greet_visitor(),
❸     None => println!("You are not on the visitor list. Please leave.")
}
```

❶ List the variable on which you want to match.

❷ Matching Some(visitor) checks to see if the option has data, and makes the contents of the option available to the code in this clause as visitor. The fat arrow ('=>') denotes the code to execute for this match—in this case, greeting the visitor. Separate match options with commas.

❸ None denotes that the option has no data—find didn't locate the visitor's name. Politely ask the the visitor to leave.

_____

8.   https://medium.com/@hinchman_amanda/null-pointer-references-the-billion-dollar-mistake-1e616534d485

Iterators: Rust's Unsung Heroes

 Iterators are amazing. The syntax takes some getting used to, but if you are familiar with LINQ in the *.NET* world or *ranges* in C++20, it's similar. They are *very* powerful—most Rust code makes heavy use of them. Iterators are also very fast, often faster than writing equivalent loops yourself. The compiler can be *certain* that you aren't trying dangerous operations such as reading beyond the end of an array. It's able to make a number of optimizations as a result.

Running the program with cargo run produces the following:

```
⇒ cargo run
❮ Hello, what's your name?
⇒ Bert
❮ Hello Bert, enjoy your treehouse.

⇒ cargo run
❮ Hello, what's your name?
⇒ Steve
❮ Hi Steve. Your milk is in the fridge.

⇒ cargo run
❮ Hello, what's your name?
⇒ bob
❮ You are not on the visitor list. Please leave.
```

You can't really predict how many visitors you will have—they may cancel or they may bring friends. Arrays are *fixed-length*—they can't grow beyond their original size. Rust's *vector* collection lets you add as many visitors as you like.

Storing a Variable Amount of Data with Vectors

Instead of turning away people who aren't on the visitor list, you decide to let them in and store their names for the next party.

Arrays can't change size. *Vectors* (Vec) are designed to be dynamically resizable. They can be used like arrays, but you can add to them with a method named push().[9] Vectors can keep growing—you are limited only by the size of your computer's memory.

Deriving Debug

When you were just storing names as strings, printing them was easy. Send them to println! and you're done. You want to be able to print the contents of

---

9.   https://doc.rust-lang.org/1.18.0/book/first-edition/vectors.html

a Visitor structure. The *debug* placeholders ({:?} —for raw printing—and {:#?}, for "pretty" printing) print any type that supports the Debug trait. Adding debug support to your Visitor structure is easy, and makes use of another convenient feature of Rust: the *derive macro*.

FirstStepsWithRust/treehouse_guestlist_vector/src/main.rs
```
#[derive(Debug)]
struct Visitor {
    name: String,
    greeting: String
}
```

Derive macros are a very powerful mechanism to save you from typing repetitive boilerplate code. You can derive a lot of things—you'll use derive statements regularly throughout the book. Deriving requires that every member field in the structure support the feature you are deriving. Fortunately, Rust primitives such as String support it out of the box. Once you've derived Debug, you can use the println! placeholder {:?} to print your entire struct.

Using a Vector Instead of an Array

Now that you can print visitors, you need to replace the visitor's array with a vector. You'd like to store newcomers on the visitor list, so you can greet them appropriately when they return for your next party. Arrays won't let you do that—they can't grow beyond their original size. Rust provides Vec (short for "vector") for this purpose.

Rust vectors are similar to arrays in operation, making it relatively easy to replace one with the other. Rust provides a helpful macro, vec!, to assist with this.[10] vec! lets you initialize a vector with similar syntax to array initialization:

FirstStepsWithRust/treehouse_guestlist_vector/src/main.rs
```
let mut visitor_list = vec![
    Visitor::new("Bert", "Hello Bert, enjoy your treehouse."),
    Visitor::new("Steve", "Hi Steve. Your milk is in the fridge."),
    Visitor::new("Fred", "Wow, who invited Fred?"),
];
```

vec! converts vector creation into similar syntax to array declaration. You could also write:

```
let mut visitor_list = Vec::new();
visitor_list.push(
  Visitor::new("Bert", "Hello Bert, enjoy your treehouse.")
);
// Keep pushing list members
```

---

10. https://doc.rust-lang.org/std/macro.vec.html

This is a lot longer and more unwieldy. Using the macro is a better choice.

Generic Types

 Vectors are a *generic* type. You can store almost anything in a vector. When you add a String to a vector, Rust deduces that you have created a vector of strings. It lists this type as Vec<String>. The angle brackets indicate that you are specifying a type to use in a generic type. Vector is declared as Vec<T>. The T is substituted for the type you specify or that Rust infers.

Looping Until You Call Break

You want to keep adding visitors to the list as they arrive, rather than having the program exit after each visitor. Rust provides a mechanism to keep running code until you tell it to stop, called loop.[11] loop runs the code inside its block over and over until it encounters a break;. At that point, it instantly jumps to the end of the loop. In your main function, wrap your user input in a loop like this:

```
loop {
  println!("Hello, what's your name? (Leave empty and press ENTER to quit)");
  ...
  break; // Execution continues after the loop
}
// Execution resumes here on break
```

Adding New Vector Entries

After a visitor registers, you need to:

1. See if the user entered a blank name, and if so, break out of the loop.
2. If they're a new visitor, use push to add them to the visitor list.

Replace your rejection message code with the following:

FirstStepsWithRust/treehouse_guestlist_vector/src/main.rs
```
match known_visitor {
    Some(visitor) => visitor.greet_visitor(),
    None => {
        if name.is_empty() {
            break;
        } else {
            println!("{} is not on the visitor list.", name);
            visitor_list.push(Visitor::new(&name, "New friend"));
        }
    }
}
```

---

11. https://doc.rust-lang.org/1.29.0/book/first-edition/loops.html

❶ is_empty is a method implemented by String. It returns true if the String is empty, false otherwise. It's more efficient than checking name.len() == 0, which also works. Clippy will remind you about this optimization.

❷ break immediately jumps to the end of the loop.

Lastly, right before the program exits, make use of the Debug annotation attached to the Visitor to print out the final visitor list:

```
println!("The final list of visitors:");
println!("{:#?}", visitor_list);
```

The Iterators Didn't Change

 Did you notice that when switching from an array to a vector, the iterator code didn't change at all? Iterators don't care what the underlying collection is, as long as it implements iterator access. You can even use iterators to transform one type of collection into another. You'll learn more ways to use iterators throughout this book.

Run the program now, and your session will look something like this:

```
⇒ cargo run
❰ Hello, what's your name? (Leave empty and press ENTER to quit)
⇒ bert
❰ Hello Bert. Enjoy your treehouse.
  Hello, what's your name? (Leave empty and press ENTER to quit)
⇒ steve
❰ Hi Steve. Your milk is in the fridge.
  Hello, what's your name? (Leave empty and press ENTER to quit)
⇒ Joey
❰ joey is not on the visitor list.
  Hello, what's your name? (Leave empty and press ENTER to quit)
⇒
❰ The final list of visitors:
  [
      Visitor {
          name: "bert",
          greeting: "Hello Bert. Enjoy your treehouse.",
      },
      Visitor {
          name: "steve",
          greeting: "Hi Steve. Your milk is in the fridge.",
      },
      Visitor {
          name: "fred",
          greeting: "Wow, who invited Fred?",
      },
      Visitor {
```

```
        name: "joey",
        greeting: "New friend",
    },
]
```

Categorizing with Enumerations

The bouncer would like even more functionality. They'd like to know how to treat different visitors and if they can drink alcohol. The final set of improvements to the visitor list are:

- Store an action associated with a visitor: admit them, admit them with a note, refuse entry, or mark them as probationary treehouse members.

- Store the visitor's age, and forbid them from drinking if they're under 21.

Enumerations

Rust lets you define a type that can only be equal to one of a set of predefined values. These are known as *enumerations*, and are declared with the enum keyword. You are going to define an enumeration listing each of the four actions associated with a visitor. Rust enumerations are very powerful, and can include data—and even functions—for each enumeration entry.[12]

Towards the top of the file—outside of any functions—create a new enumeration with the following code:

FirstStepsWithRust/treehouse_guestlist_enum/src/main.rs
```
❶ #[derive(Debug)]
❷ enum VisitorAction {
❸   Accept,
❹   AcceptWithNote { note: String },
    Refuse,
    Probation,
❺ }
```

❶ Enumerations can derive functionality, just like structs. Deriving Debug allows Rust formatters to print the enumeration's values by name.

❷ Declare a new enumeration with the enum keyword. The declaration syntax is just like other type declarations.

❸ Accept is a simple enumeration option, with no associated data. VisitorAction variables may be assigned as let visitor_action = VisitorAction::Accept;.

---

12. https://doc.rust-lang.org/std/keyword.enum.html

❹ AcceptWithNote contains data: a note string. You can assign this value with let visitor_action = VisitorAction::AcceptWithNote{ note: "my note".to_string() };.

❺ Like struct declarations, enumeration declarations do *not* end with a semi-colon.

Using Enumerations and Integer Data Members

With the type declared, it's time to include it in your Visitor structure. You'll also want to include a field for the visitor's age; it's a treehouse for grown-ups now, complete with alcohol service.

FirstStepsWithRust/treehouse_guestlist_enum/src/main.rs
```
#[derive(Debug)]
struct Visitor {
  name: String,
❶  action: VisitorAction,
❷  age: i8
}
```

❶ Declare a field named *action*, of the type *VisitorAction* you just created. You can use any type inside a struct, including enums and other structs.

❷ Declare a field named *age*, of type i8. This is an 8-bit signed integer, meaning it can hold values from -128 to 127. Rust provides i32 and i64 if you need larger integers, but it's unlikely that anyone over 127 years old will visit your treehouse.

You also need to extend the constructor to initialize these fields. Not initializing fields in a struct results in a compilation error:

FirstStepsWithRust/treehouse_guestlist_enum/src/main.rs
```
❶  fn new(name: &str, action: VisitorAction, age: i8) -> Self {
    Self {
❷      name: name.to_lowercase(),
❸      action,
      age
    }
}
```

❶ The function follows the constructor pattern: it accepts parameters describing the desired contents of the struct and returns Self.

❷ List fields by name and then a colon before the data. The function to_lowercase() converts the static string (&str) into a String in all lowercase.

❸ When you don't need to manipulate data, if the function variable is the same as the struct's field name, you can omit the colon and value—Rust will use the contents of the variable of the same name.

Now that you have a set of actions for the bouncer to perform, let's instruct them on what to do with the new options.

Assigning Enumerations

You can access the members of an enumeration with the :: operator, in the format Enumeration::Member. For example, VisitorAction::Accept. Assigning a variable or struct member to equal an enumeration member follows the form my_field = Enumeration::Member. Enumerations that contain data are slightly more complicated. You assign them with the same syntax that you would use for assigning a struct with members: my_field = Enumeration::Member{value : my_value}. You could assign a visitor action with a note as follows:

```
let my_action = VisitorAction::AcceptWithNote{ note: "Give them a taco"};
```

Replace your visitor list initialization with the following:

FirstStepsWithRust/treehouse_guestlist_enum/src/main.rs
```
fn main() {
  let mut visitor_list = vec![
    Visitor::new("Bert", VisitorAction::Accept, 45),
    Visitor::new("Steve", VisitorAction::AcceptWithNote{
        note: String::from("Lactose-free milk is in the fridge")
    }, 15),
    Visitor::new("Fred", VisitorAction::Refuse, 30),
  ];
```

Matching Enumerations

Once you have data stored inside an enumeration, you need to be able to act based upon the selection. Enumerations can be a complex type—comparing with an if statement might not make sense if you also want to consider wrapped values. Instead, you need to use *pattern matching*. Pattern matching serves two basic purposes: it checks to see if a condition is true and runs the associated code, and it can *extract* fields from complicated types (such as your enum's note). You used a match statement in Searching with Iterators, on page 32, to match against an Option.

The syntax of a match statement is shown in the image on page 41.

```
                              Point to action with a "fat arrow"        Separate cases with a comma
    match visitor_action {            ↓                               ↓
        VisitorAction::Accept => println!("Welcome to the tree house."),
        VisitorAction::Probation => {  ←———————— Longer actions can be
            do_something_more_involved();      wrapped in { .. }
        }                                               ————————— Capture enum-wrapped variables
        VisitorAction::AcceptWithNote { note } => {
            println!("{}", note);
        }                                               ————————— Use the captured variable
```
Match all other
values with _ ——————→ `_ => println!("Go away!"),`
```
    }
```

Rust pattern matching can become very complicated, and has a *lot* of advanced options available. Don't worry about the advanced usages yet—focus on understanding the basic idea that match is used to decide what to do when presented with multiple options.[13]

Matches Aren't Just for Enums (or Fires)

You can match on almost any type. If you match on a numeric type, make sure you include an underscore _ to match all other choices —otherwise you will have to type every possible number as an option. Typing 4,294,967,295 options for a 32-bit unsigned integer will take a while.

The greet_visitor function is the perfect place to match on the new visitor action enum:

FirstStepsWithRust/treehouse_guestlist_enum/src/main.rs

```rust
fn greet_visitor(&self) {
  match &self.action {
    VisitorAction::Accept => println!("Welcome to the tree
        house, {}", self.name),
    VisitorAction::AcceptWithNote { note } => {
        println!("Welcome to the treehouse, {}", self.name);
        println!("{}", note);
        if self.age < 21 {
            println!("Do not serve alcohol to {}", self.name);
        }
    }
    VisitorAction::Probation => println!("{} is now a
        probationary member", self.name),
    VisitorAction::Refuse => println!("Do not allow {} in!", self.name),
  }
}
```
❶ ❷ ❸ ❹

---

13. https://doc.rust-lang.org/reference/expressions/match-expr.html

❶ If action is equal to VisitorAction::Accept, greet the user.

❷ If you're matching against an enumeration option that contains data, include the fields in curly brackets. This is called *destructuring*. The fields are then available within the match operation's scope by name. Notice that instead of a single expression, the code contains a scope block. You can use either in match statements.

❸ The variable note is extracted from the pattern matching line above, and used as a local variable.

❹ Integer math is similar to other languages: if age is less than 21, print a warning about not serving alcohol.

You'll be using pattern matching throughout this book. Don't worry if it seems complicated for now—it will make more sense when you use it in more complicated examples.

Lastly, you need to adjust your visitor_list.push line to create new visitors with probationary status:

```
visitor_list.push(Visitor::new(&name, VisitorAction::Probation, 0));
```

The remainder of the program remains the same. If you run the program with cargo run, you'll encounter something similar to this:

```
⇒ cargo run
❰ Hello, what's your name? (Leave empty and press ENTER to quit)
⇒ bert
❰ Welcome to the treehouse, bert
  Hello, what's your name? (Leave empty and press ENTER to quit)
⇒ steve
❰ Welcome to the treehouse, steve
  Lactose-free milk is in the fridge
  No alcohol for you!
  Hello, what's your name? (Leave empty and press ENTER to quit)
⇒ fred
❰ Do not allow this person in!
  Hello, what's your name? (Leave empty and press ENTER to quit)
⇒ joebob
❰ joebob is not on the visitor list.
  Hello, what's your name? (Leave empty and press ENTER to quit)
⇒ <keystroke>ENTER</keystroke>
❰ The final list of visitors:
  [
      Visitor {
          name: "bert",
          action: Accept,
          age: 45,
      },
```

```
    Visitor {
        name: "steve",
        action: AcceptWithNote {
            note: "Lactose-free milk is in the fridge",
        },
        age: 15,
    },
    Visitor {
        name: "fred",
        action: Refuse,
        age: 30,
    },
    Visitor {
        name: "joebob",
        action: Probation,
        age: 0,
    },
]
```

Wrap-Up

You achieved a lot in this chapter and put to use many of Rust's basic concepts, enough to write useful and fun programs. In particular, you learned:

- Printing and formatting text
- Working with strings
- Using for and loop for program flow
- Using if for conditional execution
- Arrays
- Structures
- Vectors
- Enumerations
- Match statements

In the next chapter, you'll put this knowledge to work and make your first Rust game.

CHAPTER 3

Build Your First Game with Rust

The previous chapters set down a solid foundation for installing and working with Rust. This chapter puts that knowledge to use and walks you through developing your first game, *Flappy Dragon*—a Flappy Bird clone.[1]

You'll start by adding a game engine to your project dependencies, which you'll use to implement your game loop. You'll then test the game loop with a simple "Hello" program. From there, you'll implement basic program flow with a *state machine*, add a player, simulate gravity, and make the player's dragon flap its wings. Finally, you'll add obstacles and scorekeeping to the game. By the end of this chapter, you'll have a complete game—completely built in Rust.

Before you begin building Flappy Dragon, you first need to understand the game loop.

Understanding the Game Loop

The terminal-based programs you wrote in Chapter 2, First Steps with Rust, on page 19, operate and execute top to bottom through the main() function, pausing for user input. Most games won't stop or pause whenever the player wants to press a key. In Flappy Dragon, the player's dragon continues to fall even if the player isn't touching the keyboard. For games to operate smoothly, they instead run a *game loop*.

The game loop initializes windowing, graphics, and other resources. It then runs every time the screen is refreshed—often 30, 60, or more times per second. Each pass through the loop, it calls your game's tick() function. A closer look at the game loop and what each step does is shown on page 46.

---

1.   https://flappybird.io/

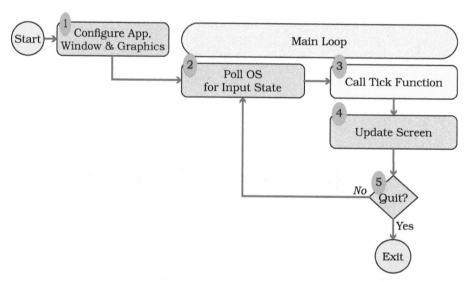

1. *Configure App, Window, and Graphics*: Configuring an application to work with your Operating System is no small undertaking and varies by platform. Displaying graphics can be an enormous endeavor—*Vulkan* or *OpenGL* can require hundreds of lines of code before the system is ready to draw a single triangle.

2. *Poll OS for Input State*: Polling for input state is also platform specific. Most Operating Systems provide a series of *events* representing what the user did with the mouse, keyboard, and window elements. The game engine translates these events into a standard format so that you don't need to worry about what type of computer you're targeting.

3. *Call Tick Function*: The tick() function provides your gameplay. bracket-lib, the game engine you'll use in this chapter, calls the tick() function on each pass through the main loop ("frame" and "tick" both represent this). Most game engines provide tick functionality in some form. *Unreal Engine* and *Unity* can attach tick functionality to objects—leading to hundreds of tick functions. Other engines provide only one and leave it to the developer to separate functionality. You'll implement your tick() function in Storing State, on page 49.

4. *Update Screen*: Once the game has updated, the game engine updates the screen. Again, the details vary by platform.

5. *Quit (Yes/No)*: Finally, the loop checks to see if the program should exit. If so, execution terminates and exits the game—again, the mechanism for this is Operating System specific. If the game should continue, the loop ensures that other programs continue to run smoothly by yielding

control back to the OS. The game loop then returns to step 2, displaying another frame.

A common problem for game developers is getting bogged down with platform-specific engine details, and running out of time and motivation to write a fun game. Most game developers use an *engine* to take care of the platform-specific parts, allowing them to focus on writing a fun game. In this chapter, you'll use *bracket-lib*.

What are Bracket-Lib and Bracket-Terminal?

bracket-lib is a Rust game programming library. It's designed as a simplified learning tool, abstracting the more complicated aspects of game development while retaining the concepts required for more complex games. It is a family of libraries, including random number generation, geometry, path-finding, color handling, and common game-development algorithms.

bracket-terminal is the display portion of bracket-lib. It provides an emulated console, and can work with various rendering platforms—ranging from text consoles to Web Assembly, including OpenGL, Vulkan, and Metal. In addition to consoles, it supports sprites and native OpenGL development. You can use bracket-lib to make graphical games, and console games like this:

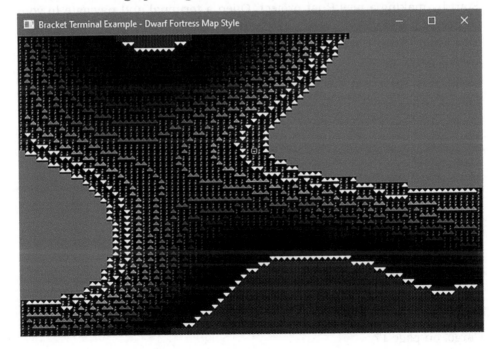

Herbert says:
Bracket-Lib is Open Source

I'm the primary author of the bracket-lib library family, but like many open source projects, this library rests upon the shoulders of giants—many users have contributed to its success.[a]

———————
a.   https://github.com/thebracket/bracket-lib

Create a New Project that Uses Bracket-Lib

When you create a game that uses a game loop, the first step is to create the program's basic structure. That means you:

1.   Create a project.
2.   Connect the project to the game engine.
3.   Display "Hello, World" text.

Creating the basic structure ensures that you have a solid game loop foundation on which to build.

Start by making a new Rust project. Open a terminal and navigate to your source code directory. Type cargo new flappy—as you did before in Starting a New Project with Cargo, on page 8. This command creates a basic "Hello, World" program.

Next, you need to add a dependency for bracket-lib, the engine you'll use in this project. You read about dependency handling in Package Management with Cargo, on page 17. Open Cargo.toml, and add a dependency for bracket-lib:

FirstGameFlappyAscii/hello_bterm/Cargo.toml
```
[package]
name = "hello_bterm"
version = "0.1.0"
authors = ["Herbert Wolverson <herberticus@gmail.com>"]
edition = "2018"

[dependencies]
bracket-lib = "~0.8.1"
```

The tilde (~) in the version number means "favor version 0.8.1, but accept patches from the 0.8 base." If bugs appear in 0.8.1, Cargo will download bug-fixes. You read about crate version options in Package Management with Cargo, on page 17.

Adding the bracket-lib library to your Cargo.toml file makes it available, but you still need to *use* it.

Hello, Bracket Terminal

Add this line to the top of your main.rs file:

FirstGameFlappyAscii/hello_bterm/src/main.rs
```
use bracket_lib::prelude::*;
```

The asterisk (*) is a *wildcard*. It means "use everything from bracket-lib." Everything you need from bracket-lib is exported via the prelude. This is a common convention for Rust crates but not mandatory. Using the prelude saves you from prefixing every call into the library with bracket-lib::prelude::. You'll learn more about preludes, and you'll make your own—in Organizing Your Imports With a Prelude, on page 78.

Now that you are using bracket-lib, you need to extend your program to store what it's doing. Data describing maps, progress, stats, and everything else you need to keep between frames is the game's *state*.

Storing State

The game loop runs by calling your application's tick() function with every frame. The tick() function doesn't know anything about your game, so you need a way to store the game's current status, known as the *game state*. Everything you need to preserve between frames is in your game's state. The state represents a snapshot of the current game.

Create a new, empty struct named State:

FirstGameFlappyAscii/hello_bterm/src/main.rs
```
struct State {}
```

Displaying "Hello, World" doesn't require any data storage, so there's no need to put variables inside your game state—yet.

Implementing Traits

Traits are a way to define shared functionality for objects.[2] Traits are similar to *interfaces* found in other languages, which you use to define a contract. If a trait is implemented, its functionality is available, and the structure meets trait requirements. You'll learn more about traits in Creating Traits, on page 204. Don't worry about the finer details yet.

---

2. https://doc.rust-lang.org/book/ch10-02-traits.html

Bracket-lib defines a trait for games state structures named GameState. GameState requires that the object implement a tick() function. You implement traits similarly to how you implement a method for a struct. Add the following to your program:

FirstGameFlappyAscii/hello_bterm/src/main.rs

```
❶ impl GameState for State {
❷     fn tick(&mut self, ctx: &mut BTerm) {
❸         ctx.cls();
❹         ctx.print(1, 1, "Hello, Bracket Terminal!");
    }
}
```

❶ This is similar to implementing functions for a structure, but you implement the trait for your struct.

❷ GameState requires that you implement a function named tick() with this signature. &mut self allows the tick function to access and change your State instance. ctx provides a window into the currently running bracket-terminal—accessing information like mouse position and keyboard input, and sending commands to draw to the window. You can think of the tick() function as the bridge between the game engine and your game.

❸ The ctx—short for "context"—provides functions for interacting with the game display. cls() clears the window. Most frames start by clearing the screen, ensuring that no residual data from previous frames gets rendered.

❹ print() provides an interface for printing text to your game window. It's similar to the println! you used in previous chapters but accepts a String rather than a format specifier. You can still format your strings by calling ctx.print(format!("{}", my_string)). [3]

You sent the print() function 1,1 as parameters. These are *screen-space coordinates*, representing where you want the text to appear. Bracket-lib defines 0,0 as the top-left of the window. In an 80x50 window, 79x49 is the bottom right. The coordinate system works like the image shown on page 51.

Now that you know how to put text on the screen, you need to *make* the screen! This doesn't always go as planned, so you need to implement some error handling.

---

3. https://doc.rust-lang.org/std/macro.format.html

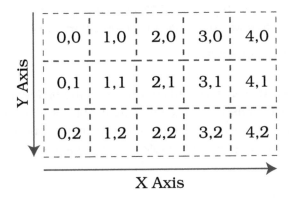

Handling Errors in the Main Function

The main() function needs to initialize bracket-lib, describing the type of window and game loop you want to create. Setup can fail, so the initialization returns a Result type.

Results are Rust's standard method for handling errors. Results are an enumeration—just like Option and the enumerations you made before. You can handle a Result in three major ways:

```
match my_result {
    Ok(a) => do_something_useful(a),
    Err(a) => handle_error(a),
}
```

Result is an enumeration - you can use match to select a response.

```
my_result.unwrap()
```

Unwrap like an option - and crash if an error occurred.

```
fn my_function() -> BError {
    ...
    my_result()?;
}
```

Pass errors to the parent function via ?

Calling unwrap is easy, but your program will crash if any error occurs. When you are using many functions that potentially return an error, littering your code with unwrap() calls can also make your code hard to read. Adding match statements for every function that might fail also makes for big, hard-to-read code. The ? mark operator can greatly simplify your code and keep it easy to read. The only requirement to use ? is that your function *must* return a Result type.

Bracket-lib provides a Result type named BError. Making your main function return a BError allows you to take advantage of the question mark operator:

FirstGameFlappyAscii/hello_bterm/src/main.rs
```
fn main() -> BError {
```

You're ready to set up bracket-lib. This library uses the *builder pattern*—a common Rust idiom is constructing complicated objects. The builder pattern takes advantage of function chaining to separate many options into individual function calls, providing more readable code than a giant list of parameters to a single function.

Using the Builder Pattern

Builders start with an initial constructor function that returns the builder. It's common to provide frequently used starting points. For example, bracket-terminal provides simple80x50() as a starting point because this is a frequently requested display mode.

Successive calls to the builder object add information to the build request. For example, with_title() adds text to the window's title bar, and with_font() lets you specify a display font.

When you've finished describing the object you want to create, call a build() function. This returns the completed object—or an error—containing your desired system.

Next, add the following to your main() function, replacing println!:

FirstGameFlappyAscii/hello_bterm/src/main.rs
```
❶ let context = BTermBuilder::simple80x50()
❷     .with_title("Flappy Dragon")
❸     .build()?;
```

❶ Start by requesting an 80x50 terminal.

❷ Request that the window be titled "Flappy Dragon."

❸ Call build() to finalize initialization, and store the resulting context in your context variable. The ? operator works because you changed main() to return a BError.

Now that you've created a terminal instance, you need to tell bracket-lib to start executing the game loop, and link the engine with your State so that bracket-lib knows where the tick() function is located:

FirstGameFlappyAscii/hello_bterm/src/main.rs
```
main_loop(context, State{})
```

You don't need a semicolon at the end of the call to main_loop—it returns a BError. Since main returns the same type, you can let Rust return the function result. Any error that occurs will be passed out of main—causing your program to crash and display the provided error message. main_loop starts the game loop and begins calling your tick() function on every frame.

Run the project with cargo run, and you'll see a window with the words "Hello, Bracket Terminal!" displayed in white on black:

```
Hello, Bracket Terminal!
```

In standard input/output programs, you can print most characters with the println! command. Bracket-lib is translating your characters into graphical sprites, and provides a more limited character set. The characters displayed are pictures—the library picks the one that matches up with the character you sent it, defined by the Codepage 437 character set.

Codepage 437: The IBM Extended ASCII Character Set

By default, bracket-lib uses a character set known as *Codepage 437*. This was the original font on DOS-based PCs and is commonly used for terminal output. In addition to letters and numbers, it provides a few symbols useful for representing simple games. The complete character set is listed in Appendix 1, ASCII/Codepage 437 Chart, on page 295.

The print() function automatically converts your text into the appropriate sprites, including Unicode representations of special characters.

Let's get started on game functionality.

Creating Different Game Modes

Games typically run in *modes*. Modes specify what the game should do on the current tick, for example, displaying the main menu or the game over screen. In computer science, this is often formalized as a *state machine*. It's a good idea to start by defining your game's basic mode structure, which acts as an outline for the rest of the program.

Flappy Dragon requires three modes:

1. Menu: The player is waiting at the main menu.
2. Playing: Game play is in progress.
3. End: The game is over.

Transitions between these modes are relatively straightforward:

Game modes are best represented as an enum. Enumerations allow you to limit the value of a variable to one of a set of possible states. Underneath the prelude import, add a GameMode enumeration to represent the available game modes:

FirstGameFlappyAscii/flappy_states/src/main.rs

```
❶ enum GameMode {
❷     Menu,
       Playing,
       End,
   }
```

❶ GameMode is an enum, like the ones you used in the treehouse example.

❷ Each possible game state is enumerated as an entry within the enum. Flappy Dragon is either displaying the menu, playing the game, or displaying the "game over" screen.

You need to store the current mode in your State. Extend the empty State struct to include a GameMode variable, and create a constructor to initialize it—as you did in Categorizing with Enumerations, on page 38:

FirstGameFlappyAscii/flappy_states/src/main.rs

```
struct State {
    mode: GameMode,
}

impl State {
    fn new() -> Self {
        State {
            mode: GameMode::Menu,
        }
    }
}
```

Replace your state initialization in main with a call to the new constructor:

FirstGameFlappyAscii/flappy_states/src/main.rs

```
main_loop(context, State::new())
```

According to the current game mode, knowing what mode you are in provides half the picture; the other half is to act differently.

Reacting to the Current Mode

Your game's tick() function should act like traffic police, directing program flow based upon the current mode. The match statement is perfect for this. Your tick function no longer needs to clear the screen—individual modes will handle this. Replace your tick function with the following code:

```
FirstGameFlappyAscii/flappy_states/src/main.rs
impl GameState for State {
    fn tick(&mut self, ctx: &mut BTerm) {
        match self.mode {
            GameMode::Menu => self.main_menu(ctx),
            GameMode::End => self.dead(ctx),
            GameMode::Playing => self.play(ctx),
        }
    }
}
```

You'll write *stub* versions of the functions used by the tick() function. "Stubbing" parts of your program is helpful when developing a larger program. It lets you concentrate on developing basic program flow, rather than diving too deeply into the complex details of implementation. When you create a stub, remember to fill it in later. Adding a // TODO comment can help with that.

Play Function Stub

The stub version of play() instantly ends the game by setting the program mode to End. Implement a new method in State:

```
impl State {
  ...
  fn play(&mut self, ctx: &mut BTerm) {
      // TODO: Fill in this stub later
      self.mode = GameMode::End;
  }
```

Main Menu

The main menu is a little more complicated. It needs to display the menu and respond to user input. It also needs to be able to change the mode to Playing and reset all game states, making the game ready to play again with a fresh copy.

Then, it implements another method in State that restarts the game. For now, it only sets the game's mode to Playing:

```
impl State {
  ...
  fn restart(&mut self) {
      self.mode = GameMode::Playing;
  }
```

Add a main_menu function to your State implementation (inside the impl State block). The main menu function starts by clearing the screen and printing menu options:

FirstGameFlappyAscii/flappy_states/src/main.rs
```
fn main_menu(&mut self, ctx: &mut BTerm) {
    ctx.cls();
    ctx.print_centered(5, "Welcome to Flappy Dragon");
    ctx.print_centered(8, "(P) Play Game");
    ctx.print_centered(9, "(Q) Quit Game");
```

print_centered() is an extended version of print() that centers text on a line, given only a y position.

Now that the player is offered some menu options, you need to check for input that triggers them. The BTerm object includes a Key variable that holds keyboard input state. The player may be pressing a key—or they may not. This is represented in Rust with an Option type.

Rust provides a shortened version of match for matching against a single case named if let. Option can only contain None or Some(data) so the shorthand can save you some typing. if let and match work the same way:

```
match my_option {
    Some( my_value ) => do_something_with(my_value),
    _ => {} ◀——— Do nothing
}
```
=
```
if let Some(my_value) = my_option {
    do_something_with(my_value);
}
```

You can use an else statement at the end of an if let, just like an if statement.

Use if let to extract the value of Key if there is one, and a match expression to determine what key was pressed and act accordingly. _ => {} directs Rust to ignore any options you didn't list. Rust treats _ as "anything"—you can use it to ignore variables or indicate a default option in a match. Finish your main_menu function with this code:

FirstGameFlappyAscii/flappy_states/src/main.rs
```
❶     if let Some(key) = ctx.key {
          match key {
❷             VirtualKeyCode::P => self.restart(),
❸             VirtualKeyCode::Q => ctx.quitting = true,
              _ => {}
          }
      }
} // Close the function
```

❶ Use if let to run this code block if the user presses a key and extract the key's value into key.

❷ If the user pressed P, restart the game by calling the restart() function.

❸ If the user pressed Q, set ctx.quitting to true. This instructs bracket-lib that you are ready to terminate your program.

Game Over Menu

The game over menu is similar to the main menu. It prints text indicating that the game is over and offers an option to play again or quit the program. Add this function to your State implementation:

```
FirstGameFlappyAscii/flappy_states/src/main.rs
fn dead(&mut self, ctx: &mut BTerm) {
    ctx.cls();
    ctx.print_centered(5, "You are dead!");
    ctx.print_centered(8, "(P) Play Again");
    ctx.print_centered(9, "(Q) Quit Game");

    if let Some(key) = ctx.key {
        match key {
            VirtualKeyCode::P => self.restart(),
            VirtualKeyCode::Q => ctx.quitting = true,
            _ => {}
        }
    }
}
```

Completed Game Control Flow

Run the program with cargo run. The basic, mode-based flow of the game works:

```
❰ Welcome to Flappy Dragon
  (P) Play Game
  (Q) Quit Game
⇒ p
❰ You are dead!
  (P) Play Again
  (Q) Quit Game
⇒ q
```

You've completed the game mode system. The next step is to add the player and some game logic.

Adding the Player

In Flappy Dragon, the player battles gravity while trying to avoid obstacles and stay alive. To keep the dragon in flight, the player needs to press the SPACEBAR to flap the dragon's wings and gain upward momentum. For this to work, you need to store the current game attributes of the dragon. Add a new struct to your main.rs file, after the enum declaration:

FirstGameFlappyAscii/flappy_player/src/main.rs
```
struct Player {
❶    x: i32,
❷    y: i32,
❸    velocity: f32,
}
```

❶ The x position of the player. This is a *world-space* position—specified in terminal characters. The player will always render on the left of the screen. x represents progress through the level.

❷ The vertical position of the player in screen-space.

❸ The player's vertical velocity. This is an f32, a floating-point number. Unlike integer types, floating-point numbers can contain a fractional portion expressed as a decimal. A floating-point number could contain the value 1.5; an equivalent integer would be equal to 1 or 2. Using whole integers to represent velocity can work, but gives very sudden—and unfair—falls. Using a floating-point number allows you to use fractional velocity numbers—and provides a much smoother gameplay experience.

You also need to write a constructor, initializing a new Player instance to a specified starting position and a velocity of zero:

FirstGameFlappyAscii/flappy_player/src/main.rs
```
impl Player {
    fn new(x: i32, y: i32) -> Self {
        Player {
            x,
            y,
❶            velocity: 0.0,
        }
    }
}
```

❶ Floating-point types (f32) *must* be fractional—add a .0 to whole numbers.

Now that you know where the player is, let's draw them on the screen.

Rendering the Player

You are going to render the player as a yellow @ symbol, towards the left of the screen. Add a Render function to the Player implementation:

FirstGameFlappyAscii/flappy_player/src/main.rs
```
fn render(&mut self, ctx: &mut BTerm) {
❶    ctx.set(
❷        0,
```

```
❸        self.y,
❹        YELLOW,
         BLACK,
❺        to_cp437('@')
    );
}
```

❶ set() is a 'bracket-lib' function that sets a single character on the screen.

❷ The x coordinate on the *screen* at which to render the character.

❸ The y coordinate on the *screen* at which to render the character.

❹ bracket-lib includes a set of named colors for your use—derived from the HTML named color list. Alternatively, you can use RGB::from_u8() to specify red/green/blue values in the 0-254 range, or RGB::from_hex() to specify HTML-style colors.

❺ The character to render. The function to_cp437() converts a Unicode symbol from your source code to the matching Codepage 437 character number.

Now that you can draw the player, let's add gravity to the game.

Falling to Your Inevitable Death

Like death and taxes, gravity is difficult to avoid. The dragon should continually fall downward except when it has upward momentum from flapping. The velocity variable in your Player structure represents vertical momentum. Each turn, you add a value representing gravity to the velocity, unless you achieve terminal velocity. You then modify the player's y position by that amount.

Implement another function for the player:

FirstGameFlappyAscii/flappy_player/src/main.rs
```
fn gravity_and_move(&mut self) {
❶    if self.velocity < 2.0 {
❷        self.velocity += 0.2;
    }
❸    self.y += self.velocity as i32;
❹    self.x += 1;
    if self.y < 0 {
        self.y = 0;
    }
}
```

❶ Check for terminal velocity: only apply gravity if the downward momentum is less than two.

❷ The += operator means add the right-hand expression or value to the left-hand variable. Adding the current velocity moves the player up or down.

❸ Add the velocity to the player's y position. Rust won't let you add floating-point and integer numbers together, so you have to convert the velocity to an integer with an i32. This number will always round down.

❹ Even though you're not moving the character on the screen, you need to know how far it has progressed through the level. Incrementing x lets you keep track of this.

Flapping Your Wings

It's time to simulate flapping the dragon's wings. Add another method to the player struct implementation:

FirstGameFlappyAscii/flappy_player/src/main.rs
```
fn flap(&mut self) {
    self.velocity = -2.0;
}
```

The flap function sets the player's velocity to -2.0. It's a negative number, so this will move the character upward—remember that 0 is the top of the screen.

Activating the Player

Now that the player is defined, you need to add an instance of the Player to your game's state and initialize them in the constructor. You also need a variable named frame_time (an f32). This tracks the time accumulated between frames to control the game's speed.

FirstGameFlappyAscii/flappy_player/src/main.rs
```
struct State {
    player: Player,
    frame_time: f32,
    mode: GameMode,
}

impl State {
    fn new() -> Self {
        State {
            player: Player::new(5, 25),
            frame_time: 0.0,
            mode: GameMode::Menu,
        }
    }
}
```

The restart function needs to run whenever a new game starts, resetting the game state and indicating that the game is in progress. Modify the restart function to reset the player when the game restarts:

FirstGameFlappyAscii/flappy_player/src/main.rs
```
fn restart(&mut self) {
    self.player = Player::new(5, 25);
    self.frame_time = 0.0;
    self.mode = GameMode::Playing;
}
```

Constants

Magic numbers are often considered a *code smell*—a sign of a potential problem. They can be confusing to people who read your code (including yourself if you come back to it later). Your game logic will refer to the size of the console (80×50), but littering your code with these numbers has two problems: if you decide to change the terminal size, you have to find every single one to change, and it doesn't make your *intent* clear when reading the code.

Code Is like Underwear

 If your code smells, you should consider changing it—just like underwear. Clippy has a keen sense of smell and can often tell you when your code needs changing.

Rust supports *constants* to help with this.[4] A constant never changes without recompiling the program. It's a lot easier to read SCREEN_WIDTH than 80 and remember what 80 means. It's also much easier to change SCREEN_WIDTH once, rather than finding every 80 in your program. Unlike let declarations, constants must declare a type. After your enum declaration, add two constants representing the screen size, and a third that indicates the duration of a frame in milliseconds:

FirstGameFlappyAscii/flappy_player/src/main.rs
```
const SCREEN_WIDTH : i32 = 80;
const SCREEN_HEIGHT : i32 = 50;
const FRAME_DURATION : f32 = 75.0;
```

Your constants are in place—let's put them to work.

Playing the Game

Modify the play function to call the new functionality:

FirstGameFlappyAscii/flappy_player/src/main.rs
```
fn play(&mut self, ctx: &mut BTerm) {
❶    ctx.cls_bg(NAVY);
❷    self.frame_time += ctx.frame_time_ms;
    if self.frame_time > FRAME_DURATION {
```

---
4. https://doc.rust-lang.org/reference/items/constant-items.html

```
        self.frame_time = 0.0;

        self.player.gravity_and_move();
    }
❸   if let Some(VirtualKeyCode::Space) = ctx.key {
        self.player.flap();
    }
    self.player.render(ctx);
    ctx.print(0, 0, "Press SPACE to flap.");
❹   if self.player.y > SCREEN_HEIGHT {
        self.mode = GameMode::End;
    }
}
```

❶ cls_bg() is just like cls(), but it lets you specify the background color. NAVY is a named color from bracket-lib, representing navy blue.

❷ The tick() function runs as fast as it can—often 60 or more times per second. Your player doesn't have superhuman reflexes, so you need to slow the game down. The context provides a variable named frame_time_ms containing the time elapsed since the last time tick() was called. Add this to your state's frame_time. If it exceeds the FRAME_DURATION constant, then it's time to run the physics simulation and reset your frame_time to zero.

❸ If the user is pressing the SPACEBAR, call the flap() function you implemented for the player. You *aren't* restricting this by frame time—if you do, the keyboard will be unresponsive during "wait" frames.

❹ Check if the player has fallen off the bottom of the screen. If they have, change the GameMode to End.

Flapping Your Wings

Run the game now with cargo run. Press P to play the game, and you'll see a yellow @ representing the player. It falls toward the bottom and flaps upward when you press SPACEBAR. When it falls off the bottom of the window, the game mode transitions to the game over menu.

You are halfway to making Flappy Dragon. Your dragon can flap their wings—now you need to add some obstacles for them to avoid.

Creating Obstacles and Keeping Score

The other key part of Flappy Dragon is dodging obstacles. Let's add walls to the game, with gaps through which the dragon may fly. Add another struct to your program:

FirstGameFlappyAscii/flappy_dragon/src/main.rs
```
struct Obstacle {
  x: i32,
  gap_y: i32,
  size: i32
}
```

Obstacles have an x value, defining their position in *world-space* (to match the player's world-space x value). The gap_y variable defines the center of the gap through which the dragon may pass. size defines the length of the gap in the obstacle.

You'll need to define a constructor for the obstacle:

FirstGameFlappyAscii/flappy_dragon/src/main.rs
```
impl Obstacle {
  fn new(x: i32, score: i32) -> Self {
    let mut random = RandomNumberGenerator::new();
    Obstacle {
      x,
➤     gap_y: random.range(10, 40),
      size: i32::max(2, 20 - score)
    }
  }
}
```

Computers are not very good at generating genuinely random numbers. However, there are many algorithms for generating "pseudo-random" numbers. bracket-lib includes one known as xorshift, wrapped in convenient access functions.

The constructor creates a new RandomNumberGenerator and uses it to place the obstacle at a random position. range() produces a random number *exclusively* in the specified range—obstacles will have a y value between 10 and 39. The gap's size is the maximum (obtained via i32::max) of 20 minus the player's score, or 2. This ensures that the walls close in as the player progresses, but the gap never shrinks below a size of 2.

Now that you know where your obstacles are, let's add them to the screen.

Rendering Obstacles

Obstacles should render as walls using the | character.

The x screen location of the obstacle requires conversion from world-space to screen-space. The player is always at 0 in screen-space, but has a *world* position defined in player.x. The obstacle's x value is also in this world-space. You can convert to screen-space by subtracting the player's x location from the obstacle's x location.

Obstacles extend from the ceiling to the top of the gap, and then from the bottom of the gap to the floor. This is represented with two loops on the y axis: from 0 to the top of the gap, and the bottom of the gap to the screen's height. The top of the gap is the gap's y position, minus *half* of its size. Likewise, the bottom is the gap's y position plus half of its size. You can visualize the spacing like this:

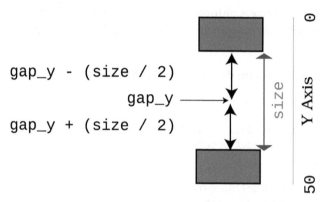

A pair of for loops is sufficient for this task. Here's the obstacle rendering function:

FirstGameFlappyAscii/flappy_dragon/src/main.rs

```rust
fn render(&mut self, ctx: &mut BTerm, player_x : i32) {
  let screen_x = self.x - player_x;
  let half_size = self.size / 2;

  // Draw the top half of the obstacle
  for y in 0..self.gap_y - half_size {
    ctx.set(
      screen_x,
      y,
      RED,
      BLACK,
      to_cp437('|'),
    );
  }

  // Draw the bottom half of the obstacle
  for y in self.gap_y + half_size..SCREEN_HEIGHT {
    ctx.set(
      screen_x,
      y,
      RED,
      BLACK,
      to_cp437('|'),
    );
  }
}
```

You won't encounter anything new in this code. You use for loops to iterate the length of the wall segments, and call ctx.set to render the wall characters. Now you have the walls rendering onscreen. Next up, you should ensure that the player can crash into them.

Crashing Into Walls

You need to calculate if the dragon has crashed into a wall. Implement a new function for Obstacle, and name it hit_obstacle:

```
FirstGameFlappyAscii/flappy_dragon/src/main.rs
fn hit_obstacle(&self, player: &Player) -> bool {
  let half_size = self.size / 2;
  let does_x_match = player.x == self.x;
  let player_above_gap = player.y < self.gap_y - half_size;
  let player_below_gap = player.y > self.gap_y + half_size;
  does_x_match && (player_above_gap || player_below_gap)
}
```

❶ If the player's x coordinate matches that of the obstacle, there might be a collision.

❷ Compare the player's y coordinate with the obstacle's upper gap.

❸ You can use parentheses to group logical checks together. In English, this comparison expands to "If the player's x coordinate matches that of the obstacle, and the player's y coordinate is either above or below the gap, then a collision has occurred."

This function receives a borrowed reference to the player as a parameter—using it to determine the player's location. It then checks whether the player's x coordinate matches the obstacle's x; if it doesn't, then no collision occurred. The second part of the comparison uses && to represent and—and places the condition in parentheses. The condition in parentheses is evaluated together. The function is checking that the x condition AND the y condition are both true.

If the player is at the obstacle, and the y value is less than the gap location minus half its size or greater than the gap location plus half its size, then the player has hit the obstacle, and this function will return true (the player has hit a wall). Otherwise, it returns false.

Keeping Score and Obstacle State

Flappy Dragon counts how many obstacles the player avoids and uses this number for the score. The State object needs to include the player's current score and the current obstacle. Extend your State struct and constructor to include these:

FirstGameFlappyAscii/flappy_dragon/src/main.rs
```
struct State {
  player: Player,
  frame_time: f32,
  obstacle: Obstacle,
  mode: GameMode,
  score: i32,
}

impl State {
  fn new() -> Self {
    State {
      player: Player::new(5, 25),
      frame_time: 0.0,
      obstacle: Obstacle::new(SCREEN_WIDTH, 0),
      mode: GameMode::Menu,
      score: 0,
    }
  }
```

Including the Obstacle and Score in the Play Function

Now that the logic for obstacles is complete, include them in the play function. Extend the function as follows:

FirstGameFlappyAscii/flappy_dragon/src/main.rs
```
   ctx.print(0, 0, "Press SPACE to flap.");
❶ ctx.print(0, 1, &format!("Score: {}", self.score));

❷ self.obstacle.render(ctx, self.player.x);
❸ if self.player.x > self.obstacle.x {
     self.score += 1;
     self.obstacle = Obstacle::new(
        self.player.x + SCREEN_WIDTH, self.score
     );
   }
   if self.player.y > SCREEN_HEIGHT ||
       self.obstacle.hit_obstacle(&self.player)
   {
     self.mode = GameMode::End;
   }
```

❶ Display the player's current score underneath the instructions. This uses the format!() macro. format!() accepts the same formatting and placeholders as println!(), but instead of sending the result to standard output, it returns a string.

❷ Call the obstacle's render() function to add it to the screen.

❸ If the player has *passed* the obstacle, then increase their score by one and replace the obstacle with a new one. The 'x' position of the obstacle is the player's current position plus the screen width—placing a new obstacle on the right-hand side of the screen.

Adding the Score to the Game Over Screen

As a finishing touch, adjust the game over screen to display the player's final score. This is the same as displaying it in the main game loop:

```
FirstGameFlappyAscii/flappy_dragon/src/main.rs
fn dead(&mut self, ctx: &mut BTerm) {
  ctx.cls();
  ctx.print_centered(5, "You are dead!");
  ctx.print_centered(6, &format!("You earned {} points", self.score));
```

Reset the Score and Obstacles When Restarting

Open the restart() method and add the following lines to reset the score and obstacle state when restarting the game:

```
FirstGameFlappyAscii/flappy_dragon/src/main.rs
fn restart(&mut self) {
  self.player = Player::new(5, 25);
  self.frame_time = 0.0;
➤ self.obstacle = Obstacle::new(SCREEN_WIDTH, 0);
➤ self.mode = GameMode::Playing;
  self.score = 0;
}
```

Flappy Dragon

Run the program and enjoy the completed game:

Wrap-Up

Congratulations, you just wrote your first game using Rust. All of the basic elements of the original *Flappy Bird* are present, and you can even compete for high scores.

You have plenty of ways to improve Flappy Dragon. Here are some exercises to try:

- Play with the gravity level, velocity changes, and game speed. Notice how different values can radically change the feel of the game.

- See if you can add graphics for the walls and dragon.

- Consider making the graphics bigger and the overall play area smaller to better match *Flappy Bird*.

- Investigate bracket-lib's "flexible console" and change the player coordinates to floating-point numbers for smoother movement.

- Add color and visual flair to the menus.

- Try animating the dragon.

A version of Flappy Dragon, including most of these enhancements, is included with the book's source code. You can find it in the flappy_bonus directory. Thanks to Bevouliin for the dragon artwork.[5] Flappy Dragon Enhanced looks like this:

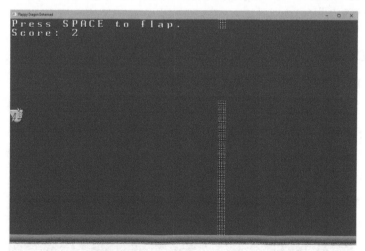

In the next chapter, you'll begin designing a more ambitious game: a roguelike dungeon crawler.

---

5. https://opengameart.org/content/flappy-dragon-sprite-sheets

Part II

Building a Dungeon Crawler

Now that you've mastered the basics of Rust and used it to make your first game, it's time for a more ambitious project: a dungeon crawler game. As you build this new game, you'll learn the core concepts required to master intermediate-level Rust.

CHAPTER 4

Design a Dungeon Crawler

Diving head first into writing a larger game is fun, but it's often a bad idea. With a little bit of planning, you can save yourself a lot of anxiety.

You don't need to create an enormous, formal *Game Design Document*, but doing some planning before you leap into writing code is always a good idea. A well-designed plan can help to keep you motivated by showing regular progress. Early planning enables you to figure out if you're biting off more than you can chew and helps you determine the structure your game will follow.

In this chapter, you'll follow the template provided in Appendix 2, Short Game Design Documents, on page 297, and outline the game you're going to make in this section of the book.

Adding Headings to Your Design Document

The Dungeon Crawler you'll create in the next few chapters is quite a small project, and it's assumed that you're either working alone or with a friend. That means the design document can be small—perfect for the *Short Game Design Document* template. In this section, you'll see all of the parts of a completed design outline for *Rusty Roguelike*.

Let's start working through the headings.

Naming Your Game

Names are difficult, and it's pretty unlikely that the first name you pick will be the name of your game. The working title for the Dungeon Crawler is *Rusty Roguelike*:

Project Name: Rusty Roguelike

Short Description

Keeping with the theme of a Dungeon Crawler, the game sees the adventurer arrive in a randomly generated dungeon. The player guides their adventurer around the dungeon, defeating monsters and collecting power-ups until they find the *Amulet of Yala* ("Yet Another Lost Amulet") and win the game.

Here's the short description for *Rusty Roguelike*:

Short Description
A dungeon crawler with procedurally generated levels, monsters of increasing difficulty, and turn-based movement.

Story

Rusty Roguelike has a very simple story. Feel free to write a better one for your game. The story entry for the short design document is as follows:

Story
The hero's hometown is suffering from a plague of monsters. Welling up from the deep, they seem unstoppable. Legend tells of the Amulet of Yala - Yet Another Lost Amulet - that can be used to stem the tide. After a long night at the tavern, the hero promises to save the day - and sets forth into the dungeon.

Basic Game Loops

The game loop for the book's Dungeon Crawler is very similar to the example in the short design document appendix. It looks like this:

Basic Game Loops
1. Enter dungeon level.
2. Explore, revealing the map.
3. Encounter enemies whom the player fights or flees from.
4. Find power-ups and use them to strengthen the player.
5. Locate the exit to the level - go to 1.

Minimum Viable Product

The Minimum Viable Product (MVP) is probably the most important part of a short design document. It tells you what you *must* accomplish to make the game—everything else is a bonus. The first chapters of this part of the book walk you through building *Rusty Roguelike's* MVP.

The MVP is shown on page 73.

Minimum Viable Product
1. Create a basic dungeon map
2. Place the player and let them walk around
3. Spawn monsters, draw them, and let the player kill them by walking into them.
4. Add health and a combat system that uses it.
5. Add healing potions.
6. Display a "game over" screen when the player dies.
7. Add the Amulet of Yala to the level and let the player win by reaching it.

Stretch Goals

Stretch goals are niceties that improve the basic game design. Once *Rusty Roguelike's* MVP is in place, you'll add these features:

Stretch Goals
1. Add Fields-of-View.
2. Add more interesting dungeon designs.
3. Add some dungeon themes.
4. Add multiple layers to the dungeon, with the Amulet on the last one.
5. Add varied weapons to the game.
6. Move to a data-driven design for spawning enemies.
7. Consider some visual effects to make combat more visceral.
8. Consider keeping score.

Wrap-Up

The MVP targets and stretch goals closely align with chapters in this book. That's deliberate: the chapter sections serve as *sprints*. The sprints are designed to be achievable in one or two sessions, and to show your progress with each section. This is important to your design so that you aren't left plodding through many sessions of development in the hopes that your final product will be fun.

A typical game development experience is that you'll read this chapter and appendix, nod sagely, and then dive into making something anyway. That's OK—we've all done it. As you gain experience, you can hammer out prototype games quickly with minimal planning. As you gain experience—and your ambitions grow—you'll realize the benefits of a bit of planning. Don't overdo it. A small plan is better than no plan, and a plan that takes more than a short session to write is overkill for hobby games. Keep it simple and your design document will help you achieve your goals.

Now that you've sketched out the design for a Dungeon Crawler, let's get started with the first sprint—drawing a map and making a player run around it.

CHAPTER 5

Build a Dungeon Crawler

In the previous chapter, you designed a dungeon crawler game. In this chapter, you'll start assembling the building blocks that make up the design, leaving you with an adventurer able to walk around a randomly generated dungeon. You'll start by dividing your code into modules, taming complexity as the program grows—and helping you isolate bugs. You'll then learn to store a map in a structure of tiles, and how this leads to an efficient and simple map rendering system. Your next step is to add a player and make them move around the map—including not walking through walls. Finally, you'll implement a random map generation system—carving out a dungeon similar to the original *Rogue* or *Nethack*. Mastering these building blocks will give you the know-how you need to make tile-based games—you can draw a tile map, and the player can navigate it.

All of your code so far has been contained in a single main.rs file. As your game grows, you'll find it easier to put similar code together in *modules*.

Dividing Your Code Into Modules

You *can* write huge programs in one file, but dividing your code into smaller sections—known as *modules* in Rust—offers significant advantages:

- It's a lot easier to find your Map functionality in a file named map.rs than it is to remember that it's somewhere around line 500 of an ever-growing main.rs.

- Cargo can compile modules concurrently, leading to much better compilation times.

- Bugs are easier to find in self-contained code that limits linkages to other sections of code.

Modules may either be a single .rs file or a directory. In this chapter, you'll use single file modules. You'll learn to create directory-based modules in Multi-File Modules, on page 111.

Crates and Modules

Rust programs are divided into *crates* and *modules*. Crates are large groups of code with their own Cargo.toml file. Your game is a crate. So is bracket-lib—every dependency you specify in Cargo is a crate. Crates are mainly independent of one another, but may each have dependencies upon other crates—and use code from them. A module is a section of code within a crate, identified by being in a separate file or directory. You can make your game code easier to navigate by grouping related code—e.g., placing all map-related code inside a map module.

Crates and modules act as *namespaces*. bracket-lib::prelude refers to the bracket-lib crate's prelude module. You can reference the current crate with crate::. For example, once you have a map module, you can refer to it through crate::map anywhere within your program. Modules form a hierarchy, with the crate at the top. Modules can contain other modules, and their namespaces grow to match. For example, map::region or map::region::chunk—you can keep nesting downwards. Crates, modules, and scopes relate to each other like this:

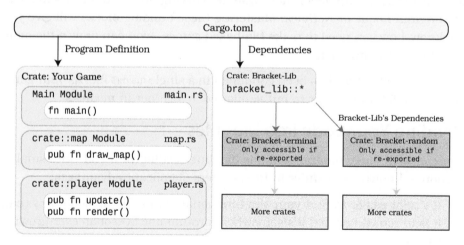

Make a Stub Map Module

Start by making a new project with cargo new dungeoncrawl. Then follow the same steps you used in Hello, Bracket Terminal, on page 49, to display "Hello, Bracket World" in a bracket-lib terminal. Make sure you include bracket-lib = "~0.8.1" in the [dependencies] section of your Cargo.toml file.

Add a new file to your src directory and name it map.rs. Leave it empty for now. This file will contain your map module.

Rust needs to know that you want to include your new module in the program compilation. The mod keyword includes a module in your project. At the top of main.rs, add the line:

```
mod map;
```

This code imports the map module into the global scope and sets up the map:: prefix. Within main.rs, items declared in map may be accessed as map::my_function(). You can also include use map::my_function and access the function as just my_function().

Module Scoping

Modules are self-contained and have their own scope. By default, everything in the module is private to that module. If you try to access an item inside the module, an error message reminds you that you don't have access. The solution is to make your shared module entries *public* with the pub keyword.

You can make most things public:

- Functions (e.g. pub fn my_function())
- Structs (e.g. pub struct MyStruct)
- Enumerations (e.g. pub enum MyEnum)
- Implemented functions (e.g. impl MyStruct { pub fn my_function() })

You can also make individual members of a structure public (they default to being private), for example:

```
pub struct MyPublicStructure {
  pub public_int : i32,
  private_int : i32
}
```

Within your module, you have complete access to private_int. From outside the module, attempting to access it directly will result in a compilation error. It's often good design to keep much of the contents of a module private, and only publish a carefully designed set of functions and structures. This is especially true when you're working with other people—the public elements of a module become the entry and exit points, and each team member does not have to learn the intricate details of how every module works.

The Law of Demeter

The *Law of Demeter* outlines this design principle: each module should have only limited knowledge about other units, and should only talk to its friends. This design promotes *loose coupling*, making it a lot easier to debug your program. If functionality is contained within a narrowly defined area, it's much easier to find the bugs.[1] *The Pragmatic Programmer [HT00]* includes an excellent discussion of this topic.

Organizing Your Imports With a Prelude

Prefixing every map access with map:: or crate::map:: is unwieldy and will get more cumbersome as you add more modules. When you access a Rust library, it's common for the library author to have placed everything you need in a convenient *prelude*. You used bracket-lib's prelude in Hello, Bracket Terminal, on page 49. You can simplify module access by making your own prelude to export common functionality to the rest of the program. Add the following to your main.rs file:

BasicDungeonCrawler/dungeon_crawl_map/src/main.rs
```
❶ mod map;

❷ mod prelude {
❸     pub use bracket_lib::prelude::*;
❹     pub const SCREEN_WIDTH: i32 = 80;
       pub const SCREEN_HEIGHT: i32 = 50;
❺     pub use crate::map::*;
   }
❻ use prelude::*;
```

❶ Add the module to your project with mod.

❷ The mod keyword can also be used to declare a new module in your source code. Because this is the top level of your crate, you don't need to make it public—modules branching from crate are visible throughout your program.

❸ Publicly using the bracket_lib prelude *re-exports* it inside your prelude. Anything that uses your prelude also uses bracket_lib.

❹ Adding pub to constants makes them public. Declaring them in your prelude makes them available to any section of code that uses your prelude.

---

1.   https://en.wikipedia.org/wiki/Law_of_Demeter

❺ You imported map into your main scope. Your module can reference the main scope as crate::. Re-export the map as a public module available from within your prelude.

❻ Finally, use your prelude to make it available to the main scope in main.rs.

Any module that uses your prelude now has access to all of bracket-lib and your map module.

Accessing Other Modules

Modules are organized as a tree. When you import access to other modules with use, you have several ways of accessing different parts of the module tree.

- super:: accesses the module immediately above your module in the tree.

- crate:: accesses the root of the tree, main.rs.

Set Up Your Map Module

Open map.rs. Add the following code to import the prelude, and create a constant defining the number of tiles in the map:

BasicDungeonCrawler/dungeon_crawl_map/src/map.rs
```
use crate::prelude::*;
const NUM_TILES: usize = (SCREEN_WIDTH * SCREEN_HEIGHT) as usize;
```

NUM_TILES is a constant that's calculated from other constants. Constants may *only* include other constants (including constant functions). This is a good way to keep your code clean; if you change SCREEN_WIDTH, the map size will automatically change when you recompile the program.

What Is a USize?

 Most types in Rust are always the same size. i32 will *always* give you a 32-bit integer. i64 will always be 64 bits in size. usize is a special case. It uses the preferred bit size for your CPU. If you have a 64-bit computer, usize will be 64 bits. Rust commonly uses usize to index collections and arrays.

Storing the Dungeon Map

Most games include a map, typically an array of *tiles*. For a dungeon crawler game, the map structure represents the dungeon layout. Platform games use maps to represent the location of ledges, platforms, and ladders. A *Minesweeper* game represents the discovered areas and the positions of mines on the map. Most two-dimensional games represent their map as a series of tiles in a grid pattern. Each tile has a *type* describing how that tile is rendered—and what happens if you try to enter it.

You'll represent your map as a vector. Each entry in the vector represents one tile, so for an 80x50 map you will have 4,000 tiles. Tiles represent portions of the map, and the same tile graphic is re-used to represent tiles of a particular type. *Entities*—such as the player or any monsters—are overlaid on top:

Each map graphic is a tile, arranged in a grid.

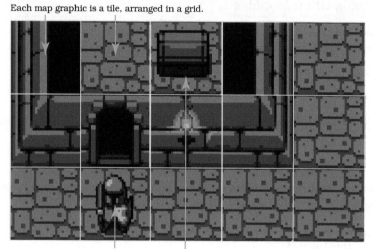

Entities—the knight and the chest— are rendered on top of the tile grid.

Represent Your Tiles

Tiles are limited to a pre-defined set of tile types, making them perfect for an enum. In map.rs, define a *public* enumeration named TileType with entries for walls and floors:

BasicDungeonCrawler/dungeon_crawl_map/src/map.rs
```
#[derive(Copy, Clone, PartialEq)]
pub enum TileType {
    Wall,
    Floor,
}
```

You'll notice that the code includes a derive list. The derivations are:

- Clone adds a clone() function to the type. Calling mytile.clone() makes a deep copy of the variable without affecting the original. If you clone a struct, everything the struct contains will also be cloned. This is useful when you want to safely work with a clone of some data with no risk of altering the original—or when you need to work around the borrow checker.

- Copy changes the default action when assigning a TileType from one variable to another. Instead of *moving* the value, it takes a copy. Smaller types are often faster when you copy them around. Clippy will warn you if you are borrowing a variable and it would be faster to copy it.

- PartialEq adds code that allows you to compare TileType values with the == operator.

You marked TileType as public, so the wildcard in your prelude means that any part of the program that uses the prelude can use the TileType enumeration.

For now, you'll represent walls with # and the player with an @ symbol—just like you did with Flappy Dragon. Now that you've defined what a map tile can contain, it's time to build a map.

Create an Empty Map

Make a new Map struct, containing a vector of tiles. Notice that the structure and the tiles member are public—accessible from outside the module:

```
BasicDungeonCrawler/dungeon_crawl_map/src/map.rs
pub struct Map {
    pub tiles: Vec<TileType>,
}
```

You also need to add a constructor for your Map type:

```
BasicDungeonCrawler/dungeon_crawl_map/src/map.rs
impl Map {
pub fn new() -> Self {
        Self {
            tiles: vec![TileType::Floor; NUM_TILES],
        }
    }
```

The constructor uses an extended form of the vec! macro to create NUM_TILES number of entries each set to TileType::Floor, creating a map consisting entirely of floors.

Index the Map

Vectors are indexed on a single dimension, so you need a way to transform map locations (x,y) into vector indices. This transformation is known as *striding*.

This book will use *row-first* encoding. Each row of the map will be stored together, in x order. The next set of entries will contain the second row. A 5x3 map would be indexed as shown in the image on page 82.

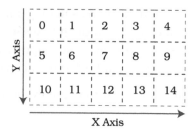

This allows you to calculate the index of a tile from x and y coordinates as follows:

```
let index = (y * WIDTH) + x;
```

You can calculate the reciprocal—the x and y coordinates represented by an index—with:

```
let x = index % WIDTH;
let y = index / WIDTH;
```

The % symbol is *modulus*—the remainder from a division. Note that dividing integers *always* rounds down.

Row-First, Column-First, or Morton Encoding

You can index your map vector in different ways. *Y-first*, illustrated above, places each *row* of data together in y-order. *X-first* reverses this, storing each column together. More esoteric systems exist, including *Morton Encoding* which tries to place adjacent tiles together in memory. [2]

Unless your encoding is causing performance problems, you probably don't need Morton Encoding; however, it's good to be aware of its existence.

Using this logic, you can implement map indexing. Add a public function to your map.rs module to calculate a tile index. Make sure you add the function *outside* of the Map implementation:

```
pub fn map_idx(x: i32, y: i32) -> usize {
  ((y * SCREEN_WIDTH) + x) as usize
}
...
impl Map {
```

Note the as usize. x and y are 32-bit integers (i32), but vectors are indexed by a variable of type usize. Adding as usize to a variable reference converts the result to a usize.

---

2.   https://en.wikipedia.org/wiki/Z-order_curve

Render the Map

The map needs to be able to draw itself to the screen. Add another function inside the map's implementation and name it render:

BasicDungeonCrawler/dungeon_crawl_map/src/map.rs
```
pub fn render(&self, ctx: &mut BTerm) {
    for y in 0..SCREEN_HEIGHT {
        for x in 0..SCREEN_WIDTH {
            let idx = map_idx(x, y);
            match self.tiles[idx] {
                TileType::Floor => {
                    ctx.set(x, y, YELLOW, BLACK,
                        to_cp437('.')
                    );
                }
                TileType::Wall => {
                    ctx.set(x, y, GREEN, BLACK,
                        to_cp437('#')
                    );
                }
            }
        }
    }
}
```

The function uses for loops to iterate through the y and x values of the map (iterating y first is faster with row-first striding due to memory cache usage), uses match to determine tile type, and calls set to render each map tile. Floors appear as a . in yellow, and walls as a # in green.

Consume the Map API

With the Map module ready to go, all that remains is to use it. Open main.rs. You need to add a Map to the State object and initialize it State's constructor. The tick() function should call the map's render() function.

BasicDungeonCrawler/dungeon_crawl_map/src/main.rs
```
struct State {
    map: Map,
}

impl State {
    fn new() -> Self {
        Self { map: Map::new() }
    }
}

impl GameState for State {
    fn tick(&mut self, ctx: &mut BTerm) {
        ctx.cls();
```

```
        self.map.render(ctx);
    }
}

fn main() -> BError {
    let context = BTermBuilder::simple80x50()
        .with_title("Dungeon Crawler")
        .with_fps_cap(30.0)
        .build()?;

    main_loop(context, State::new())
}
```

❶ fps_cap() automatically tracks your game speed, and tells your Operating System that it can rest in between frames. This prevents the player from moving too quickly and gives your CPU a rest.

Run the program now and you'll see an empty map:

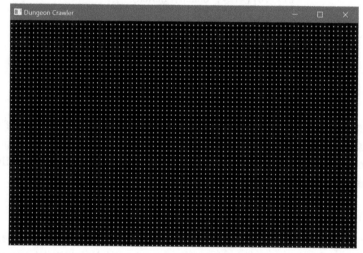

Now that you have a map, and have verified that it renders, it's time to add an adventurer.

Adding the Adventurer

The adventurer is the player's avatar in the dungeon. The player roams the dungeon, hopefully collecting loot and probably dying at the hands of vicious monsters. The game needs to know what tiles the adventurers can enter so they don't walk through walls. It also needs to store where the player is, handle moving them with the keyboard, and perform the movement. This section will address each of these requirements.

Extend the Map API

Let's add some more map functions to support player functionality. You need to determine if an x/y coordinate pair is within the bounds of the map. If you don't perform bounds-checking, the player can move off the edge of the map, and either wrap around or crash the program. Add the following to your Map implementation:

```
BasicDungeonCrawler/dungeon_crawl_player/src/map.rs
pub fn in_bounds(&self, point : Point) -> bool {
    point.x >= 0 && point.x < SCREEN_WIDTH
        && point.y >= 0 && point.y < SCREEN_HEIGHT
}
```

This function checks that the location specified in point is greater than zero on both the x and y axes, and that it is less than the screen height and width. Chaining multiple tests together with &&—short for AND—returns true if *all* the conditions are met.

You need a second function to determine if the player can enter a tile. Players can walk on floors but not through walls. This function should call the in_bounds function you just wrote, to ensure that the move is valid both dimensionally and for the TileType. Add this function to your Map implementation:

```
BasicDungeonCrawler/dungeon_crawl_player/src/map.rs
pub fn can_enter_tile(&self, point : Point) -> bool {
    self.in_bounds(point)
        && self.tiles[map_idx(point.x, point.y)]==TileType::Floor
}
```

The can_enter_tile function uses in_bounds to check that the destination is valid, and also checks that the destination tile is a floor. If both are true, the adventurer may enter the tile.

You need one more function. It would be useful to have a means of determining a tile's index coordinates, and indicate an error condition if the requested coordinates fall outside of the map boundaries. Add one more method to your Map implementation:

```
impl Map {
    ...
    pub fn try_idx(&self, point : Point) -> Option<usize> {
        if !self.in_bounds(point) {
            None
        } else {
            Some(map_idx(point.x, point.y))
        }
    }
}
```

This uses the in_bounds function you defined earlier to test if a map coordinate is valid. If it is, it returns Some(index). If it isn't, it returns None.

Your map now has the supporting code required to handle entities moving across it. It's time to build the player.

Create the Player Structure

The player is a logically distinct entity, so it belongs in its own module. Create a new file in your src directory, and name it player.rs. This will be the new player module.

Open main.rs, and add the new module to your prelude setup:

```
BasicDungeonCrawler/dungeon_crawl_player/src/main.rs
mod map;
mod player;

mod prelude {
    pub use bracket_lib::prelude::*;
    pub const SCREEN_WIDTH: i32 = 80;
    pub const SCREEN_HEIGHT: i32 = 50;
    pub use crate::map::*;
    pub use crate::player::*;
}
```

Return to player.rs, and add a new structure and constructor for the player information:

```
BasicDungeonCrawler/dungeon_crawl_player/src/player.rs
use crate::prelude::*;

pub struct Player {
    pub position: Point
}

impl Player {
    pub fn new(position: Point) -> Self {
        Self {
            position
        }
    }
}
```

Rather than storing x and y separately, you can use the Point type exported from bracket-lib. Point is an x and y value, but with additional functionality provides basic vector geometry functionality.

Render the Player

Just like the map, Player should have a render function:

BasicDungeonCrawler/dungeon_crawl_player/src/player.rs
```
pub fn render(&self, ctx: &mut BTerm) {
    ctx.set(
        self.position.x,
        self.position.y,
        WHITE,
        BLACK,
        to_cp437('@'),
    );
}
```

It's very similar to rendering a map tile: it calculates the screen position of the player and uses set to draw the @ symbol—representing the adventurer—at that screen location.

Move the Player

The player needs to be able to walk around the map in response to keyboard commands from the user.

Create a new function implementation for your Player structure:

BasicDungeonCrawler/dungeon_crawl_player/src/player.rs
```
pub fn update(&mut self, ctx: &mut BTerm, map : &Map) {
    if let Some(key) = ctx.key {
        let delta = match key {
            VirtualKeyCode::Left => Point::new(-1, 0),
            VirtualKeyCode::Right => Point::new(1, 0),
            VirtualKeyCode::Up => Point::new(0, -1),
            VirtualKeyCode::Down => Point::new(0, 1),
            _ => Point::zero()
        };
```

This function is similar to player input management in Main Menu, on page 55. You check for a key press with if let, and match on relevant key codes. The function creates a variable named delta to store the intended change in player position. A delta of zero indicates that no movement was requested.

The second half of the function calculates the player's new position: the current position plus the delta. It then calls can_enter_tile from the map—and updates the position if the move is valid:

BasicDungeonCrawler/dungeon_crawl_player/src/player.rs
```
        let new_position = self.position + delta;
        if map.can_enter_tile(new_position) {
            self.position = new_position;
        }
    }
}
```

Consume the Player API

With Player defined, you need to add it to your State and constructor, and call the update() and render() functions in your tick() function. Note that you render the player *after* you render the map—you want the player to sit on top of the map tiles:

BasicDungeonCrawler/dungeon_crawl_player/src/main.rs
```
struct State {
    map: Map,
    player: Player,
}

impl State {
    fn new() -> Self {
        Self {
            map : Map::new(),
            player: Player::new(
                Point::new(SCREEN_WIDTH / 2, SCREEN_HEIGHT / 2)
            ),
        }
    }
}

impl GameState for State {
    fn tick(&mut self, ctx: &mut BTerm) {
        ctx.cls();
        self.player.update(ctx, &self.map);
        self.map.render(ctx);
        self.player.render(ctx);
    }
}
```

Run the program now and you'll see an @ on the map (as shown in the image on page 89)—you can move it around with your cursor keys.

Building a Dungeon

You've built an empty map and have a player who can walk around it. The structure is in place to handle walls, so it's time to add a simple dungeon. In this section, you'll learn to randomly place rooms, connect them with corridors, and build a dungeon for your adventurer to explore.

Create a Map Builder Module

Make another new file named map_builder.rs. This file will contain the map building module. Add it to your prelude in main.rs:

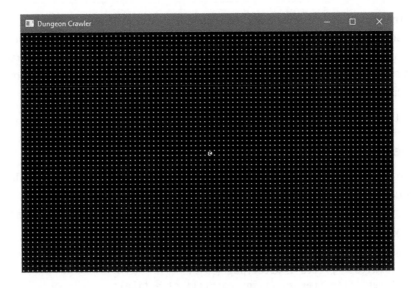

BasicDungeonCrawler/dungeon_crawl_rooms/src/main.rs
```
mod map;
➤ mod map_builder;
mod player;

mod prelude {
    pub use bracket_lib::prelude::*;
    pub const SCREEN_WIDTH: i32 = 80;
    pub const SCREEN_HEIGHT: i32 = 50;
    pub use crate::map::*;
    pub use crate::player::*;
➤    pub use crate::map_builder::*;
}
```

Open map_builder.rs. Start by importing the main prelude, and defining a constant representing the maximum number of rooms you'd like to allow in your dungeon. Twenty rooms yield a nice looking dungeon. Experiment with it:

BasicDungeonCrawler/dungeon_crawl_rooms/src/map_builder.rs
```
use crate::prelude::*;
const NUM_ROOMS: usize = 20;
```

Define a new structure to hold the MapBuilder:

BasicDungeonCrawler/dungeon_crawl_rooms/src/map_builder.rs
```
pub struct MapBuilder {
    pub map : Map,
    pub rooms : Vec<Rect>,
    pub player_start : Point,
}
```

The structure contains its own Map—it will work on its copy, and then pass the result to the game. The rooms vector is a list of the rooms that will be added to the map. Each room is represented with the Rect structure from bracket-lib. Rect is a helper for calculations involving rectangles.[3] Finally, player_start stores the location at which the player enters the map.

Let's start adding some details to the map.

Fill the Map With Walls

The previous example started with a dungeon entirely comprised of floors. A room-carving algorithm works the other way around, starting with a solid block of rock and carving rooms and corridors from the stone. Add the following to your MapBuilder implementation:

BasicDungeonCrawler/dungeon_crawl_rooms/src/map_builder.rs
```
fn fill(&mut self, tile : TileType) {
    self.map.tiles.iter_mut().for_each(|t| *t = tile);
}
```

This function obtains a mutable iterator with iter_mut(), and then uses for_each() to change every tile into a wall. The asterisk (*) before t is a *de-reference*. The iterator passes t (the tile type) as a reference—an &TileType. De-referencing indicates that you want to write to the referenced variable, not the reference itself.

Carving Rooms

Starting with a solid block of stone, you want to place rooms. Rooms shouldn't overlap, and you want to create NUM_ROOMS locations. The location of each room is random.

Add a new function to your MapBuilder implementation:

BasicDungeonCrawler/dungeon_crawl_rooms/src/map_builder.rs
```
❶ fn build_random_rooms(&mut self, rng : &mut RandomNumberGenerator) {
❷     while self.rooms.len() < NUM_ROOMS {
❸         let room = Rect::with_size(
               rng.range(1, SCREEN_WIDTH - 10),
               rng.range(1, SCREEN_HEIGHT - 10),
               rng.range(2, 10),
               rng.range(2, 10),
           );
❹         let mut overlap = false;
❺         for r in self.rooms.iter() {
               if r.intersect(&room) {
```

---

3.   https://github.com/thebracket/bracket-lib/blob/master/bracket-geometry/src/rect.rs

```
                overlap = true;
            }
        }
    }
    if !overlap {
        room.for_each(|p| {
            if p.x > 0 && p.x < SCREEN_WIDTH && p.y > 0
                && p.y < SCREEN_HEIGHT
            {
                let idx = map_idx(p.x, p.y);
                self.map.tiles[idx] = TileType::Floor;
            }
        });
        self.rooms.push(room)
    }
  }
}
```

❶ build_random_rooms() accepts a RandomNumberGenerator as a parameter. It's a good idea to use the same PRNG throughout your map generation, so if you re-use the same seed, you always get the same results.

❷ Keep generating rooms until there are NUM_ROOMS rooms on the map.

❸ Generate a randomly positioned room with random sizes. range() produces a random number within the provided minimum and maximum ranges.

❹ Test the new room against each placed room, and flag it as overlapping if rooms intersect.

❺ The Rect type includes a function named for_each(). It runs the provided closure on every x/y coordinate inside the rectangle it represents. This differs from regular iterators, but can be a handy shortcut for common tasks involving rectangles.

❻ If the rooms don't overlap, check that they are within the map boundaries and set their contents to floors.

Carving Corridors

You now have a list of non-overlapping rooms. The next step is to connect them with hallways. The basic map will use "dog-leg" corridors—corridors with a horizontal and vertical section, joined by a single corner. Create a new method in MapBuilder to create a vertical tunnel between two points on the map:

BasicDungeonCrawler/dungeon_crawl_rooms/src/map_builder.rs
```
fn apply_vertical_tunnel(&mut self, y1:i32, y2:i32, x:i32) {
    use std::cmp::{min, max};
    for y in min(y1,y2) ..= max(y1,y2) {
```

```
        if let Some(idx) = self.map.try_idx(Point::new(x, y)) {
            self.map.tiles[idx as usize] = TileType::Floor;
        }
    }
}
```

Range iterators expect that the starting value of a range will be the minimum value, and the destination the maximum. This function uses min() and max() to find the lowest and highest of a pair of values—in this case, the starting position. It then iterates y from the start to the end of the corridor, carving the tunnel along the way.

Add a second function to add horizontal tunnels in the same way, but traversing the x axis instead of the y axis:

BasicDungeonCrawler/dungeon_crawl_rooms/src/map_builder.rs
```
fn apply_horizontal_tunnel(&mut self, x1:i32, x2:i32, y:i32) {
    use std::cmp::{min, max};
    for x in min(x1,x2) ..= max(x1,x2) {
        if let Some(idx) = self.map.try_idx(Point::new(x, y)) {
            self.map.tiles[idx as usize] = TileType::Floor;
        }
    }
}
```

A third function, build_corridors, uses these functions to generate complete corridors between rooms:

BasicDungeonCrawler/dungeon_crawl_rooms/src/map_builder.rs
```
fn build_corridors(&mut self, rng: &mut RandomNumberGenerator) {
    let mut rooms = self.rooms.clone();
❶  rooms.sort_by(|a,b| a.center().x.cmp(&b.center().x));

❷  for (i, room) in rooms.iter().enumerate().skip(1) {
❸      let prev = rooms[i-1].center();
        let new = room.center();

❹      if rng.range(0,2) == 1 {
            self.apply_horizontal_tunnel(prev.x, new.x, prev.y);
            self.apply_vertical_tunnel(prev.y, new.y, new.x);
        } else {
            self.apply_vertical_tunnel(prev.y, new.y, prev.x);
            self.apply_horizontal_tunnel(prev.x, new.x, new.y);
        }
    }
}
```

❶ Vectors include a sort_by() to sort their contents.[4] It requires a closure—an inline function—that calls the cmp() function on two elements of the vector's

4. https://doc.rust-lang.org/std/vec/struct.Vec.html#method.sort_by

contents. cmp() returns an indicator if two elements are the same, or one is greater than the other. Sorting the rooms by their center point before allocating corridors makes it more likely that corridors will connect adjacent rooms and not snake across the whole map.[5]

sort_by() sends pairs of rooms to the closure. The closure receives these as a and b. a.center().x finds the x coordinate of room A. This is then compared via the cmp() function with the center of room B.

This re-orders your rooms to sort them by the x order of their central points. Doing this shortens corridors between the rooms. If you don't sort your rooms, you may find yourself with some very long corridors that almost certainly overlap with other rooms.

❷ Iterators include a lot of useful functionality. enumerate() counts items in the iterator and includes them as the first entry in a *tuple*. The (i, room) extracts the counter into the i variable. skip() allows you to ignore some entries in the iterator—in this case, you're ignoring the first one.

❸ Obtain the center position (as Point types) of the current and previous room. This is why you skipped the first entry: the previous room would be invalid.

❹ Randomly dig the horizontal and then vertical parts of the corridor, or vice versa.

Tuples

Tuples are a convenient way to pass data around without building a struct. You can use them to return multiple values from a function, or as a way to group data. Unlike structs, their fields aren't named—so you lose a bit of code readability in return for the convenience.[a]

You put data into a tuple by surrounding your data with parentheses: let tuple = (a, b, c);. You can then access each item with tuple.0, tuple.1, and so on. You can also use destructuring to extract values from a tuple into named variables: let (a, b, c) = tuple;.

---

a.   https://doc.rust-lang.org/std/primitive.tuple.html

---

5.   https://doc.rust-lang.org/std/cmp/index.html

Build the Map and Place the Player

Now that you have all the parts required to build a map, it's time to make the build constructor for your MapBuilder class. The constructor calls all of the elements you just created.

BasicDungeonCrawler/dungeon_crawl_rooms/src/map_builder.rs
```
pub fn new(rng: &mut RandomNumberGenerator) -> Self {

    let mut mb = MapBuilder{
        map : Map::new(),
        rooms : Vec::new(),
        player_start : Point::zero(),
    };
    mb.fill(TileType::Wall);
    mb.build_random_rooms(rng);
    mb.build_corridors(rng);
    mb.player_start = mb.rooms[0].center();
    mb
}
```

❶ Set player_start to the center of the first room in the rooms list. This ensures that they start in a valid, walkable tile.

Consume the MapBuilder API

Finally, it's time to use the MapBuilder. Open main.rs, and make the State::new function use the MapBuilder to generate a new dungeon:

BasicDungeonCrawler/dungeon_crawl_rooms/src/main.rs
```
fn new() -> Self {
    let mut rng = RandomNumberGenerator::new();
    let map_builder = MapBuilder::new(&mut rng);
    Self {
        map : map_builder.map,
        player: Player::new(map_builder.player_start),
    }
}
```

Run the game now, and you'll see dungeon rooms and hallways, and you can move your player around the map, as shown in the image on page 95.

Graphics, Camera, Action

ASCII is a great prototyping tool—even used for some full games such as Rogue or Nethack. Most games feature graphics, but this early in development isn't the right time to find an artist and make beautiful content—you might decide to change the game and waste hours of the artist's work. In early development, it's a much better idea to use *Programmer Art*—rough graphics designed to

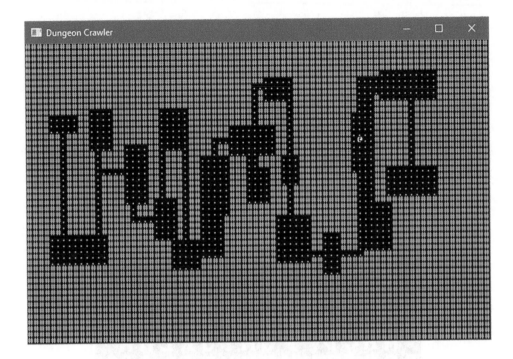

give you an idea for the feel of a game, but without requiring a significant time investment if (when) you decide to change things.

In this section, you'll implement graphical *layers*—so the player stands on top of the floor rather than replacing it. The graphics are much larger than simple ASCII glyphs, so you'll need to reduce the visible portion of the map—without sacrificing size or map quality. You'll solve this issue by creating a *camera*.

Programmer Art for the Dungeon

bracket-lib renders terminals by copying glyphs from a font file onto the terminal window. You can take advantage of this during prototyping by assigning a symbol to a tile type and replacing that character in the font file with your chosen programmer art. Any bitmap editor can do the job—I use *The Gimp.*[6]

Create a new directory named resources in your project's root directory. This directory will hold all graphical resources needed for the game. Copy dungeon-font.png into this directory. (It's already present in the example source code.) Rather than recreate this file throughout the book, the file includes all of the graphics needed for the game.

---

6.   https://www.gimp.org/

The following glyphs are defined:

Glyph	Graphic	Represents	Glyph	Graphic	Represents	Glyph	Graphic	Represents
#		Dungeon Wall	@		The Player			Amulet of Yala
.		Dungeon Floor	E		Ettin	!		Healing Potion
"		Forest Wall	O		Ogre	{		Dungeon Map
;		Forest Floor	o		Orc	s		Rusty Sword
>		Down Stairs	g		Goblin	S		Shiny Sword
						/		Huge Sword

The font file with all of the graphic elements defined looks like this:

The dungeon floor, wall, and adventurer graphics were kindly provided by Buch for free.[7] Potion and scroll graphics are from Melissa Krautheim's *Fantasy Magic Set*.[8] Weaponry is from Melle's *Fantasy Sword Set*.[9] Monster

7.   https://opengameart.org/content/unfinished-dungeon-tileset
8.   https://opengameart.org/content/fantasy-magic-set
9.   https://opengameart.org/content/fantasy-sword-set

graphics are from the game *Dungeon Crawl Stone Soup* (CC0 license), packaged by Chris Hamons.[10]

Credit Your Artists

 Even if you're using freely provided content, please credit the artists whose work you use. Making art is difficult work, just like programming. Be sure to thank the people who are giving it away.

Graphics Layers

Currently, your game renders everything to a single layer. The map is drawn and then the player is drawn on top of it. This works with graphics but tends to leave artifacts around the player's graphic. You can get much better results by using *layers*. The map is rendered to a base layer, and the player to the layer on top of it—with transparency, so the floor remains visible. Later in this book, you'll add a third layer for game information.

Start with a little housekeeping. Using large tiles makes the window *huge*—larger than many screens. Instead, render the game window as a smaller view of part of the map, centered on the player. Add some constants to your prelude in main.rs to indicate the dimensions of the smaller viewport into your world:

BasicDungeonCrawler/dungeon_crawl_graphics/src/main.rs
```
pub const DISPLAY_WIDTH: i32 = SCREEN_WIDTH / 2;
pub const DISPLAY_HEIGHT: i32 = SCREEN_HEIGHT / 2;
```

You can introduce layers to bracket-lib by changing your initialization code:

BasicDungeonCrawler/dungeon_crawl_graphics/src/main.rs
```
❶ let context = BTermBuilder::new()
      .with_title("Dungeon Crawler")
      .with_fps_cap(30.0)
❷     .with_dimensions(DISPLAY_WIDTH, DISPLAY_HEIGHT)
❸     .with_tile_dimensions(32, 32)
❹     .with_resource_path("resources/")
❺     .with_font("dungeonfont.png", 32, 32)
❻     .with_simple_console(DISPLAY_WIDTH, DISPLAY_HEIGHT, "dungeonfont.png")
      .with_simple_console_no_bg(DISPLAY_WIDTH, DISPLAY_HEIGHT,
❼         "dungeonfont.png")
      .build()?;
```

❶ Use new() to create a generic terminal and specify attributes directly.

❷ with_dimensions specifies the size of subsequent consoles you add.

---

10. https://github.com/crawl/tiles

❸ The tile dimensions are the size of each character in your font file, in this case 32x32.

❹ The directory in which you placed the graphics file.

❺ The name of the font file to load and the character dimensions. These are usually the same as tile dimensions, but can be different for some advanced forms of rendering.

❻ Add a console using the dimensions already specified and the named tile graphics file.

❼ Add a second console with no background so transparency shows through it.

This code creates a terminal with two console layers, one for the map and one for the player. You won't be rendering the whole map at once—and to limit the viewport, you use a camera.

Make a Camera

The camera acts as your game's window into the world. It defines the section of the map that is currently visible. Create a new file, camera.rs. Import your prelude, and create a structure with enough information to define the boundaries of the camera view:

BasicDungeonCrawler/dungeon_crawl_graphics/src/camera.rs
```
use crate::prelude::*;

pub struct Camera {
    pub left_x : i32,
    pub right_x : i32,
    pub top_y : i32,
    pub bottom_y : i32
}
```

You need to be able to create a camera and update it when the player moves. Because the camera is centered on the player, you need the player's position for both of these functions:

BasicDungeonCrawler/dungeon_crawl_graphics/src/camera.rs
```
impl Camera {
    pub fn new(player_position: Point) -> Self {
        Self{
            left_x : player_position.x - DISPLAY_WIDTH/2,
            right_x : player_position.x + DISPLAY_WIDTH/2,
            top_y : player_position.y - DISPLAY_HEIGHT/2,
            bottom_y : player_position.y + DISPLAY_HEIGHT/2
        }
    }
```

```
    pub fn on_player_move(&mut self, player_position: Point) {
        self.left_x = player_position.x - DISPLAY_WIDTH/2;
        self.right_x = player_position.x + DISPLAY_WIDTH/2;
        self.top_y = player_position.y - DISPLAY_HEIGHT/2;
        self.bottom_y = player_position.y + DISPLAY_HEIGHT/2;
    }
}
```

The new and on_player_move functions are essentially the same: they define the visible window as being centered on the player. The left-most visible tile is the player's x coordinate, *minus* half of the screen size. The right-most visible tile is the x coordinate *plus* one half of the screen size. The y dimensions are the same, but with screen height.

Add the camera structure to your prelude and module imports in main.rs:

```
mod camera;

mod prelude {
    ...
    pub use crate::camera::*;
}
```

Add the camera to your game's state:

BasicDungeonCrawler/dungeon_crawl_graphics/src/main.rs
```
struct State {
    map: Map,
    player: Player,
➤   camera: Camera
}
```

You also need to update your state's new function to initialize the camera:

BasicDungeonCrawler/dungeon_crawl_graphics/src/main.rs
```
fn new() -> Self {
    let mut rng = RandomNumberGenerator::new();
    let map_builder = MapBuilder::new(&mut rng);
    Self {
        map : map_builder.map,
        player: Player::new(map_builder.player_start),
➤       camera: Camera::new(map_builder.player_start)
    }
}
```

Use the Camera for Rendering the Map

You need to update map.rs with a render function that understands camera placement:

BasicDungeonCrawler/dungeon_crawl_graphics/src/map.rs

```
pub fn render(&self, ctx: &mut BTerm, camera: &Camera) {
    ctx.set_active_console(0);
    for y in camera.top_y .. camera.bottom_y {
        for x in camera.left_x .. camera.right_x {
            if self.in_bounds(Point::new(x, y)) {
                let idx = map_idx(x, y);
                match self.tiles[idx] {
                    TileType::Floor => {
                        ctx.set(
                            x - camera.left_x,
                            y - camera.top_y,
                            WHITE,
                            BLACK,
                            to_cp437('.')
                        );
                    }
                    TileType::Wall => {
                        ctx.set(
                            x - camera.left_x,
                            y - camera.top_y,
                            WHITE,
                            BLACK,
                            to_cp437('#')
                        );
                    }
                }
            }
        }
    }
}
```

The function receives a borrowed Camera, and uses the boundaries from the camera to render just the visible part of the map. Notice that it now calls in_bounds to make sure that each tile exists. The *screen* coordinates sent to the set function have left_x and top_y subtracted from them—moving them to be relative to the camera. Notice that it calls set_active_console(0)—this tells the library to render to the first console layer, the base map.

The map will now be centered on the player.

Connect the Player to the Camera

The rendered map center is determined by the player's position, so you need to extend the update() function in player.rs to use it. Update the function signature as follows:

BasicDungeonCrawler/dungeon_crawl_graphics/src/player.rs

```
pub fn update(&mut self, ctx: &mut BTerm, map : &Map, camera: &mut Camera)
{
```

Notice that it receives a *mutable* camera—it will use it to send updates if the player moves:

BasicDungeonCrawler/dungeon_crawl_graphics/src/player.rs

```
if map.can_enter_tile(new_position) {
  self.position = new_position;
  camera.on_player_move(new_position);
}
```

Lastly, for the player, you need to update the render() function to take into account camera placement:

BasicDungeonCrawler/dungeon_crawl_graphics/src/player.rs

```
pub fn render(&self, ctx: &mut BTerm, camera: &Camera) {
  ctx.set_active_console(1);
  ctx.set(
    self.position.x - camera.left_x,
    self.position.y - camera.top_y,
    WHITE,
    BLACK,
    to_cp437('@'),
  );
}
```

Just like the map, this subtracts left_x and top_y from the player's coordinates when rendering. Notice the call to set_active_console. This specifies that you want to use the second layer for the player.

Clear Layers, Connect Functions

Finally, you need to update the tick function in main.rs to send the camera to the updated functions—and to clear all layers.

BasicDungeonCrawler/dungeon_crawl_graphics/src/main.rs

```
fn tick(&mut self, ctx: &mut BTerm) {
    ctx.set_active_console(0);
    ctx.cls();
    ctx.set_active_console(1);
    ctx.cls();
    self.player.update(ctx, &self.map, &mut self.camera);
    self.map.render(ctx, &self.camera);
    self.player.render(ctx, &self.camera);
}
```

Run the game now and you have a graphical dungeon:

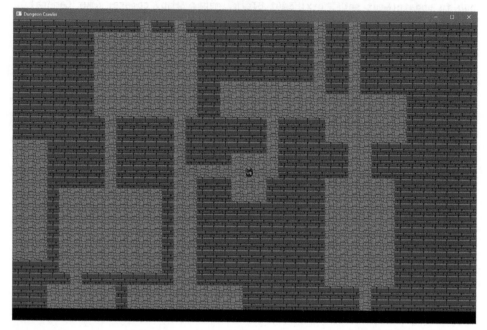

Wrap-Up

In this chapter, you made a map and a player to explore it. You randomly generated a dungeon and verified that your movement code works. You added programmer art to get a better idea of the finished product. In the next chapter, you'll add monsters and learn to use entities, components, and systems to share common functionality between your dungeon's residents.

CHAPTER 6

Compose Dungeon Denizens

In the previous chapter, you created the beginnings of a dungeon crawler. You added a random map, an adventurer to roam the dungeon, and collision detection to prevent the player from walking through walls. You also took your first steps into programmer art and layered graphics. In this chapter, you'll learn a popular approach to managing *game state*—the data that represents your game's world simulation.

Games can have a *lot* of data: every monster, every item, every little graphical effect needs to be stored somewhere in your computer's memory. In the past, games employed various techniques to handle the resulting combinatorial explosion of data. An increasingly popular approach to managing game data is the *Entity Component System* (ECS) architecture. It efficiently handles large amounts of data and is becoming the de facto standard for large engines such as Unity and Godot (Unreal Engine uses a similar system with components, but without separate systems). Rust is a great fit for ECS-driven game development, and you can find several great ECS systems available in the crates system. For this book, you'll use *Legion*—an open source, high-performance ECS included for free in the Rust crates library.[1]

Understanding Terminology

ECS uses a common set of terms to denote its different parts:

- An *entity* can be anything: an adventurer, an orc, or a pair of shoes. The game map is an exception—it's usually not an entity, but rather a resource entity's reference to travel. Entities don't have logic associated with them; they are little more than an identification number.

---

1. https://github.com/amethyst/legion

- A *component* describes a property an entity may have. Entities typically have lots of components attached to them, serving as a description—and adding functionality through systems. For example, a goblin might have a Position component describing where it is on the map, a Render component describing how to render it, a MeleeAI component indicating that it attacks with hand-to-hand combat, and a Health component describing how many hit points it has left. A sword might also have a Position component describing its location on the map, and a Render component indicating what it looks like. It would differ from the goblin by having an Item component to indicate that it's an item. Components don't have logic associated with them, either.

- *Systems* query the entities and components and provide one element of game-play/world simulation. For example, a Render system might draw everything with a Render component and a Position component onto the map. A Melee system might handle hand-to-hand combat. Systems provide the "game logic" that makes your game function. Systems read entity/component data and make changes to them—providing the powerhouse that makes the game function.

- *Resources* are shared data available to multiple systems.

This diagram illustrates the relationship between these terms.

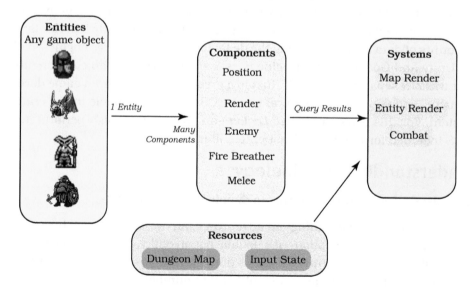

Composing Entities

Entities are composed of combined components that describe them. Whenever you add a component type (and systems that use it), you're offering that functionality to *any entity*. You can use it for everything, or you may restrict it to a small number of special creatures—but every time you add a component, you are giving yourself options. You can now add that functionality to anything you like. Some combinations may not make sense, but with a little thought, you can quickly add realism and fun to your game.

One advantage of using component composition is that it becomes easier to translate from an English description of a monster to a set of components. You might write that a goblin is "a small, green, angry humanoid. They roam the dungeon, preying upon unsuspecting adventurers. They prefer to attack from a distance, and are cowardly and quite weak." Reading a description like this gives you some valuable clues as to what components your goblin may require:

- It's a small humanoid requiring the same Render components as other humanoids.

- It has a Position on the map.

- It's angry, so you need an AI component denoting that it attacks on sight.

- It prefers ranged attacks, so your AI components should indicate that.

- It is cowardly, so maybe that needs a component when you implement running away.

- It is quite weak, implying that while it has a Health component, the number of hit points is quite low.

As you add components, entity design becomes a checklist. What components properly describe this new creature? For example:

Component Composition
Monster entity has the following components:

	Goblin	Goblin Archer	Goblin Sorcerer	Dragon
Render	✔	✔	✔	✔
Position	✔	✔	✔	✔
Name	✔	✔	✔	✔
Melee AI	✔			✔
Ranged AI		✔		
Spellcaster			✔	✔

Now that you understand the concepts of an ECS, it's time to install one.

Installing and Using Legion

Legion is included in Rust's crates system, so installing it is very similar to installing bracket-lib. Open Cargo.toml in your dungeoncrawl project, and add Legion to the dependency list:

```
[dependencies]
bracket-lib = "~0.8.1"
legion = "=0.3.1"
```

Note that you're using an *exact* version number for Legion with the equals (=) sign. Legion is rapidly improving, which guarantees that your code will work with that published version.

Pin Your Dependencies

When you're working on a project, it's a good idea to pin your dependencies with the equals (=) sign once you progress beyond initial planning. This guarantees that your project won't break because a library upgraded and changed part of its API.

Add Legion to Your Prelude

You'll be using Legion a lot throughout your program. Rather than type use legion::* everywhere you can re-export it in your prelude, much as you did with bracket-lib. Open main.rs in your project, and add Legion to your prelude:

```
mod prelude {
    pub use bracket_lib::prelude::*;
    pub use legion::*;
    pub use legion::world::SubWorld;
    pub use legion::systems::CommandBuffer;
    ...
}
```

Any module that imports your prelude now has access to Legion.

Remove Old Code

You'll need to replace some code from the previous version with ECS-enabled versions. You're no longer treating the player as a special case—they are just another entity. Delete player.rs from your project, and remove mod player; from your prelude in main.rs. In the same file, remove it from your State and reduce your tick function to a simple stub:

```
impl GameState for State {
    fn tick(&mut self, ctx: &mut BTerm) {
        ctx.set_active_console(0);
        ctx.cls();
        ctx.set_active_console(1);
        ctx.cls();
        // TODO: Execute Systems
        // TODO: Render Draw Buffer
    }
}
```

You also need to delete the render() function from your map.rs file.

Create the World

Legion stores all entities and components in a structure it calls a World. Your game needs to create a world in which to place the game entities. Change State in main.rs to include a World, a Schedule to hold your systems, and remove the camera and map:

```
struct State {
    ecs : World,
    resources : Resources,
    systems: Schedule
}
```

The map is no longer part of your game state. Instead, it's now a *resource*—a shared piece of data, available to all systems that need it. Map creation remains the same, but instead of storing it in your State, it's inserted into Legion's resource list—which you also have to initialize. The Camera also becomes a resource. Note that you aren't storing the map_builder—just the map it creates. Update your State's new() function to create a world and resources. Then inject the map and camera as resources:

```
fn new() -> Self {
    let mut ecs = World::default();
    let mut resources = Resources::default();
    let mut rng = RandomNumberGenerator::new();
    let map_builder = MapBuilder::new(&mut rng);
    resources.insert(map_builder.map);
    resources.insert(Camera::new(map_builder.player_start));
    Self {
        ecs,
        resources,
        systems: build_scheduler()
    }
}
```

Note that build_scheduler() doesn't exist yet. You'll build it in Multi-File Modules, on page 111.

The World and Resources are created with a simple constructor called Default. The map builder is set up the same way as before, but rather than storing it in State, it's injected into the world's resources with insert().

Now that you have an ECS, it's time to describe the player with components.

Composing the Player

Rather than coding everything player related into a single module, the ECS approach is to *describe* a player in terms of what components they use. Looking at the Player module from the previous chapter, you can deduce some components that meet your needs:

- A Player component indicating that the player *is* a Player. Components don't have to contain any fields. An empty component is sometimes called a "tag"—it serves to flag that a property exists.

- A Render component describing how the player appears on the screen.

- A Position component indicating where the entity is on the map. The Point structure from bracket-lib is ideal for this; it contains an x and a y component, and it also provides several point-related math functions that will prove useful.

Create a new file, src/components.rs. This creates a new module named components. You're going to use components throughout your game, so it makes sense to add it to your prelude in main.rs:

```
mod components;
mod prelude {
    ...
    pub use crate::components::*;
}
```

Legion components are usually structs, but can also be enum types such as options. They don't have to derive any functionality, but when you can, it's a good idea to derive Clone. This allows you to make a copy of the component if you need it. It's often helpful to also derive Debug to print debugging information when things aren't working as intended. Open components.rs, and add Player and Render components:

EntitiesComponentsAndSystems/playerecs/src/components.rs
```
pub use crate::prelude::*;

#[derive(Clone, Copy, Debug, PartialEq)]
pub struct Render {
❶    pub color : ColorPair,
❷    pub glyph : FontCharType
}

#[derive(Clone, Copy, Debug, PartialEq)]
❸ pub struct Player;
```

❶ ColorPair is a helper class from bracket-lib that stores both a foreground and background color in a single struct.

❷ FontCharType is defined in bracket-lib to store a single character or glyph.

❸ Player is an empty struct containing no data. It serves as a "tag" indicating that an entity with this component is the player.

Add the Player to the World

Create another new file, src/spawner.rs—a module that handles spawning entities. Add your new module to your prelude in main.rs:

```
mod spawner;
...

mod prelude {
  ...
  pub use crate::spawner::*;
}
```

Now open spawner.rs and add a function that spawns a player:

EntitiesComponentsAndSystems/playerecs/src/spawner.rs
```
use crate::prelude::*;

❶ pub fn spawn_player(ecs : &mut World, pos : Point) {
❷    ecs.push(
        (
❸            Player,
❹            pos,
❺            Render{
                color: ColorPair::new(WHITE, BLACK),
                glyph : to_cp437('@')
            }
        )
    );
}
```

❶ The function requires a mutable reference to the World and the location to spawn the player.

❷ You create components by calling push, just like a vector. The components are separated in a tuple. Calling push() creates a new Entity composed of the listed components.

❸ Add a tag component, indicating that this is the player. Tag components are treated like other components.

❹ The player's position, the Point passed to the function as a parameter. Legion can accept most types as components—here, you are using bracket-lib's structure.

❺ A Render component containing the player's appearance.

Calling spawn_player() adds the player and their components to the ECS. You only need one player, so add it to your State constructor:

```
impl State {
    fn new() -> Self {
        ...
        let map_builder = MapBuilder::new(&mut rng);
        spawn_player(&mut ecs, map_builder.player_start);
        ...
}
```

The world now contains a single player entity who possesses Point and Render components. Now you need to create some systems to use the data.

Managing Complexity with Systems

Systems are a special type of function that *queries* the ECS for data and performs operations with the results. An ECS game may have a *lot* of systems (my *Nox Futura* project has over a hundred systems). Systems can run concurrently and are managed by a Scheduler. Legion builds a schedule by examining the systems you give to it, and determines data dependencies between them. Many systems can read data at once, but only a single system can safely write to it. The order in which you present systems is also considered: Legion will run systems in the order in which they are presented, unless they can be grouped together to run concurrently. The good news is that you usually don't need to worry too much about this—Legion has your back.

As your game grows, you'll keep adding systems. You need a way to organize your systems to make adding new ones relatively painless. Generally, systems can't see the innards of other systems—making them ideal for module-based organization.

Multi-File Modules

Rust modules don't have to be limited to a single file—they can also be a directory containing a mod.rs file. That directory can then contain sub-modules—which may be single files or directories. This is a powerful way to organize your code, but it can require a little planning.

Create a new directory in your src folder, and name it systems. Create a new file in that folder and name it mod.rs. Leave it blank for now. Open main.rs, and add your new module to the prelude, just like other modules:

```
mod systems;
...

mod prelude {
  ...
  pub use crate::systems::*;
}
```

You're going to take advantage of Rust's nested modules to keep your system's functionality separated from the rest of the program, but still logically grouped together. Before you implement any systems, you need a stub schedule builder that returns an empty Legion schedule. Add the following to systems/mod.rs:

```
use crate::prelude::*;

pub fn build_scheduler() -> Schedule {
    Schedule::builder()
        .build()
}
```

This function creates a Legion Schedule—an execution plan for your systems. It follows the builder pattern: Schedule::builder starts the system-building process, and build() finishes it. For now, it creates an empty schedule—it does nothing.

Open main.rs, and add your system scheduler to State and its constructor:

```
struct State {
    ecs : World,
    systems: Schedule,
}
impl State {
    fn new() -> Self {
      ...
      Self {
          ecs,
          systems: build_scheduler()
      }
    }
}
```

You also want the tick() function to execute your systems. You can do this with the execute() function provided by the schedule, which requires a mutable borrow of the ECS world:

```
impl GameState for State {
    fn tick(&mut self, ctx: &mut BTerm) {
        ctx.set_active_console(0);
        ctx.cls();
        ctx.set_active_console(1);
        ctx.cls();
        self.resources.insert(ctx.key);
        self.systems.execute(&mut self.ecs, &mut self.resources);
        // TODO - Render Draw Buffer
    }
}
```

You added ctx.key (which holds the keyboard state) as a resource in your tick() function. This makes the current keyboard state available to any system that requests it. When you insert a resource into Legion's resource handler, it replaces any existing resource of the same type—you don't need to worry about making duplicates.

Mutable Borrows

 There are two types of borrowing in Rust. A regular borrow (&var_to_borrow) lets the recipient of the borrowed reference see the contents of the borrowed variable. A mutable borrow (&mut var_to_borrow) lets the recipient change the value. Any changes they make are applied to the borrowed variable directly—they are visible to any other part of the program that reads that variable.

Rust's safety features make a mutable borrow *exclusive*. If a variable is mutably borrowed, it cannot be borrowed—mutably or immutably—by other statements while the borrow remains. It can "sub-lease" the borrow by passing it to functions, but you *cannot* keep a borrowed mutable variable in scope and lend it again.

Most systems require queries to help them access the data stored in the ECS.

Understanding Queries

Queries take a list of components as input. Every entity in the world is then matched against these components—and only entities that have *all* of the components will be included in the results. Queries provide their results as an iterator, allowing you to use them in the same way as the iterators you've encountered before. A query is declared in the form <(Component1, Component2)>::query(). They work as shown in the image on page 113.

Components to include   Create the query

```
<(Point, MeleeAI)>::query()
```
                        <>::() is a "turbofish"
```
.iter(ecs)
```
← Connect the query to the ECS World

Query iterator matches as follows:

	Point	MeleeAI	Included in query?
Goblin	✓	✓	✓
Goblin Archer	✓	X	X
Goblin Sorceror	✓	X	X
Dragon	✓	✓	✓

The iterator returns:

```
(point, melee)
(point, melee)
```
← A tuple containing the requested components

One entry for each matching Entity

A query is similar to a JOIN when working with databases: it returns references to components—grouped by entity—that have *all* of the components you requested.

You can further refine a query with a *filter*. Query filters aren't quite the same as iterator filters—but you can use them together to great effect. A query filter lets you specify additional requirements for an Entity to appear in the query results. For example:

```
<(Point, MeleeAI)>::query().filter(component::<Render>())
```

The query will only match entities that have Point, MeleeAI and Render components. The query results won't include the Render component. This is useful when you want to test that a component exists—but don't care what value it has.

Now that you know about queries, let's make some systems. Your Dungeon Crawler needs three systems: an input handler, a map renderer, and an entity renderer.

Player Input as a System

Create a new file named src/systems/player_input.rs. This is your first *nested module*—the module is inside your systems module. Rather than adding it to your prelude in main.rs, open systems/mod.rs and add mod player_input; as the first line. Within the systems module, you can now access the module as player_input::*—and since you didn't add a pub to make it public, you can't access it from elsewhere in your code.

Procedural Macros

Legion systems are quite complicated internally. It uses *Procedural Macros* (commonly referred to as "proc macros") to save you from writing a lot of repetitive boilerplate code for each system.

You've already used some proc macros. #[derive(...)] is a proc macro. Legion's macros use a similar format. You annotate a system with #[system] to trigger the macro. The system macro does a lot of work. It appends _system to the name of your function—player_input() becomes player_input_system(). It wraps your system in boilerplate to make it work, and handles injecting resources and components. For now, focus on "this is how systems work"—the intricacies of procedural macros are a very advanced Rust topic.

Open the new player_input.rs file. Import the main prelude, and create a stub function to make a system:

```
use crate::prelude::*;

#[system]
pub fn player_input() {
}
```

The #[system] line annotates the player_input function with a procedural macro named system. This macro transforms your function name into player_input_system, and wraps it with all of the extra code Legion requires to construct a system.

Your player_input system needs access to some of the resources you inserted into Legion's Resources manager, and some of the components you have defined. You can request access to these by extending the player_input function signature:

```
#[system]
#[write_component(Point)]
#[read_component(Player)]
pub fn player_input(
    ecs: &mut SubWorld,
    #[resource] map: &Map,
    #[resource] key: &Option<VirtualKeyCode>,
    #[resource] camera: &mut Camera
) {}
```

The other two annotations on the system function's header define the system's component access:

- write_component requests *writable* access to a component type, in this case, the Point component. You must request write access if you intend to change the contents of a component in your system.

- read_component requests *read-only* access to a component type. You must request read access to use the values stored in a component of this type—but you cannot make changes to the stored value.

Legion's scheduler needs to know what types of component you are accessing, and how you need to access them. Multiple systems can access a read-only component at once, but only a single system can write to a component type at once (and prevents read-only access from running until it is finished—preventing a system from encountering data that changed partway through system execution).

The function has also gained some parameters:

- The first function parameter requests a SubWorld. A SubWorld is like a World—but can only see the components you requested.

- #[resource] requests access to types you stored in Legion's Resource handler. It is also a procedural macro.

- You access the map by listing map: &Map after the resource annotation. This is just like borrowing elsewhere—you are requesting a read-only reference to the map.

- You access the camera with &mut Camera. This is just like a mutable borrow—you are requesting a mutable reference to the camera. Your code can change the contents of the Camera struct, and the global resource is updated with the new values.

Now that resource access and your query are in place, it's time to build the system function's body. This is very similar to the player input handler you built in Move the Player, on page 87. Here's the completed system with the changes highlighted:

EntitiesComponentsAndSystems/playerecs/src/systems/player_input.rs
```rust
use crate::prelude::*;

#[system]
#[write_component(Point)]
#[read_component(Player)]
pub fn player_input(
    ecs: &mut SubWorld,
    #[resource] map: &Map,
    #[resource] key: &Option<VirtualKeyCode>,
    #[resource] camera: &mut Camera
)
{
    if let Some(key) = key {
        let delta = match key {
```

```
                VirtualKeyCode::Left => Point::new(-1, 0),
                VirtualKeyCode::Right => Point::new(1, 0),
                VirtualKeyCode::Up => Point::new(0, -1),
                VirtualKeyCode::Down => Point::new(0, 1),
                _ => Point::new(0, 0),
            };

            if delta.x != 0 || delta.y != 0 {
❶              let mut players = <&mut Point>::query()
❷                  .filter(component::<Player>());
❸              players.iter_mut(ecs).for_each(|pos| {
                    let destination = *pos + delta;
                    if map.can_enter_tile(destination) {
                        *pos = destination;
                        camera.on_player_move(destination);
                    }
                });
            }
        }
    }
```

❶ You access components with a query. Queries list one or more components, and return references—mutable if you use &mut—to each instance of that component type. If you request more than one component type, only entities with *all* of those components will be returned. The components will be grouped together to ensure that each returned set of components only operates on the entity that owns the components.

❷ You don't want to update *all* Point components—just the player. Otherwise, when you begin to add monsters and items, they would move when the player moves. Legion queries include a filter() function to further refine the set of components required for a query to match an entity. This line specifies that only entities with a Point component and a Player tag component should be included in the query.

Note that this isn't the same as using filter() on an iterator. The query doesn't become an iterator until you call iter() or iter_mut()—it's still a query. Adding filters before the iterator call limits the types included in the query. Query filters can require that a component exists—but can't refer to its content. If you need to filter on the component's content, you can use the iterator's filter() function instead.

This may be confusing at first, and that's OK. You'll be using queries throughout the remainder of this book and will have plenty of time to understand how they work.

❸ Calling iter_mut() runs the query you have defined and places the results in an iterator. It's just like the other iterators you have used, with all of Rust's iterator functionality included.

Finally, you need to include the new system in your scheduler. Modify the build_scheduler() function in systems/mod.rs to include it in the schedule builder. Using the module names as a namespace clarifies what you are doing:

```
mod player_input;

pub fn build_scheduler() -> Schedule {
    Schedule::builder()
        .add_system(player_input::player_input_system())
        .build()
}
```

Batched Rendering

Using systems automatically turns your game into a multi-threaded program. If you have more than one CPU core (most computers do now), systems will execute *at the same time*. This presents a problem with the context-based rendering you used in the previous chapter. Two systems writing to the console at the same time can produce bizarre results, sometimes displaying parts of the output from each system. Bracket-lib could implement a locking system directly in the context, allowing it to be directly shared as a system resource, but this would add a lot of complexity to your program. You'd need to lock (and remember to unlock) the context each time you used it. Repeated locking/unlocking performs poorly and makes for overly complicated code.

Instead, bracket-lib offers a batching service. At any time—and from any thread—you can request a new draw batch by calling DrawBatch::new(). This creates a buffer of deferred rendering commands. Your draw commands aren't executed immediately; instead, they're stored for presentation all at once. When you're finished adding to a batch, you call draw_batch.submit(sort_order) to finalize it. The sort_order specifies the order in which the command batches are executed, with zero going first.

When all of your batches are ready to render, in your tick() function, you tell bracket-lib to render them with a call to render_draw_buffer(ctx). Extend your tick() function (in main.rs) to include this:

```
...
self.systems.execute(&mut self.ecs, &mut self.resources);
render_draw_buffer(ctx).expect("Render error");
```

Data Races

 One of Rust's selling points is that it protects you from "data races." The borrow checker will not allow you to concurrently access a shared resource without implementing locks. This can prevent a whole class of common bugs found in other languages.

Map Rendering System

Let's make a system to draw the map. Create a new file named src/systems/map_render.rs. Add mod map_render; to the top of src/systems/mod.rs. The system builder for Map only needs read access to the Map—and no queries. The system code is almost the same as the previous chapter's render() function in Map. Here's the entire system with changes highlighted:

`EntitiesComponentsAndSystems/playerecs/src/systems/map_render.rs`
```
use crate::prelude::*;

#[system]
pub fn map_render(#[resource] map: &Map, #[resource] camera: &Camera) {
    let mut draw_batch = DrawBatch::new();
    draw_batch.target(0);
    for y in camera.top_y ..= camera.bottom_y {
        for x in camera.left_x .. camera.right_x {
            let pt = Point::new(x, y);
            let offset = Point::new(camera.left_x, camera.top_y);
            if map.in_bounds(pt) {
                let idx = map_idx(x, y);
                let glyph = match map.tiles[idx] {
                    TileType::Floor => to_cp437('.'),
                    TileType::Wall => to_cp437('#'),
                };
                draw_batch.set(
                    pt - offset,
                    ColorPair::new(
                        WHITE,
                        BLACK
                    ),
                    glyph
                );
            }
        }
    }
    draw_batch.submit(0).expect("Batch error");
}
```

❶ Your system doesn't use any components, but does need access to the map and camera. It requests these as parameters to the map_render() function and uses the #[resource] annotation to indicate that they are resources.

❶ Instead of immediate-mode rendering, the system starts a drawing batch. DrawBatch::new() starts a new batch. Draw commands are appended to the batch in the order that you want them to occur.

❷ You add draw commands to a batch with the same commands as immediate mode, but calling the batch rather than the context.

❸ Submitting the batch adds it to the global command list. It accepts a single integer parameter, serving as a sort order. Zero renders first, ensuring that your map is drawn at the beginning of the render cycle.

Finally, you need to add the map rendering to your systems builder. In systems/mod.rs, modify the build_scheduler() function to include it:

```
mod map_render;
mod player_input;

pub fn build_scheduler() -> Schedule {
    Schedule::builder()
        .add_system(player_input::player_input_system())
        .add_system(map_render::map_render_system())
        .build()
}
```

Render Entities in a System

A third system renders all entities with both a Point and Render component. The player has both, so it'll be included in the render cycle—but if you add more entities with both components, they will automatically be rendered. Make a new file, src/systems/entity_render.rs, and add a mod entity_render; to your systems/mod.rs file.

Open entity_render.rs, and add a stub builder function to it:

```
use crate::prelude::*;

#[system]
#[read_component(Point)]
#[read_component(Render)]
pub fn entity_render(ecs: &SubWorld, #[resource] camera: &Camera) {
}
```

The system requests read-only access to Point and Render components, and read-only access to the Camera resource. The camera is used to calculate the offset to apply to your entity's screen position, just like you did in the previous chapter. The Point component tells you where the entity is, and the Render component describes its appearance.

You can perform a query with multiple types with the following syntax:

```
<(&Point, &Render)>::query()
```

The outer < and > denotes that the contents contain *types*. The parentheses indicate a tuple—a collection of data accessed together. Then you list each of the component types you want as a reference separated by commas. This query looks for entities that contain both a Point and a Render component—only returning entities that have both. Once you call iter(), the query transforms into an iterator containing each matching entity's components grouped together.

You can use this query to obtain a list of every entity that can be rendered and draw them to the map as follows:

EntitiesComponentsAndSystems/playerecs/src/systems/entity_render.rs
```
use crate::prelude::*;

#[system]
#[read_component(Point)]
#[read_component(Render)]
pub fn entity_render(ecs: &SubWorld, #[resource] camera: &Camera) {
①    let mut draw_batch = DrawBatch::new();
    draw_batch.target(1);
    let offset = Point::new(camera.left_x, camera.top_y);

②    <(&Point, &Render)>::query()
③        .iter(ecs)
④        .for_each(|(pos, render)| {
⑤            draw_batch.set(
                *pos - offset,
                render.color,
                render.glyph
            );
        }
    );
⑥    draw_batch.submit(5000).expect("Batch error");
}
```

❶ Remember to start a new DrawBatch in each system that writes to the terminal.

❷ Query for all entities that have a Point and Render component.

❸ Transform the query into an iterator. You have to specify which SubWorld to use.

❹ for_each() works the same on a query as it does on a vector. Each call receives the query's components in a tuple. Destructure these to use the components by name.

❺ Set the screen character at the position in pos to the glyph and color specified in the Render component.

❻ Submit the render batch: 5,000 is used as a sort order because the map may include 4,000 elements. It's a good idea to leave some room in case that changes or you add some user interface elements.

Once again, you need to add your new system to the scheduler in systems/mods.rs:

```
mod map_render;
mod player_input;
mod entity_render;

pub fn build_scheduler() -> Schedule {
    Schedule::builder()
        .add_system(player_input::player_input_system())
        .add_system(map_render::map_render_system())
        .add_system(entity_render::entity_render_system())
        .build()
}
```

Run your game now, and you can move around the map just like before. If you watch closely in a debugger, you'll notice that your program is now multi-threaded. That's a great example of *fearless concurrency*, one of Rust's major selling points. Your game is now using many threads (the number will depend upon your hardware):

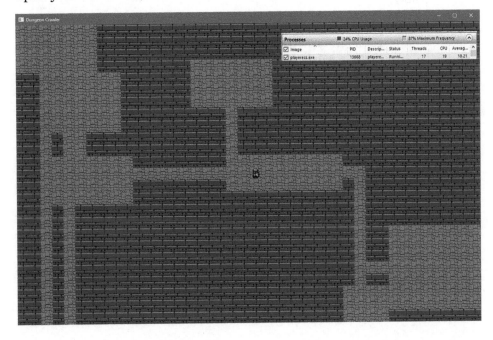

To see the real benefit of using an ECS, let's add some monsters that use most of the same components as the player.

Adding Monsters

Monsters have a lot in common with the player. They have a position and render information. They aren't keyboard controlled and they shouldn't have a Player tag. Instead, monsters need an Enemy tag component. Open components.rs, and add an Enemy tag:

EntitiesComponentsAndSystems/dungeonecs/src/components.rs
```
#[derive(Clone, Copy, Debug, PartialEq)]
pub struct Enemy;
```

An empty structure is all that's required for a tag class. You still need a way to spawn monsters. Open spawner.rs, and add a spawn_monster() function. It's very similar to the player spawning code:

EntitiesComponentsAndSystems/dungeonecs/src/spawner.rs
```
pub fn spawn_monster(
    ecs: &mut World,
    rng: &mut RandomNumberGenerator,
    pos : Point
) {
    ecs.push(
        (Enemy,
            pos,
            Render{
                color: ColorPair::new(WHITE, BLACK),
                glyph : match rng.range(0,4) {
                    0 => to_cp437('E'),
                    1 => to_cp437('O'),
                    2 => to_cp437('o'),
                    _ => to_cp437('g'),
                }
            }
        )
    );
}
```

To spice things up a bit, the spawning code randomly selects one of four monster types. E for ettin (a two-headed giant), O for ogre, o for orc and g for goblin. You'll differentiate monsters more in later chapters. For now, this shows how changing the Render component data can change the appearance of an entity without changing any other code.

Add Monsters to the Map

In your State constructor, you need to spawn some monsters. Let's spawn one per room, except in the first room with the player. The Rect structure you used to place rooms includes a center() function—you can combine this with a bit of iterator magic to efficiently place a random monster in each room:

```
EntitiesComponentsAndSystems/dungeonecs/src/main.rs
spawn_player(&mut ecs, map_builder.player_start);
map_builder.rooms
    .iter()
    .skip(1)
    .map(|r| r.center())
    .for_each(|pos| spawn_monster(&mut ecs, &mut rng, pos));
resources.insert(map_builder.map);
resources.insert(Camera::new(map_builder.player_start));
```

This is a good example of an iterator chain simplifying a procedure. The code includes some new iterator functions, so let's walk through the steps performed in the iterator chain:

1. Obtain an iterator with iter().

2. Skip the first room, with skip(1).

3. Transform each entry from a room to the result of center() (a Point) using map(). Mapping an iterator passes each entry into a closure, which can then return a different type of result. You can use map() to transform one type of iterator into another. After this call, you are iterating a list of Point data—representing the center of each room.

4. Call for_each to run a closure on each location. The closure receives the point as pos, and calls your spawn_monster() function with the location.

The monster graphics used are already in the dungeonfont.png file. Run the program now, and you'll see a monster in every room other than the player's starting point as shown in the image on page 124.

Notice that you didn't touch the rendering system at all. The system already knows how to render any entity with both a Point and a Render component. You can make entities with other combinations of components. If they have a Point and a Render component, the system will render them. This is a key benefit of Entity Component Systems—you can add functionality without affecting other systems.

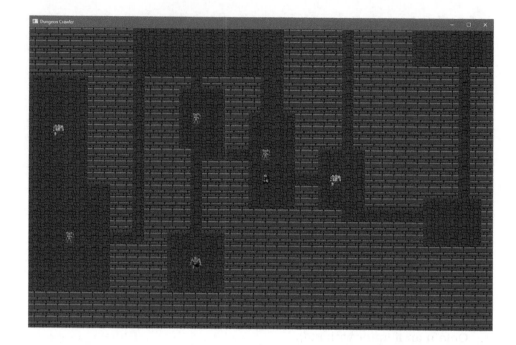

Collision Detection

If you run around the map, you'll notice that nothing happens when you hit a monster. Let's change that by adding *collision detection*. You'll write a combat system in Chapter 8, Health and Melee Combat, on page 141—for now, walking into a monster will remove it from the dungeon.

Collision detection will be its own system. Add a new file to your project, src/systems/collisions.rs. Don't forget to add mod collisions; to your src/systems/mod.rs file.

Start collisions.rs with a similar pattern:

EntitiesComponentsAndSystems/dungeonecs/src/systems/collisions.rs
```
use crate::prelude::*;

#[system]
❶ #[read_component(Point)]
#[read_component(Player)]
#[read_component(Enemy)]
❷ pub fn collisions(ecs: &mut SubWorld, commands: &mut CommandBuffer) {
```

❶ This system requires access to Point, Player, and Enemy.

❷ Legion can give your system a CommandBuffer. This is a special container to insert instructions for Legion to perform after the system is finished. You'll use the command buffer to remove entities from the game.

Next, create a variable named player_pos to store the player's position. You then create the same players query you used in player_input to find just the player's position. You then iterate the new query, storing the position you find in the new player_pos variable. Calculating the player's position once saves you from re-calculating it on each iteration of the second query.

EntitiesComponentsAndSystems/dungeonecs/src/systems/collisions.rs
```
let mut player_pos = Point::zero();
let mut players = <&Point>::query()
    .filter(component::<Player>());
players.iter(ecs).for_each(|pos| player_pos = *pos);
```

Next, you need a query that detects only enemies. This is very similar to the players query:

```
let mut enemies = <(Entity, &Point)>::query()
   .filter(component::<Enemy>());
```

You can use this query to find all enemy positions, check to see if the player has moved on top of them, and remove the enemy if the player has collided with them:

EntitiesComponentsAndSystems/dungeonecs/src/systems/collisions.rs
```
let mut enemies = <(Entity, &Point)>::query()
    .filter(component::<Enemy>());
enemies
    .iter(ecs)
❶    .filter(|(_,pos)| **pos == player_pos)
❷    .for_each(|(entity, _)| {
❸        commands.remove(*entity);
    }
);
```

❶ Filter removes iterator entries that don't meet criteria. Here, you're filtering only positions that match the player's position. The _ ignores the entity— you don't need it for the filter. By the time pos reaches the filter function, it has the type &&Point. It entered the query as a reference, and the iterator references it again. You want to compare with its actual value—so '**' removes the references.

❷ The first tuple entry is the Entity. You can ignore the position; you only need it for the filter.

❸ ECS commands provide the ability to create and delete entities from within systems. Calling commands.remove() instructs Legion to remove the specified entity from the world at the end of the frame.

Finally, you need to include the collisions system in your systems scheduler. Open systems/mod.rs and include the collision system in your scheduler:

EntitiesComponentsAndSystems/dungeonecs/src/systems/mod.rs
```
Schedule::builder()
    .add_system(player_input::player_input_system())
➤   .add_system(collisions::collisions_system())
    .add_system(map_render::map_render_system())
    .add_system(entity_render::entity_render_system())
    .build()
```

If you run your game now, you can remove monsters from the dungeon by running into them.

ECS and Code Reuse

One of the benefits of the Entity Component System model is code reuse. By creating a component and system to manage it, *any* entity can now have the component you created. You could use it for triggering alarms, mapping explosions, or making a talking sword greet anyone who approaches it.

It's a great idea to implement components and systems in this way. If you suddenly realize that your game needs to be able to set things on fire, you can implement OnFire—and possibly Flammable—and your game has gained a complete pyromania implementation.

Wrap-Up

In this chapter, you migrated your Dungeon Crawler to a modern ECS system. You learned concepts that apply to most professional game engines, including Unity, Unreal, and Godot. You also saw how it can help you—systems provide generic functionality to any entity with matching components. This allowed you to implement different rendering for monster types without changing your systems code. In the next chapter, you'll implement turn-based movement—you take your turn, and then the monsters move.

Take Turns with the Monsters

In the previous chapter, you extended your game to use an Entity Component System (ECS). You added monsters and a simple collision detection system to remove monsters from the dungeon when you bump into them. The monsters remained static, quietly awaiting their demise. In this chapter, you'll make the monsters move randomly. The game is then too fast to play, so you'll implement a turn-based game flow—similar to *Nethack*[1] or *Dungeon Crawl: Stone Soup*.[2] You'll learn to selectively schedule systems execution based upon turn state, and move to an intent-based system allowing for greater complexity such as movement being canceled by being stunned.

Making Monsters Wander Randomly

Let's start by making the monsters do something: move randomly through the dungeon. This isn't the overall behavior you'll keep for the finished game, but it can still be useful later. For example, adding *Confusion* effects may force an entity to move randomly. Bats and other irritants might flap randomly around the map. Like most ECS systems, the random movement system provides an option for you to use when adding functionality to your game.

You need a way to indicate that an entity moves randomly. This is best accomplished with a simple component—anything that has the component will wander aimlessly around the map. In components.rs, create a new tag component:

TurnBasedGames/wandering/src/components.rs
```
#[derive(Clone, Copy, Debug, PartialEq)]
pub struct MovingRandomly;
```

---

1.   https://www.nethack.org/
2.   https://crawl.develz.org/

Now that the component exists, you need a system that uses it.

Random Movement System

Create a new file and name it random_move.rs. Place this new file in your src/systems directory. Like the other systems, the new file is a module. The basic structure of the system is similar to the systems you created in Chapter 6, Compose Dungeon Denizens, on page 103:

`TurnBasedGames/wandering/src/systems/random_move.rs`
```
use crate::prelude::*;

#[system]
#[write_component(Point)]
#[read_component(MovingRandomly)]
❶ pub fn random_move(ecs: &mut SubWorld, #[resource] map: &Map) {
❷     let mut movers = <(&mut Point, &MovingRandomly)>::query();
       movers
           .iter_mut(ecs)
           .for_each(|(pos, _)| {
               let mut rng = RandomNumberGenerator::new();
❸             let destination = match rng.range(0, 4) {
                   0 => Point::new(-1, 0),
                   1 => Point::new(1, 0),
                   2 => Point::new(0, -1),
                   _ => Point::new(0, 1),
               } + *pos;

❹             if map.can_enter_tile(destination) {
❺                 *pos = destination;
               }
           }
       );
}
```

❶ Obtain read-only access to the Map resource.

❷ Create a new Query with writable access to Point and read-only access to MovingRandomly.

❸ Randomly choose a direction to move and store the delta. Add pos (the position) to it to determine the destination.

❹ Check that the destination tile is accessible.

❺ If the entity can enter the tile, move their position to the destination.

There's no intelligence behind this movement—it's completely random. Don't forget to register the new system in systems/mod.rs:

TurnBasedGames/wandering/src/systems/mod.rs
```
use crate::prelude::*;

mod map_render;
mod entity_render;
mod player_input;
mod collisions;
mod random_move;

pub fn build_scheduler() -> Schedule {
    Schedule::builder()
        .add_system(player_input::player_input_system())
        .add_system(collisions::collisions_system())
        .flush()
        .add_system(map_render::map_render_system())
        .add_system(entity_render::entity_render_system())
        .add_system(random_move::random_move_system())
        .build()
}
```

The flush() call is new. When a system executes commands—your collision detection code did in Collision Detection, on page 124—they don't take effect immediately. A hidden flush at the end of the systems tells Legion—the ECS library—to apply changes immediately. Flushing after collision detection ensures that any deleted entities are gone before they are rendered. Flushing also guarantees that all systems up to that point have finished executing before the next one runs. This is a handy way to tame multi-threading issues and ensure that subsequent systems use up-to-date information. It's a good idea to flush() your systems after you make changes—or at least before you rely on them.

Finally, you need to add the component to monsters so that they move randomly. Open spawner.rs, and add the new MovingRandomly component to the vector of components that describe new monsters:

TurnBasedGames/wandering/src/spawner.rs
```
    pos,
    Render{
        color: ColorPair::new(WHITE, BLACK),
        glyph : match rng.range(0,4) {
            0 => to_cp437('E'),
            1 => to_cp437('O'),
            2 => to_cp437('o'),
            _ => to_cp437('g'),
        }
    },
    MovingRandomly{}
)
```

Run the program now, and you'll see that a problem is immediately apparent. The monsters are zooming around the screen—so fast that they're a flickering blur. It's a good thing you didn't include a mechanism for them to kill the adventurer—the game would be over in the blink of an eye. You could implement a timing code—similar to what you used in Flappy Dragon, or you could implement a turn-based game. Your design document talked about making a turn-based game, which also solves the issue.

Moving Entites in a Turn-Based Game

Most traditional roguelike games (e.g. Nethack, Rogue, and Cogmind) are turn-based. You move, and then the enemies move. Even Diablo started as a turn-based game—the real-time movement aspect was added after play testing. Turn-based play provides for very tactical game play—you win games based on careful positioning and movement, and not with your reflexes. It's also required by the game design document you wrote in Chapter 4, Design a Dungeon Crawler, on page 71.

For a "you move, they move" cycle, you need three states: player moving, monsters moving, and waiting for input. You don't need to do much while you wait for input other than poll the keyboard and mouse, so save someone's laptop battery and do less. Separating input from action allows the game to be sure what you want to do before simulating your action—but generally allows the player to be treated just like other entities in the game.

The turn structure looks like this:

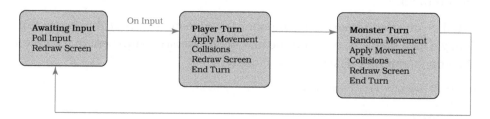

Storing Turn State

In your game, turn state represents exactly one of three states, so it's a natural fit for an enum. Create a new file named src/turn_state.rs, and define your enumeration:

```
TurnBasedGames/turnbased/src/turn_state.rs
#[derive(Copy, Clone, Debug, PartialEq)]
pub enum TurnState {
    AwaitingInput,
    PlayerTurn,
    MonsterTurn
}
```

Open main.rs and register the module:

```
mod turn_state;

mod prelude {
    ...
    pub use crate::turn_state::*;
}
```

In your State initialization, add an initial turn state—AwaitingInput—to your ECS resources:

```
...
resources.insert(TurnState::AwaitingInput);
Self {
    ecs,
    resources,
    systems: build_scheduler()
}
```

The game now knows what turn phase it is—let's use that information to implement a turn-based game.

Taking Turns

You need a way to transition to the next turn phase, once you are sure that the turn is complete. A new system can take care of this. Make a new file named systems/end_turn.rs. Add the new module to systems/mod.rs with mod end_turn;, after use crate::prelude::*. Place the following in the new file:

```
TurnBasedGames/turnbased/src/systems/end_turn.rs
use crate::prelude::*;

#[system]
❶ pub fn end_turn(#[resource] turn_state: &mut TurnState) {
    let new_state = match turn_state {
❷        TurnState::AwaitingInput => return,
❸        TurnState::PlayerTurn => TurnState::MonsterTurn,
❹        TurnState::MonsterTurn => TurnState::AwaitingInput
    };

❺    *turn_state = new_state;
}
```

❶ Obtain writable access to the TurnState resource.

❷ If the game is awaiting input, there's nothing to do—so exit the function immediately with return.

❸ If it's currently the player's turn, the next phase will be the monsters' turn.

❹ If the monsters' turn is ending, it's time to go back to waiting for input.

❺ Set the turn resource to the chosen value. The asterisk (*) de-references the variable, allowing you to write directly to the stored resource.

Don't add it to the list of running systems yet—the next task is to divide systems execution up by turn phase.

Keep Borrows Short

Rust's borrow/lending system makes it easy to share data. It's always tempting to store the borrowed data in case you need it later. Rust's borrow checker makes your life difficult when you do this—it has to be able to *prove* that no unsafe behavior occurs. Keeping your borrows as short as they can be prevents this frustration—and also avoids a whole class of common bugs that Rust was designed to prevent.

Dividing the Scheduler

It doesn't make sense to run every system in every phase. Nothing can move while the game is waiting for input. Monsters can't move while the player is moving. Input can't be accepted during any phase other than AwaitingInput. You still want to share a lot of functionality—make monsters and the player obey the same rules—but you can constrain which systems run in each phase by creating a separate scheduler for each turn state.

Open systems/mod.rs, and divide the build_scheduler() function into three functions—one for each input state.

TurnBasedGames/turnbased/src/systems/mod.rs
```
use crate::prelude::*;

mod map_render;
mod entity_render;
mod player_input;
mod collisions;
mod random_move;
mod end_turn;

pub fn build_input_scheduler() -> Schedule {
```

```
    Schedule::builder()
        .add_system(player_input::player_input_system())
        .flush()
        .add_system(map_render::map_render_system())
        .add_system(entity_render::entity_render_system())
        .build()
}
pub fn build_player_scheduler() -> Schedule {
    Schedule::builder()
        .add_system(collisions::collisions_system())
        .flush()
        .add_system(map_render::map_render_system())
        .add_system(entity_render::entity_render_system())
        .add_system(end_turn::end_turn_system())
        .build()
}
pub fn build_monster_scheduler() -> Schedule {
    Schedule::builder()
        .add_system(random_move::random_move_system())
        .flush()
        .add_system(collisions::collisions_system())
        .flush()
        .add_system(map_render::map_render_system())
        .add_system(entity_render::entity_render_system())
        .add_system(end_turn::end_turn_system())
        .build()
}
```

This is very similar to your build_scheduler function—but now you have three schedulers. Note that flush() is called when a system makes changes to the ECS dataset. The systems in each phase are carefully divided by what makes sense:

- While awaiting input, the screen still needs to display the map and entities. It also calls the player_input system.

- When it's the player's turn, the game doesn't accept input—but does check for collisions, as well as rendering everything. It finishes with end_turn.

- The monsters' turn is very similar to the player's, but adds random movement.

You need to adjust State in main.rs to include these separate schedulers instead of the single scheduler:

TurnBasedGames/turnbased/src/main.rs
```
struct State {
    ecs : World,
    resources: Resources,
```

```
    input_systems: Schedule,
    player_systems: Schedule,
    monster_systems: Schedule
}
```

You also need to adjust the state's constructor to initialize all three schedules:

TurnBasedGames/turnbased/src/main.rs
```
resources.insert(TurnState::AwaitingInput);
Self {
    ecs,
    resources,
    input_systems: build_input_scheduler(),
    player_systems: build_player_scheduler(),
    monster_systems: build_monster_scheduler()
}
```

Finally, replace the call to execute the single scheduler with a match statement calling the appropriate scheduler based upon the current turn state:

TurnBasedGames/turnbased/src/main.rs
```
let current_state = self.resources.get::<TurnState>().unwrap().clone();
match current_state {
    TurnState::AwaitingInput => self.input_systems.execute(
        &mut self.ecs,
        &mut self.resources
    ),
    TurnState::PlayerTurn => {
        self.player_systems.execute(&mut self.ecs, &mut self.resources);
    }
    TurnState::MonsterTurn => {
        self.monster_systems.execute(&mut self.ecs, &mut self.resources)
    }
}
render_draw_buffer(ctx).expect("Render error");
```

The line let current_state = self.resources.get::<TurnState>().unwrap().clone(); is a little strange, so let's unpack it:

- self.resources.get::<TYPE> requests a resource of a given type (in this case TurnState) from the ECS's resources.

- The result is returned as an Option, so you need to unwrap() it to access the contents. You know for sure that a turn state exists, so you can skip error checking for once.

- The final call to clone() duplicates the state. This ensures that the resource is no longer borrowed—you're looking at a copy of the current turn state, rather than the original. This is another example of working around Rust's borrow checker.

Ending the Player's Turn

The last thing to do is to advance the turn state when user input is submitted. Open systems/player_input.rs. Amend the header to retrieve the TurnState resource:

```
pub fn player_input(
    ecs: &mut SubWorld,
    #[resource] map: &Map,
    #[resource] key: &Option<VirtualKeyCode>,
    #[resource] camera: &mut Camera,
➤    #[resource] turn_state: &mut TurnState
)
{
```

You also need to update TurnState to PlayerTurn when the player has acted. You can do this by adding one line to your movement handler:

```
if map.can_enter_tile(destination) {
    *pos = destination;
    camera.on_player_move(destination);
➤    *turn_state = TurnState::PlayerTurn;
}
```

Run the game now. You can move around the dungeon and the monsters move once after each of your moves, as shown in the image on page 136.

Now that you have a working turn-based game, let's improve upon it a bit. You can reduce the number of systems that modify overall game state. Introduce opportunities for future improvements by moving away from systems directly modifying state and towards messages of intent.

Sending Messages of Intent

Currently, the PlayerInput and RandomMovement systems load the map and check for tile access. As you add more game-play elements, you don't want to remember to update both of them—and any other system that can produce movement. Instead, you can share a lot of the functionality by having systems that produce movement send a message indicating that an entity *intends* to move. A later system can then process all of the movement requests and apply them if possible. This is very powerful. Suppose you add a stun mechanic—stunned monsters can't move. Your system that handles stun could remove movement intention from any entity, and you wouldn't have to change a line of the other systems.

Move near monster.

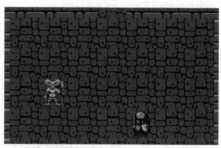

Skip turn (space),
Monster moves.

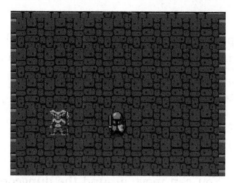

Move north (up arrow)
Monster moves, too.

Messages Can Be Entities Too

Games often feature elaborate messaging systems. Message queuing and efficient handling of messages could easily fill its own book—so this book will keep it simple. You can build an efficient messaging system inside an ECS by treating each message as its own entity. You'll need a new component type for the message. Open components.rs and create two new component structures:

TurnBasedGames/intent/src/components.rs
```
#[derive(Clone, Copy, Debug, PartialEq)]
pub struct WantsToMove {
    pub entity : Entity,
    pub destination : Point
}
```

These are just like the other components you have built—simple Rust structs that derive Copy, Clone, PartialEq, and Debug. In WantsToMove you are storing an Entity. This is what it sounds like: a reference to an entity inside Legion.

Receiving Messages and Moving

You need a new system to receive WantToMove messages and apply the movement. Create a new file named src/systems/movement.rs. Add the following code to the file:

TurnBasedGames/intent/src/systems/movement.rs
```
use crate::prelude::*;

❶ #[system(for_each)]
   #[read_component(Player)]
   pub fn movement(
       entity: &Entity,
       want_move: &WantsToMove,
       #[resource] map: &Map,
       #[resource] camera: &mut Camera,
       ecs: &mut SubWorld,
       commands: &mut CommandBuffer
   ) {
       if map.can_enter_tile(want_move.destination) {
❷          commands.add_component(want_move.entity, want_move.destination);

❸          if ecs.entry_ref(want_move.entity)
❹              .unwrap()
❺              .get_component::<Player>().is_ok()
           {
❻              camera.on_player_move(want_move.destination);
           }
       }
❼      commands.remove(*entity);
   }
```

❶ Legion provides a shorthand for systems that only run a single query. Declaring a system as system(for_each) derives the query from the system parameters—and runs the system once for every matching entity. This is the same as declaring a query that reads Entity and WantsToMove and iterating it as you have with other systems.

❷ It's safer and more efficient to use commands, rather than directly modifying the component. Legion can batch the updates and perform them all at once very quickly. Adding a component that already exists replaces the old one.

❸ Accessing components on an entity outside of your query is a little more complicated. You can access the details of another component with the entry_ref() method. This returns a Result, indicating if the entity is available to the sub-world. Entities are only available if you've specified the components that they use in your read_component or write_component declarations for the system.

❹ You know the entity that wishes to move exists, so you can unwrap() the Option to access its contents.

❺ With the entry, you then call get_component() to access the entity's component. This returns a Result. You can check if the component exists by calling is_ok().

❻ To reach this point, you've determined that the moving entity exists and is a player. You can now call on_player_move() to update the player's camera information.

❼ It's important to remove messages once they are processed. If you don't, they will be processed again on the next turn.

The movement system iterates all entities with a WantsToMove component. It then checks that the move is valid, and if it is, replaces the Point component of the target entity. If the entity is a player, it also updates the camera.

Register the new system in src/systems/mod.rs with mod movement;, and add it to the list of systems executed in the player's and monsters' turns:

```
TurnBasedGames/intent/src/systems/mod.rs
pub fn build_player_scheduler() -> Schedule {
    Schedule::builder()
➤       .add_system(movement::movement_system())
➤       .flush()
        .add_system(collisions::collisions_system())
        .flush()
        .add_system(map_render::map_render_system())
        .add_system(entity_render::entity_render_system())
        .add_system(end_turn::end_turn_system())
        .build()
}

pub fn build_monster_scheduler() -> Schedule {
    Schedule::builder()
        .add_system(random_move::random_move_system())
        .flush()
➤       .add_system(movement::movement_system())
➤       .flush()
        .add_system(map_render::map_render_system())
        .add_system(entity_render::entity_render_system())
        .add_system(end_turn::end_turn_system())
        .build()
}
```

Notice that the new code is calling flush() after the movement system executes—this immediately applies the changes it made in its command buffer.

Simplified Player Input

The player_input system can be simplified to take advantage of these changes. Rather than checking move validity and directly editing the Point component, it can create a WantsToMove message. The first part of systems/player_input.rs is simplified to no longer need write-access to Point, and no longer need access to the map:

TurnBasedGames/intent/src/systems/player_input.rs
```
#[system]
#[read_component(Point)]
#[read_component(Player)]
pub fn player_input(
    ecs: &mut SubWorld,
    commands: &mut CommandBuffer,
    #[resource] key: &Option<VirtualKeyCode>,
    #[resource] turn_state: &mut TurnState
) {
    let mut players = <(Entity, &Point)>::query()
        .filter(component::<Player>());
```

Generating the "delta" for movement remains unchanged:

TurnBasedGames/intent/src/systems/player_input.rs
```
if let Some(key) = *key {
    let delta = match key {
        VirtualKeyCode::Left => Point::new(-1, 0),
        VirtualKeyCode::Right => Point::new(1, 0),
        VirtualKeyCode::Up => Point::new(0, -1),
        VirtualKeyCode::Down => Point::new(0, 1),
        _ => Point::new(0, 0),
    };
```

Instead of checking the map, and writing to Point, the program now emits a WantsToMove message:

TurnBasedGames/intent/src/systems/player_input.rs
```
players.iter(ecs).for_each(| (entity, pos) | {
    let destination = *pos + delta;
    commands
        .push(((), WantsToMove{ entity: *entity, destination }));
});
*turn_state = TurnState::PlayerTurn;
```

You can add new entities with the commands buffer in systems. It follows the same syntax as the world.push system you used in spawner.rs. Note that you insert type tuple ((), WantsToMove{..}). Legion's push function doesn't work with single-component insertions.

The player now uses the same movement system as the monsters.

Monster Movement Messages

Updating the random_move system to use WantsToMove components is very similar. Instead of checking the map and writing directly to Point, you create a WantsToMove message:

```
TurnBasedGames/intent/src/systems/random_move.rs
use crate::prelude::*;

#[system]
#[read_component(Point)]
#[read_component(MovingRandomly)]
pub fn random_move(ecs: &SubWorld, commands: &mut CommandBuffer) {
    let mut movers = <(Entity, &Point, &MovingRandomly)>::query();
    movers.iter(ecs).for_each(| (entity, pos, _) | {
        let mut rng = RandomNumberGenerator::new();
        let destination = match rng.range(0, 4) {
            0 => Point::new(-1, 0),
            1 => Point::new(1, 0),
            2 => Point::new(0, -1),
            _ => Point::new(0, 1),
        } + *pos;

        commands
            .push(((), WantsToMove{ entity: *entity, destination }));
    });
}
```

The system hasn't changed very much, and the message creation code is almost exactly the same as it was in the player action system.

Run the program now, and you have a turn-based Dungeon Crawler. You move—or press another key to wait—and then the monsters move. If they move into you—or you move into them—they are destroyed.

Wrap-Up

In this chapter, you extended the ECS system to allow monsters to move. You implemented a turn-based game by tracking current turn state, and dividing the System scheduler into multiple parts. You also moved beyond directly writing to the game state by implementing messages—indicating intent—so that later systems can process them. Using an intent-based messaging system removed duplicate code, reduced dependencies between systems, and grants future flexibility. In the next chapter, you'll add another intent—the intent to attack (or be attacked by) a monster.

CHAPTER 8

Health and Melee Combat

The brave protagonist rounds a corner in the dungeon and spots a vile goblin. Charging forward, she exchanges blows with the creature until she emerges victorious. Suddenly conscious of her wounds, she stumbles back into the corridor to rest—hoping that the other goblin won't find her.

This scene is typical of fantasy novels and roleplaying games like *Dungeons & Dragons*. Implementing this scene in-game requires several elements. The hero can move and fight the goblin. The goblin can fight back. The hero is conscious of their status and realizes that they need healing. They heal by hiding in a corner and waiting.

In the previous chapter, you made the monsters move randomly. This chapter focuses on making the introductory scene a reality in your game. You'll add hit points to entities, both the monsters and the player. You'll also introduce a Heads-Up Display to show the player's health, and tool-tips to show the monsters' names and health. Moving into a monster will attack it, reducing the monster's health and slaying them if their health reaches zero—likewise, monsters who move into the player will damage the player. Finally, you'll add the ability for the player to heal by waiting—enabling more strategic play.

Giving Entities Hit Points

Adding hit points to entities requires a new component type. This is a common theme in ECS design patterns—whenever you want to represent something new about entities, you add a component type. Open src/components.rs and add another component type to the file:

HealthSimpleMelee/health/src/components.rs
```
#[derive(Clone, Copy, Debug, PartialEq)]
pub struct Health {
    pub current: i32,
    pub max: i32
}
```

This component stores both the current and max (maximum) hit points of an entity. It's important to store the maximum hit points because health bars are scaled to show how much health an entity is missing. When an entity is healed, you can use the maximum hit points to ensure it's not healed above its maximum.

Now that you have a Health component, let's add it to the player.

Adding Health to the Player

Open src/spawner.rs and locate the spawn_player() function. Extend it to include a health component for the player:

HealthSimpleMelee/health/src/spawner.rs
```
ecs.push(
    (Player,
        pos,
        Render{
            color: ColorPair::new(WHITE, BLACK),
            glyph : to_cp437('@')
        },
➤        Health{ current: 20, max: 20 }
    )
);
```

You've giving the player 20 hit points. That's quite a few hit points, but you can tweak it later. Picking a large number is helpful during development because it lets you debug the game without worrying about instantly dying when you hit the wrong key.

The player now has hit points but no way to see the current value. Don't worry, though, you're about to fix that.

Adding a Heads-up Display

Most games display information onscreen about the players, such as their health, names, any power-ups they may have, or other useful information. This data usually displays near the top of the main game display in what's known as a *Heads-Up Display (HUD)*—named after some really cool military hardware that lets pilots see data about their aircraft without looking down at an instrument panel.

You need the Heads-Up Display to render on top of the map, in a smaller font so that it is both easier to read and can contain more detail than you would fit on a layer with huge graphical tiles.

Adding Another Rendering Layer

The game currently has two layers: the map and entities. The HUD lives on a third layer, rendered on top of the main display. It's helpful to use smaller font in the HUD than what you're using to display the game tile—with smaller font, you can display more information without overly cluttering the screen.

The layers are arranged like this:

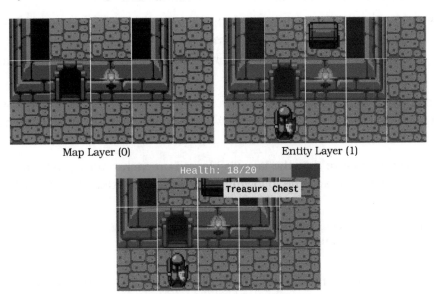

Map Layer (0) Entity Layer (1)

Heads-Up Display Layer (2)

Open main.rs and navigate to the initialization in the main() function. Change the initialization as follows:

HealthSimpleMelee/health/src/main.rs
```
let context = BTermBuilder::new()
    .with_title("Dungeon Crawler")
    .with_fps_cap(30.0)
    .with_dimensions(DISPLAY_WIDTH, DISPLAY_HEIGHT)
    .with_tile_dimensions(32, 32)
    .with_resource_path("resources/")
❶   .with_font("dungeonfont.png", 32, 32)
❷   .with_font("terminal8x8.png", 8, 8)
❸   .with_simple_console(DISPLAY_WIDTH, DISPLAY_HEIGHT,
        "dungeonfont.png")
```

```
    .with_simple_console_no_bg(DISPLAY_WIDTH, DISPLAY_HEIGHT,
        "dungeonfont.png")
    .with_simple_console_no_bg(SCREEN_WIDTH*2, SCREEN_HEIGHT*2,
        "terminal8x8.png")
    .build()?;
```

❹

Much of this should be familiar from previous chapters. The highlighted lines indicate changes:

❶ When using multiple fonts, you have to load every font explicitly. dungeon-font.png contains the map and monster tiles you used in previous chapters.

❷ terminal8x8.png contains regular ASCII/CP437 characters.

❸ Each simple console specifies the font it should use.

❹ Note that you're specifying SCREEN_WIDTH * 2 as the size. There's room on the screen for twice as many characters as the underlying terminal. This lets you be verbose in your descriptions. bracket-lib takes care of scaling for you.

This code creates the layers. You selected the previous layers with set_active_console() set to 0 or 1. The new layer is on top of them, so it becomes layer 2.

You need to ensure that the layer is cleared on each render pass. Open the tick() function, and add the following code to your existing set_active_console/cls cycle:

HealthSimpleMelee/health/src/main.rs
```
ctx.set_active_console(2);
ctx.cls();
```

This is the same as the cls() calls to the other consoles—it just clears the new console layer as well.

With the layer cleared, you have a blank slate upon which to draw the HUD.

Rendering the HUD

HUD rendering requires its own system. Create a new file, src/systems/hud.rs. Place the following into the file:

HealthSimpleMelee/health/src/systems/hud.rs
```
use crate::prelude::*;

#[system]
#[read_component(Health)]
#[read_component(Player)]
pub fn hud(ecs: &SubWorld) {
    let mut health_query = <&Health>::query().filter(component::<Player>());
```
❶

```
    let player_health = health_query
        .iter(ecs)
        .nth(0)
        .unwrap();

    let mut draw_batch = DrawBatch::new();
    draw_batch.target(2);
    draw_batch.print_centered(1,
        "Explore the Dungeon. Cursor keys to move.");
    draw_batch.bar_horizontal(
        Point::zero(),
        SCREEN_WIDTH*2,
        player_health.current,
        player_health.max,
        ColorPair::new(RED, BLACK)
    );
    draw_batch.print_color_centered(
        0,
        format!(" Health: {} / {} ",
            player_health.current,
            player_health.max
        ),
        ColorPair::new(WHITE, RED)
    );
    draw_batch.submit(10000).expect("Batch error");
}
```

The general system layout and boilerplate are similar to the systems you've already created, and there's only one new command: bar_horizontal()—a helper function that assists with health bars. Health bars are a common enough game element that most major engines provide some assistance with them.

❶ Define a query that reads Health components, filtered to show only the Player.

❷ nth() is another Rust iterator feature. It retrieves a single entry from an iterator as an option. You know that there is a player, so it's safe to unwrap() the option—extracting the player's health component.

❸ Draw to the HUD console layer.

❹ Greet the player and give them an idea of how to play.

❺ bar_horizontal() is a helper method in bracket-lib designed to help with the common task of drawing health bars.

❻ The first parameter specifies where the bar should start.

❼ The second parameter states how wide (in characters) the bar should be.

❽ The *current* value of the bar.

❾ The *maximum* value of the bar. Bracket-lib will divide the current value into this one (as 'f32' to preserve decimals) and fill the appropriate portion of the bar to match the resulting percentage.

❿ A pair of colors specifying the color of the full and empty health bar.

Don't forget to register the system. Add mod hud; to your systems/mod.rs file, and add .add_system(hud::hud_system()) to each of the systems builders before end_turn. You'll see the completed code in Register Your Systems, on page 150, after you've added some more information about monsters.

Registering Modules

 When you create a new file, it's a good idea to immediately add it to the parent mod.rs or main.rs file. Your IDE's code analysis plugin (Rust, or Rust Analyzer) will ignore the new file until you do so. Add it early, and your development environment can immediately begin to offer advice and assistance as you write the module.

Naming Monsters

The HUD provides a golden opportunity to tell the player about the entities on the map via *tooltips*. Tooltips are text that pops up when you hover the mouse over an icon.

Names are another component type. Add the following code to components.rs:

```
HealthSimpleMelee/health/src/components.rs
#[derive(Clone, PartialEq)]
pub struct Name(pub String);
```

Notice that the syntax is different here. Structs can also be tuples. If you only have one piece of information to store inside a struct, you can replace the named fields with (pub type)—in this case, String. You can then access the structure's contents just like a tuple - mystruct.0 contains the string. This can be a convenient shorthand when your structure only contains one or two items, but it's less readable. An in-development (at the time of writing) extension to Rust will allow you to mark single-entry structures as "transparent" and directly access the contents.[1]

Having created a name component, let's add it to the monsters—along with some health.

---

1.   https://doc.rust-lang.org/1.26.2/unstable-book/language-features/repr-transparent.html

Giving Monsters Names and Hit Points

Open spawner.rs, and navigate to the spawn_monster function. Currently, monsters only vary by the glyph they are assigned. As the game grows in complexity, you want more variety of monsters. For now, you'll vary their name and hit points. Create a new function named goblin():

HealthSimpleMelee/health/src/spawner.rs
```
fn goblin() -> (i32, String, FontCharType) {
    (1, "Goblin".to_string(), to_cp437('g'))
}
```

This is a straightforward function. It returns a tuple containing a hit point count, a name, and a FontCharType (reference to an ASCII character) for the goblin. Add another function, this time name it orc():

HealthSimpleMelee/health/src/spawner.rs
```
fn orc() -> (i32, String, FontCharType) {
    (2, "Orc".to_string(), to_cp437('o'))
}
```

This function returns a tuple describing the orc. Notice that the orc has more hit points and uses the o character (which maps to an orc in the font file).

You can now change spawn_monster() to randomly create an orc or a goblin, and assign a name and health component to it:

HealthSimpleMelee/health/src/spawner.rs
```
pub fn spawn_monster(
    ecs: &mut World,
    rng: &mut RandomNumberGenerator,
    pos : Point
) {
```
❶
❷
```
    let (hp, name, glyph) = match rng.roll_dice(1,10) {
        1..=8 => goblin(),
        _ => orc()
    };

    ecs.push(
        (Enemy,
            pos,
            Render{
                color: ColorPair::new(WHITE, BLACK),
                glyph,
            },
            MovingRandomly{},
```
❸
❹
```
            Health{current: hp, max: hp},
            Name(name)
        )
    );
}
```

❶ The orc() and goblin() functions return a tuple. You can destructure data out
of tuples using this syntax. let (a, b, c) = function_returns_three_values. This lets
you name your variables, rather than remembering that .0 is hit points,
.1 is the name, etc.

❷ You want more of the easy monsters—goblins—and fewer of the tougher
orcs. The game creates a random number between 1 and 10, and spawns
a goblin for 1..8—otherwise, it spawns an orc. Match can only match on
inclusive ranges, requiring the equals (..=) symbol.

❸ Add the new health component like other components.

❹ The name component syntax is slightly different because it's a tuple struct.

Now that you have monsters with names and hit points, let's display that
data as tooltips.

Identifying Monsters with Tooltips

Before you can pop up information at the mouse location, you need to know
where the mouse is. Bracket-lib provides this information with a function named
mouse_pos(), associated with the context data. In main.rs, find where you inserted
ctx.key as a resource and do the same with the mouse position:

HealthSimpleMelee/health/src/main.rs
```
self.resources.insert(ctx.key);
ctx.set_active_console(0);
self.resources.insert(Point::from_tuple(ctx.mouse_pos()));
```

Virtual consoles can have different resolutions, and the mouse position is
provided in terminal coordinates. You should call set_active_console before
requesting the mouse_pos to ensure that you receive coordinates for the correct
terminal layer.

Rather than use Point::new, use a constructor named from_tuple(). It's a common
Rust convention that when one type can be created from another type, the
constructor is named from_x(). The mouse_pos() function returns a tuple containing x and y screen positions. Converting it to a Point helps retain consistency,
since you're already using Point types for locations.

Displaying the tooltips should be done in another system. Create a new file
named systems/tooltips.rs. It's a large system, so let's step through each section:

HealthSimpleMelee/health/src/systems/tooltips.rs
```
use crate::prelude::*;

#[system]
#[read_component(Point)]
```

```
    #[read_component(Name)]
    #[read_component(Health)]
    pub fn tooltips(
        ecs: &SubWorld,
❶      #[resource] mouse_pos: &Point,
❷      #[resource] camera: &Camera
    ) {
❸      let mut positions = <(Entity, &Point, &Name)>::query();
```

❶ Request read-only access to the mouse position you inserted as a Point.

❷ Request read-only access to the camera.

❸ Including Entity in the query includes the parent entity (that owns the components) in the query. This query returns the Entity and the Point and Name components from entities that have both of these components.

With the system boilerplate done, let's draw the tooltips:

HealthSimpleMelee/health/src/systems/tooltips.rs

```
        let offset = Point::new(camera.left_x, camera.top_y);
❶      let map_pos = *mouse_pos + offset;
        let mut draw_batch = DrawBatch::new();
        draw_batch.target(2);
        positions
            .iter(ecs)
❷          .filter(|(_, pos, _)| **pos == map_pos )
            .for_each(|(entity, _, name) | {
❸              let screen_pos = *mouse_pos * 4;
❹              let display = if let Ok(health) = ecs.entry_ref(*entity)
                    .unwrap()
                    .get_component::<Health>()
                {
❺                  format!("{} : {} hp", &name.0, health.current)
❻              } else {
                    name.0.clone()
                };
                draw_batch.print(screen_pos, &display);
            });
        draw_batch.submit(10100).expect("Batch error");
    }
```

❶ The current position plus the left and top of the screen—the offset—gives you the screen position of an entity.

❷ Filtering is the same as including an if statement in your code, but it's often slightly faster. Many also consider it easier to read. The filter call reduces the contents of the iterator to *only* include elements whose Point position is equal to the current mouse cursor position stored in map_pos.

❸ The mouse position is in coordinates that align with the monsters layer. The tooltips layer is four times larger—so multiply the mouse position by four to get the screen position for the tooltip layer.

❹ You still need to use entry_ref() to access an entity's components from outside of a query. Start by requesting the entry and unwrapping it. On the resulting entry, use get_component() to retrieve a component from the ECS without a query. It returns a Result, so if let provides an easy way to read the component's contents if there is one—and ignore it if there isn't.

❺ Use the format! macro to build the string "Monster Name: X hp."

❻ if let is like other if statements—if there's no match, you can run code in the else block. If the player is examining something that doesn't have a health component—maybe it's a table or amulet—return just the name. Clone is used to make a copy of the string—rather than borrowing it.

Now that your systems are created, you need to register them with the scheduler.

Register Your Systems

You need to register both tooltips and hud in your systems module, and add them to the systems execution:

```
...
mod movement;
➤ mod hud;
➤ mod tooltips;

pub fn build_input_scheduler() -> Schedule {
    Schedule::builder()
        ..
➤       .add_system(hud::hud_system())
➤       .add_system(tooltips::tooltips_system())
        .build()
}

pub fn build_player_scheduler() -> Schedule {
    Schedule::builder()
        ..
➤       .add_system(hud::hud_system())
➤       .add_system(end_turn::end_turn_system())
        .build()
}

pub fn build_monster_scheduler() -> Schedule {
    Schedule::builder()
        ..
➤       .add_system(hud::hud_system())
```

```
➤        .add_system(end_turn::end_turn_system())
         .build()
}
```

Run the program now. You'll see a greeting and health bar, and tooltips when you hover the mouse over a monster:

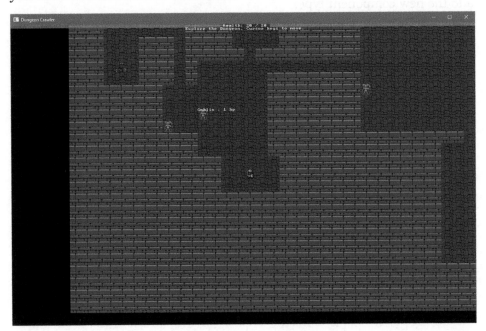

With the health component in place, and tooltips to show you what's going on, it's time to engage some monsters in melee.

Implementing Combat

Combat plays a large part in most games—so it's worth the effort to develop a flexible system. You now have all of the elements required to implement combat. Monsters and the player have health, you know where they are, and you display the results. Let's implement "bump to attack" melee combat.

Remove the Collision System

You need to start by removing the existing collision system. It served its purpose, but you need something more advanced to handle combat. Remove the file systems/collision.rs and all references to it and remove calls to the collision system in systems/mod.rs.

Indicating Intent to Attack

The WantsToMove component indicates that an entity intends to move into a tile. You can indicate that an entity wishes to attack another entity in a similar fashion—by creating a WantsToAttack component. Open components.rs and add the new component type:

```
HealthSimpleMelee/combat/src/components.rs
#[derive(Clone, Copy, Debug, PartialEq)]
pub struct WantsToAttack {
    pub attacker : Entity,
    pub victim : Entity
}
```

The component stores both the attacker and the victim as Entity types. You'll need to track the attacker later, when you start offering rewards for ridding the dungeon of vile monsters.

Player Move to Attack

Open systems/player_input.rs. You determine the destination tile as before, but rather than blindly issuing a *move* instruction, you should check the destination tile for monsters. If a monster is present, you issue an attack order.

Let's refactor the player_input system to use the new approach. The start of the system can stay the same—it does what you need. Navigate to the end of the let delta = match section.

The first refactor replaces the players iterator. You'll need a copy of the destination and player entity, so it's a good idea to obtain them efficiently up front:

```
HealthSimpleMelee/combat/src/systems/player_input.rs
let (player_entity, destination) = players
        .iter(ecs)
        .find_map(|(entity, pos)| Some((*entity, *pos + delta)) )
        .unwrap();
```

This is similar to code you've written before, and uses some Rust tricks for brevity. player_entity and destination are de-structured from the iterator results. find_map() is an extension to the map process you used before. Like map, it transforms iterator data into other iterator data—the entity and calculated destination. Unlike map, it stops the first time you return Some data as an option. Calling unwrap as the final step retrieves your tuple from the iterator chain, and it's then stored in the two variables you listed at the beginning.

The next step is to ensure that the player tried to move (delta is non-zero), and check if an enemy is in the destination tile:

```
HealthSimpleMelee/combat/src/systems/player_input.rs
let mut enemies = <(Entity, &Point)>::query().filter(component::<Enemy>());
if delta.x !=0 || delta.y != 0 {
    let mut hit_something = false;
    enemies
        .iter(ecs)
        .filter(|(_, pos)| {
            **pos == destination
        })
```

This code has two important parts. It sets hit_something to false—a flag you'll use to indicate if combat was initiated.

It then runs a for_each on the remaining entities (if any matched; an empty iterator will skip this step):

```
HealthSimpleMelee/combat/src/systems/player_input.rs
.for_each(|(entity, _) | {
    hit_something = true;

    commands
        .push(((), WantsToAttack{
            attacker: player_entity,
            victim: *entity,
        }));
});
```

This is quite straightforward: if the loop executes, then you already know that you're targeting an enemy who is standing in the destination tile. So you set hit_something to true, and send a command to Legion (the ECS) to create a WantsToAttack message entity with the attacker (the player) and victim listed in it.

Finally, the system handles the case in which you *didn't* hit something:

```
HealthSimpleMelee/combat/src/systems/player_input.rs
    if !hit_something {
        commands
            .push(((), WantsToMove{
                entity: player_entity,
                destination
            }));
    }
}
*turn_state = TurnState::PlayerTurn;
```

If you didn't initiate an attack, it sends a WantsToMove just like it did before—and advances the turn phase to the processing phase.

Now that you're requesting attacks, it's time to kick some monster butt!

Creating a Combat System

You'll handle combat calculations in their own system. Create a new file named systems/combat.rs. Don't forget to add mod combat; to your systems/mod.rs file.

The system starts with the usual system boilerplate before you define a query:

HealthSimpleMelee/combat/src/systems/combat.rs
```
use crate::prelude::*;

#[system]
#[read_component(WantsToAttack)]
#[write_component(Health)]
pub fn combat(ecs: &mut SubWorld, commands: &mut CommandBuffer) {
    let mut attackers = <(Entity, &WantsToAttack)>::query();
```

The query reads WantsToAttack—providing a list of entities that wish to initiate combat.

You then build a list of victims. Add the following code to your function:

HealthSimpleMelee/combat/src/systems/combat.rs
```
❶ let victims : Vec<(Entity, Entity)> = attackers
    .iter(ecs)
❷  .map(|(entity, attack)| (*entity, attack.victim) )
❸  .collect();
```

❶ At the end of the iteration, you will call collect() to take the iterator's results and put them into a vector. collect() doesn't know what type of collection you'd like to use. Specifying that victims are a vector of (Entity, Entity) tuples tells the compiler your intended type. collect() can then gather your results into the correct type of collection.

❷ When you map() an iterator, you translate it into different data. Map takes a closure as its parameter. The closure receives entity and attack as inputs. It returns a tuple containing the entity (de-references, because iterating turned it into a reference) and the attack.victim.

❸ collect() gathers the current data from an iterator and creates a new collection containing the iterator's results. It can deduce the required collection type from the let statement at the beginning of the iterator, or you can use a turbofish to specify the collection type you require.

The Turbofish Is Your Friend

When you declare a type with one or more associated types, you are using Rust's *generics*. You can declare a vector that holds any type you want with the syntax Vec<MyType>.

The Turbofish Is Your Friend

Sometimes a function needs a type annotation too. The turbofish lives to help with that. You can add a turbofish to a function call with the syntax function::<Type>(). For example, collect::<Vec<MyType>>().

If you have trouble remembering the turbofish, you can find a website dedicated to them.[2]

If you were to modify the attack victims inside the query, you would run into two issues:

- Modifying a collection while you iterate it is a bad idea. You can invalidate the iterator, and Rust will do its best to prevent you from doing that.

- You will run into *borrow checker* problems because you are simultaneously borrowing the data to iterate and to update.

In Rust, it's generally a better idea to obtain the list of data on which you will act—and then modify it in a separate loop.

Now that you have gathered pairs of attackers and defenders into your victims list, it's time to check if the victim has a Health component. If they do, you damage them by reducing their hit points:

```
HealthSimpleMelee/combat/src/systems/combat.rs
victims.iter().for_each(|(message, victim)| {
    if let Ok(mut health) = ecs
        .entry_mut(*victim)
        .unwrap()
        .get_component_mut::<Health>()
    {
        println!("Health before attack: {}", health.current);
        health.current -= 1;
        if health.current < 1 {
            commands.remove(*victim);
        }
        println!("Health after attack: {}", health.current);
    }
    commands.remove(*message);
});
```

This code iterates the victims collection you just created. Then it uses if let to activate only if the victim has health (once again, preventing you from mindlessly beating up inanimate objects). It then reduces the victim's current

---

2. https://turbo.fish/

health by one. If the victim's hit points are less than one, the victim is deleted from the game. Finally, it deletes the WantsToAttack message.

Printing Is a Great Debugging Tool

You'll notice that this system contains println! statements. They print the victim's health before and after the attack. You'll want to delete or comment out these lines before sharing them with your friends, but it's a great way to double check that your program is working as intended.

Many programmers call this printf debugging, named after the equivalent in C. It can be a lot easier than attaching your debugger, setting a breakpoint, and watching the code execute.

Now that your player can defeat enemies, it's time to make the enemies fight back.

The Monsters Strike Back

Fighting hordes of monsters is a lot more fun when they can fight back. Random movement isn't ideal for this—and the monsters will start to behave intelligently very soon—but implementing it completes combat. Open your systems/random_move.rs system. A lot of the system won't change, but you need to incorporate attacking the player. Start by adjusting the system to be able to read Player and Health—and no longer require the map:

HealthSimpleMelee/combat/src/systems/random_move.rs
```
#[system]
#[read_component(Point)]
#[read_component(MovingRandomly)]
➤ #[read_component(Health)]
➤ #[read_component(Player)]
pub fn random_move(ecs: &SubWorld, commands: &mut CommandBuffer) {
```

In addition to the Point/MovingRandomly query, add a second query that gets the positions of any entity with a health component:

HealthSimpleMelee/combat/src/systems/random_move.rs
```
let mut movers = <(Entity, &Point, &MovingRandomly)>::query();
let mut positions = <(Entity, &Point, &Health)>::query();
```

The random destination code remains the same, but instead of immediately issuing a move instruction, you need to check the destination for potential targets. Insert the following code inside the for_each iterator, immediately after you assign destination:

HealthSimpleMelee/combat/src/systems/random_move.rs

```
let mut attacked = false;
positions
    .iter(ecs)
    .filter(|(_, target_pos, _)| **target_pos == destination)
    .for_each(|(victim, _, _)| {
        if ecs.entry_ref(*victim)
        .unwrap().get_component::<Player>().is_ok()
        {
            commands
                .push(((), WantsToAttack{
                    attacker: *entity,
                    victim: *victim
                }));
        }
        attacked = true;
    }
);
```

This code is very similar to the code you used in the player's movement system. It queries all entities and filters to only list ones in the destination tile. If the destination contains an entity, it checks to see if the target has the Player component. If it does, it sends a WantsToAttack command.

Notice that attacked is set to true even if no attack was launched. This prevents the monster from moving into a tile containing another monster. Nobody needs to be harassed by goblin-cheerleading pyramids, and the game doesn't have a way to render it correctly if it happens.

Finally, the system wraps the creation of a WantsToMove command in a check that no attack was launched:

HealthSimpleMelee/combat/src/systems/random_move.rs

```
if !attacked {
    commands
        .push(((), WantsToMove{ entity: *entity, destination }));
}
```

This ensures that if the monster attacked someone, it won't also move onto their tile.

Running the Systems

Before you run the game, you need to make sure that the systems scheduler includes calls to the new systems. The input scheduler needs to call all of the rendering code and none of the game logic other than player_input:

HealthSimpleMelee/combat/src/systems/mod.rs
```
pub fn build_input_scheduler() -> Schedule {
    Schedule::builder()
        .add_system(player_input::player_input_system())
        .flush()
        .add_system(map_render::map_render_system())
        .add_system(entity_render::entity_render_system())
        .add_system(hud::hud_system())
        .add_system(tooltips::tooltips_system())
        .build()
}
```

The player and monster scheduler need to call the combat systems:

HealthSimpleMelee/combat/src/systems/mod.rs
```
pub fn build_player_scheduler() -> Schedule {
    Schedule::builder()
        .add_system(combat::combat_system())
        .flush()
        .add_system(movement::movement_system())
        .flush()
        .add_system(map_render::map_render_system())
        .add_system(entity_render::entity_render_system())
        .add_system(hud::hud_system())
        .add_system(end_turn::end_turn_system())
        .build()
}

pub fn build_monster_scheduler() -> Schedule {
    Schedule::builder()
        .add_system(random_move::random_move_system())
        .flush()
        .add_system(combat::combat_system())
        .flush()
        .add_system(movement::movement_system())
        .flush()
        .add_system(map_render::map_render_system())
        .add_system(entity_render::entity_render_system())
        .add_system(hud::hud_system())
        .add_system(end_turn::end_turn_system())
        .build()
}
```

Run the game now. You can attack monsters and sometimes they'll fight back. Your health bar and monsters' tooltips will show damage, and monsters will vanish when slain.

After the monsters have chewed on the player, they currently have no way to recover their hit points. Let's rectify that and add some strategy to the game at the same time.

Waiting as a Strategy

You can make the game a little more strategic by allowing the player to *deliberately* wait and receive some healing as a benefit. The player licks their wounds, possibly staunches some bleeding, and hit points are restored. Waiting while adjacent to a monster is a poor choice, usually resulting in a painful blow to the noggin. If the player wants to give it a try, that is their prerogative—dying is often the best way to learn to play a game.

Deliberate waiting and healing on inaction is handled entirely within the systems/player_input.rs system. Open the file and let's tweak it a little.

Start by adding an Enemy and Health to the system:

HealthSimpleMelee/healing/src/systems/player_input.rs
```
#[system]
#[read_component(Point)]
#[read_component(Player)]
➤ #[read_component(Enemy)]
➤ #[write_component(Health)]
pub fn player_input(
    ecs: &mut SubWorld,
    commands: &mut CommandBuffer,
    #[resource] key : &Option<VirtualKeyCode>,
    #[resource] turn_state : &mut TurnState
) {
```

This attribute gives the system write access to the Health component. You need that if you're going to increase the player's health through healing.

Before you check for "delta" showing any requested movement, introduce a new variable named did_something:

HealthSimpleMelee/healing/src/systems/player_input.rs
```
let mut did_something = false;
if delta.x !=0 || delta.y != 0 {
```

When you set hit_something, *also* set did_something to true:

HealthSimpleMelee/healing/src/systems/player_input.rs
```
.for_each(|(entity, _) | {
    hit_something = true;
    did_something = true;
```

You also want to set it to true if the player moved:

HealthSimpleMelee/healing/src/systems/player_input.rs
```
if !hit_something {
    did_something = true;
    commands
```

Finally, at the end of the system, if the player didn't do anything, grant them some health back:

HealthSimpleMelee/healing/src/systems/player_input.rs
```
if !did_something {
    if let Ok(mut health) = ecs
        .entry_mut(player_entity)
        .unwrap()
        .get_component_mut::<Health>()
    {
        health.current = i32::min(health.max, health.current+1);
    }
}
*turn_state = TurnState::PlayerTurn;
```

This code uses if let with get_component to obtain the player's health component. It then uses i32::min—the *minimum* of two 32-bit signed integers—to set the player's health to either their maximum or the current health plus one. That prevents the player from healing beyond their maximum health.

Run the game now. You can move the player around and hit a non-movement key (I use SPACEBAR) to wait. The monsters move and if you are damaged you regain health. Combat is now much more tactical—you can withdraw, heal, and then re-enter the fray.

Wrap-Up

You've added a lot of functionality in this chapter. The monsters and the player now have hit points, displayed as a health bar and tooltips. You can also attack and slay monsters, and they can fight back. Sure, they're still dumb as rocks, and there's no way to win or lose the game, but the building blocks continue to stack up, giving you an increasingly fun game. The next chapter will address winning and losing the game, and start to provide the monsters with some intelligence.

CHAPTER 9

Victory and Defeat

After hours of searching the twisting dungeon halls, our brave hero notices the glistening Amulet of Yala in a corner. Raising the amulet in triumph, the hero slips its chain around their neck. Power courses through them and the darkness that threatened their home is repelled. They have achieved a great victory and can rest—knowing that their friends and families are once again safe.

Meanwhile, in an alternate universe, our hero is surrounded by enemies. Fatigue weighs the hero down as they hew at a seemingly never-ending wave of monsters. Orcs and goblins fall, but the hero suffers increasingly devastating injuries as they fight to forestall the end. Finally, a vicious orc lands a telling blow and our hero sinks to the ground—defeated.

What you've just read are common endings in roleplaying games: the player has either won or lost the game. The two go hand in hand; victory with no chance of failure isn't a game and failure with no chance of winning is just depressing.

In this chapter, you'll give the monsters some intelligence, introducing the real possibility of failure. You'll add a game over screen with an option to try again.

Once you have that working, you'll add the code necessary to spawn the *Amulet of Yala* somewhere within the dungeon, and as far away from the player as possible. You'll also add a victory screen that shows up after the player reaches the amulet.

Building a Smarter Monster

Monsters that move randomly aren't much of a threat, and monsters with too much intelligence can make a game unplayable. Finding a nice balance is the key to making a fun yet challenging game.

In this chapter, you'll give the monsters perfect knowledge of the dungeon's floor plan. You'll also provide the monsters with the player's location and a relentless need to pursue that player. This creates a "gauntlet" effect in which monsters constantly beset the player until the level is clear.

You'll begin to turn this "heat-seeking" behavior into more realistic behavior in Chapter 10, Fields of View, on page 185, but for now, the goal is to create an action-packed challenge.

You'll start by tagging monsters with the new behavior. You'll then learn about *Dijkstra maps* (sometimes also called *flow maps*) and how you can use them to efficiently help your monsters navigate toward the player.

Tagging the New Behavior

Start by adding another component to indicate that the monster is chasing the player. In components.rs, add the following component:

WinningAndLosing/gauntlet/src/components.rs
```
#[derive(Clone, Copy, Debug, PartialEq)]
pub struct ChasingPlayer;
```

This component is similar to the other "tag" components you've added. It doesn't contain any data as the tag's existence serves only as a flag indicating that a behavior should occur.

Open spawner.rs, and replace all of the MovingRandomly tags with ChasingPlayer:

WinningAndLosing/gauntlet/src/spawner.rs
```
pub fn spawn_monster(
    ecs: &mut World,
    rng: &mut RandomNumberGenerator,
    pos : Point
) {
    let (hp, name, glyph) = match rng.roll_dice(1,10) {
        1..=8 => goblin(),
        _ => orc()
    };

    ecs.push(
        (Enemy,
            pos,
            Render{
```

```
            color: ColorPair::new(WHITE, BLACK),
            glyph,
        },
        ChasingPlayer{},
        Health{current: hp, max: hp},
        Name(name)
      )
   );
}
```

This code ensures that you replace the random movement behavior with the new chasing behavior you are about to create. If you feel like some variety, you can always leave some monster types moving randomly. A drunken goblin or two can only enhance the fun of a dungeon.

Now, let's create a system to implement the player-chasing behavior.

Supporting Pathfinding with Traits

The general term in game development for an algorithm that helps an entity find its way from point A to point B is *pathfinding*. Many different pathfinding algorithms are available, some of which are provided by bracket-lib.

The bracket-lib library is designed to be generic, so it doesn't know the exact details of how your game works. bracket-lib offers map-related services through traits. You've touched on traits several times before.

When you #[derive(..)] services, you're using Rust shorthand to *implement* traits. Your tick() function is part of the implementation of the GameState trait. Pathfinding requires that you implement two traits for your map: Algorithm2D and BaseMap. Let's take a moment to learn a bit more about traits. You'll be writing your own traits soon, in Creating Traits, on page 204.

The Rust documentation defines a trait as follows:

> A *trait* tells the Rust compiler about functionality a particular type has and can share with other types. You can use traits to define shared behavior in an abstract way. You can use trait bounds to specify that a generic can be any type that has certain behavior.[1]

In practical terms, this means that a trait offers functionality to anything that meets its requirements without having to know about the specifics of your program. GameState doesn't know anything about your game other than it promises that a tick() function will be available. The Algorithm2D and BaseMap

---

1. https://doc.rust-lang.org/book/ch10-02-traits.html

traits take this a step further in that they offer map services without understanding how your map works.

Mapping the Map

Algorithm2D translates between your map and generic map services offered by bracket-lib. The library can't assume that you're storing your map in a row-first format (or even a vector), so it requires that you implement a trait that maps your system to bracket-lib's internal map services. The Algorithm2D trait includes the following functions:

- dimensions provides the size of the map.

- in_bounds determines if an x/y coordinate is valid and contained within the map.

- point2d_to_index is the same as your map_idx function; it converts a 2D x/y coordinate to a map index.

- index_to_point2d is the reciprocal of point2d_to_index; given a map index, it returns the x/y coordinates of that point.

That's a lot of functions to implement. Fortunately, Rust traits support *default implementations*. Bracket-lib can automatically define all of these functions except dimensions() and in_bounds() if you are using its preferred map storage system.

Open map.rs and add an implementation of dimensions():

WinningAndLosing/gauntlet/src/map.rs
```
impl Algorithm2D for Map {
    fn dimensions(&self) -> Point {
        Point::new(SCREEN_WIDTH, SCREEN_HEIGHT)
    }

    fn in_bounds(&self, point: Point) -> bool {
        self.in_bounds(point)
    }
}
```

dimensions() is a straightforward function. It returns a single Point containing the x and y size of the map. You're storing these in your SCREEN_WIDTH and SCREEN_HEIGHT constants, so the function puts them into a Point and returns them. That's sufficient data for bracket-lib to derive the other trait functions, so you don't need to implement them.

Navigating the Map

The second trait—BaseMap—tells bracket-lib how one may travel across the map. It requires that you write two functions: get_available_exits() and get_pathing_distance(). The former looks at a tile and provides an itemized list of possible exits from that tile. The second estimates distance between any two points.

Let's start by creating a function that determines if an exit from a tile is valid. Add the following to your impl Map block:

WinningAndLosing/gauntlet/src/map.rs

```
❶ fn valid_exit(&self, loc: Point, delta: Point) -> Option<usize> {
❷     let destination = loc + delta;
❸     if self.in_bounds(destination) {
❹         if self.can_enter_tile(destination) {
❺             let idx = self.point2d_to_index(destination);
               Some(idx)
           } else {
❻             None
           }
       } else {
           None
       }
   }
```

❶ The function signature takes a Point representing the tile from which you are considering moving, and a second Point indicating the movement delta (change). It returns an Option. If the option is None, you can't go that way. If it's Some, it contains the tile index of the destination.

❷ Calculate the destination by adding the current position to the delta.

❸ Check that the destination is on the map. Always do this first to ensure you don't read past the end of the map array, crashing your program.

❸ Determine if you can enter the tile with the can_enter_tile() function you created earlier.

❺ If you can enter the tile, determine its array index with point2d_to_index() and return Some(idx).

❻ If you're not able to enter the tile, return None.

This function gives you a quick way to check any tile and delta combination for accessibility. You can now implement get_available_exits():

WinningAndLosing/gauntlet/src/map.rs

```
impl BaseMap for Map {
    fn get_available_exits(&self, idx: usize)
❶     -> SmallVec<[(usize, f32); 10]>
```

```
    {
❷       let mut exits = SmallVec::new();
❸       let location = self.index_to_point2d(idx);

❹       if let Some(idx) = self.valid_exit(location, Point::new(-1, 0)) {
❺           exits.push((idx, 1.0))
        }
❻       if let Some(idx) = self.valid_exit(location, Point::new(1, 0)) {
            exits.push((idx, 1.0))
        }
        if let Some(idx) = self.valid_exit(location, Point::new(0, -1)) {
            exits.push((idx, 1.0))
        }
        if let Some(idx) = self.valid_exit(location, Point::new(0, 1)) {
            exits.push((idx, 1.0))
        }

❼       exits
    }
```

❶ Bracket-lib uses a small optimization for lists of exits. Rust's Vec type can be quite resource intensive. A tile will never have many exits, so the library uses a type named SmallVec. SmallVec is more efficient for small lists of data. Don't worry about the details unless you find yourself needing a small vector in your own code.

The SmallVec syntax is a little confusing. Smallvec takes an array as its type parameter. The first element is the type to store; in this case, a tuple containing a usize and an f32. The second parameter tells the small vector how much memory to use before falling back to acting like a normal vector.

The usize represents a tile index. The f32 represents a *cost* to travel there —generally 1.0.

❷ new doesn't require the type parameters. Rust is smart enough to figure out what you specified them, as in the function signature, and will use the definition from there.

❸ Use the Algorithm2D function index_to_point2d() to translate a map index into an x/y value for the tile being examined.

❹ Call your new valid_exit() function with the current tile and a delta, in this case, moving west, a value of (-1,0). If it returns Some value, add the exit to the SmallVec of exits.

❺ Push the exit to the exits list. Use a cost of 1.0. If you want your navigator to prefer certain routes, you can use a lower cost to make them more likely to be chosen. Likewise, a higher cost makes a tile less likely to be chosen. For example, a swamp might have a high cost to traverse, while a road might have a lower cost.

Cost is particularly important if you implement diagonal movement. Moving diagonally covers approximately 1.4 times as much ground as a straight move, so using a cost of 1.0 will give "optimal" paths that bounce diagonally rather than moving naturally.

6 Repeat the process for the other three possible exit directions (east, north, and south).

7 Finish by returning the populated exits list.

The other function used in pathfinding is get_pathing_distance. Many algorithms optimize based upon the remaining distance to the exit; they look first in directions that approach the exit, often saving a ton of work. Add this short function to your BaseMap implementation:

WinningAndLosing/gauntlet/src/map.rs
```
    fn get_pathing_distance(&self, idx1: usize, idx2: usize) -> f32 {
        DistanceAlg::Pythagoras
            .distance2d(
                self.index_to_point2d(idx1),
                self.index_to_point2d(idx2)
            )
    }
}
```

The function passes two points to DistanceAlg::Pythagoras.distance2d(), which returns the Pythagorean distance between the two points. DistanceAlg is an enum. Bracket-lib also supports other distance algorithms, but you don't need to worry about those yet.

Now that your map supports pathfinding and your enemies are tagged as wanting to chase the player, it's time to build a smarter monster.

Heat-Seeking Monsters

You'll need another system to handle chasing the player. Create a new file, and name it src/systems/chasing.rs. Add the following system boilerplate:

WinningAndLosing/gauntlet/src/systems/chasing.rs
```
use crate::prelude::*;

#[system]
#[read_component(Point)]
#[read_component(ChasingPlayer)]
#[read_component(Health)]
#[read_component(Player)]
```

```
pub fn chasing(
    #[resource] map: &Map,
    ecs: &SubWorld,
    commands: &mut CommandBuffer
) {
    let mut movers = <(Entity, &Point, &ChasingPlayer)>::query();
    let mut positions = <(Entity, &Point, &Health)>::query();
    let mut player = <(&Point, &Player)>::query();
```

You've seen this sort of thing before. The system defines three queries:

1. The first query (movers) finds only entities with Point positions and Chasing-Player tags.

2. The second query (positions) lists all entities with Point and Health components. It's the same as the query you used in the random movement system to find other entities.

3. A final query (player) finds only entities with Point positions and the Player tag and returns the player's position.

The system also requests read access to the game map.

Finding the Player

Navigating toward the player requires knowing where they are within the map. You can use an iterator to open the player query and extract a single value from it to locate the player, exactly as you did before:

WinningAndLosing/gauntlet/src/systems/chasing.rs
```
let player_pos = player.iter(ecs).nth(0).unwrap().0;
let player_idx = map_idx(player_pos.x, player_pos.y);
```

You store the player's position and tile index for future reference. You'll need them in the next section.

Dijkstra Maps

Edsger W. Dijkstra was one of the great minds behind modern Computer Science.[2] He created many of the algorithms and theories that drive modern software development. One of his creations was a pathfinding algorithm that can reliably find a path between any two points in a graph. This, in turn, spawned many other algorithms. You'll be using *Dijkstra Maps*—sometimes also called "flow maps."

---

2. https://en.wikipedia.org/wiki/Edsger_W._Dijkstra

Dijkstra maps are incredibly useful. You can use them for everything from AI to making your game automatically play itself. They power a large part of the popular roguelike *Brogue*.[3] You'll start by using them to help the monsters find the player.

A Dijkstra map represents your map as a grid of numbers. You indicate "starting points" and these are set to zero. The rest of the map is set to a large number indicating that you can't go there. Each starting point is scanned, and tiles to which you can travel from that point are given a value of 1. On the next iteration, open tiles that you haven't already visited get a value of 2. This is repeated until every available tile on the map has a value, and that value tells you how far away you are from the starting point:

With this information, you can find the player from any tile on the map. Examine your neighboring tile values, and the lowest distance leads you to the target. Likewise, if your goal is to run away, pick the highest.

Bracket-lib includes a suite of Dijkstra map functions so you don't have to write it yourself. Add the following code to your system to obtain a map with the player as the starting point:

WinningAndLosing/gauntlet/src/systems/chasing.rs
```
❶ let search_targets = vec![player_idx];
let dijkstra_map = DijkstraMap::new(
❷    SCREEN_WIDTH,
    SCREEN_HEIGHT,
    &search_targets,
❸    map,
❹    1024.0
);
```

3. http://roguebasin.roguelikedevelopment.org/index.php?title=The_Incredible_Power_of_Dijkstra_Maps

❶ Create a vector containing the tile index of the player as your starting point.

❷ The first two parameters define your map size. These are *not* derived from the map, in case you want to limit the scope of the search to a portion of the map.

❸ The map is already a borrowed reference (retrieved as &Map)—so you don't need to borrow it.

❹ Building a Dijkstra map for a *huge* map can be slow. The algorithm lets you specify a maximum distance at which point it will stop calculating the map. You want to pick a number large enough to cover as much of the map as you consider relevant—but small enough to be sure that the algorithm won't take too long to run. 1,024 is large enough to cover most of the map, but not so huge as to slow your computer down.

Now that you have created a Dijkstra map, it's available to help monsters hunt down the player.

Chasing the Player

The majority of what's required to chase the player may be found in the random movement system you created in Making Monsters Wander Randomly, on page 127. Checking for stacking/cheerleading pyramids, and generating attack or movement commands is the same. New code checks if the player is adjacent to the monster by calculating the distance between the entity and the player. If the monster is adjacent, it will always attack the player. If the player is not adjacent to the monster, it will follow the Dijkstra map towards the player:

WinningAndLosing/gauntlet/src/systems/chasing.rs

```
❶  movers.iter(ecs).for_each(| (entity, pos, _) | {
        let idx = map_idx(pos.x, pos.y);
        if let Some(destination) = DijkstraMap::find_lowest_exit(
            &dijkstra_map, idx, map
        )
❷      {
❸
❹          let distance = DistanceAlg::Pythagoras.distance2d(*pos, *player_pos);
            let destination = if distance > 1.2 {
                map.index_to_point2d(destination)
            } else {
                *player_pos
            };
```

❶ Iterate all entities with the Chasing tag and only apply the systems' logic to matching entities.

❷ The DijkstraMap type includes a helpful function to find the exit with the lowest distance to your target point. It returns an Option, so you use if let to process the contents if there's an exit.

❸ Use Pythagoras's algorithm to determine the distance to the player.

❹ If the player is more than 1.2 tiles away, set the destination to the result of the Dijkstra map search.

There are two interesting things here:

1. Floating-point numbers can be imprecise. It isn't always guaranteed that my_float == 1.0 will work, because my_float may have quietly changed to 0.99999 internally. It's always safer to use greater than or less than when comparing floating-point numbers.

2. 1.2 is guaranteed to be larger than 1.0, so greater than checks will work. It is also less than 1.4, the approximate distance of a diagonal move. This ensures that monsters won't attack diagonally. The player can't do that, so it's only fair not to let the monster do that either.

The rest of the chasing system is the same as the code you used in the random movement system:

WinningAndLosing/gauntlet/src/systems/chasing.rs
```
let mut attacked = false;
positions
    .iter(ecs)
    .filter(|(_, target_pos, _)| **target_pos == destination)
    .for_each(|(victim, _, _)| {
        if ecs.entry_ref(*victim).unwrap().get_component::<Player>()
            .is_ok() {
                commands
                    .push(((), WantsToAttack{
                        attacker: *entity,
                        victim: *victim
                    }));
        }
        attacked = true;
    });

if !attacked {
    commands
        .push(((), WantsToMove{ entity: *entity, destination }));
}
}
```

Finally, don't forget to register the system. Add mod chasing; to systems/mod.rs, and call the system alongside random_movement:

WinningAndLosing/gauntlet/src/systems/mod.rs
```
pub fn build_monster_scheduler() -> Schedule {
    Schedule::builder()
        .add_system(random_move::random_move_system())
➤       .add_system(chasing::chasing_system())
        .flush()
        .add_system(combat::combat_system())
        .flush()
        .add_system(movement::movement_system())
        .flush()
        .add_system(map_render::map_render_system())
        .add_system(entity_render::entity_render_system())
        .add_system(hud::hud_system())
        .add_system(end_turn::end_turn_system())
        .build()
}
```

Now that the monsters can hunt for the player, let's make the player a little easier to defeat.

Reducing the Player's Health

Open spawner.rs, and reduce the player's starting hit points (both current and maximum) from 20 to 10. This makes it more likely that the player will fall victim to the onslaught of monsters.

WinningAndLosing/gauntlet/src/spawner.rs
```
pub fn spawn_player(ecs : &mut World, pos : Point) {
    ecs.push(
        (Player,
            pos,
            Render{
                color: ColorPair::new(WHITE, BLACK),
                glyph : to_cp437('@')
            },
➤           Health{ current: 10, max: 10 }
        )
    );
}
```

Run your game now, and the monsters will head toward the player like a heat-seeking missile, providing a gauntlet for the player to navigate. It's still possible to win—by finding a choke point to defend and rest to heal between monsters—but there's now a very real chance of death, because fighting off hordes of monsters requires some skill, as shown in the image on page 173.

When a monster finally slays you, the game crashes. That's not an ideal way to end the game.

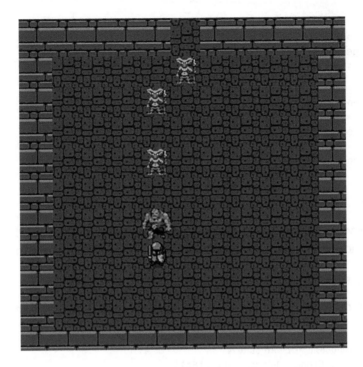

Implementing a Game Over Screen

You need to let the player know when the game ends. This can be as simple or elaborate as you like. Some games display detailed statistics about the game, some wish you better luck next time. The game over screen is an opportunity to engage with your player and encourage them to come back for more. It should also provide an easy transition to restarting the game—you always want to encourage player engagement.

Let's start improving the game over scenario by fixing the crash when the player dies. Open systems/combat.rs and notice that you're deleting whatever entity died. That includes the player, and when the player ceases to exist, the Heads-Up Display system crashes when it tries to find the player's status. In the system's component declarations, add a request for a Player component:

```
#[read_component(WantsToAttack)]
➤ #[read_component(Player)]
#[write_component(Health)]
```

Then amend the victim's loop as follows:

WinningAndLosing/losing/src/systems/combat.rs
```
victims.iter().for_each(|(message, victim)| {
    let is_player = ecs
```

```
        .entry_ref(*victim)
        .unwrap()
        .get_component::<Player>()
        .is_ok();
    if let Ok(mut health) = ecs
        .entry_mut(*victim)
        .unwrap()
        .get_component_mut::<Health>()
    {
        health.current -= 1;
        if health.current < 1 && !is_player {
            commands.remove(*victim);
        }
    }
```

Now that your game doesn't crash when the player is defeated, let's handle the situation gracefully by adding a state to indicate that the game is over.

Adding a Game Over Turn State

The game needs a way to know if it should display a game over screen. Open turn_state.rs, and add another game state:

WinningAndLosing/losing/src/turn_state.rs
```
#[derive(Copy, Clone, Debug, PartialEq)]
pub enum TurnState {
    AwaitingInput,
    PlayerTurn,
    MonsterTurn,
➤   GameOver
}
```

Once you've made this change, your development environment may warn you of errors. match statements *must* include every possible state—or a catch-all _. This is often helpful in avoiding errors (unimplemented options are a code smell)—but it can be alarming when you change your code and other parts of the source code light up in red. Two places in your game require game state handling: the tick function and the end_game state. Let's start by fixing the end_turn system.

Detecting When the Game Has Ended

At the end of a turn, the game should check to see if the player has run out of hit points, ending the game. Open systems/end_turn.rs and edit as follows:

WinningAndLosing/losing/src/systems/end_turn.rs
```
use crate::prelude::*;

#[system]
#[read_component(Health)]
```

```
    #[read_component(Player)]
    pub fn end_turn(
        ecs: &SubWorld,
        #[resource] turn_state: &mut TurnState
    ) {
❶      let mut player_hp = <&Health>::query().filter(component::<Player>());
        let current_state = turn_state.clone();
❷      let mut new_state = match current_state {
            TurnState::AwaitingInput => return,
            TurnState::PlayerTurn => TurnState::MonsterTurn,
            TurnState::MonsterTurn => TurnState::AwaitingInput,
❸          _ => current_state
        };
❹      player_hp.iter(ecs).for_each(|hp| {
            if hp.current < 1 {
                new_state = TurnState::GameOver;
            }
        });

        *turn_state = new_state;
    }
```

❶ Add a query that returns an entity's health, and filter it to only include the player.

❷ Change current_state to be mutable because you might want to change it later.

❸ Using _ to match is a catch-all. Everything that wasn't already matched will take this branch. Return current_state to do nothing.

❹ Iterate the player health query. If the player's current hit points are less than one, change the new game state to GameOver.

Now that you've fixed the end_turn system, it's time to teach tick() to render a game over screen.

Displaying a Game Over Screen

Open main.rs. At the end of the impl State block, add a new function:

WinningAndLosing/losing/src/main.rs
```
fn game_over(&mut self, ctx: &mut BTerm) {
❶  ctx.set_active_console(2);
❷  ctx.print_color_centered(2, RED, BLACK, "Your quest has ended.");
    ctx.print_color_centered(4, WHITE, BLACK,
        "Slain by a monster, your hero's journey has come to a \
        premature end.");
    ctx.print_color_centered(5, WHITE, BLACK,
        "The Amulet of Yala remains unclaimed, and your home town \
        is not saved.");
```

```
        ctx.print_color_centered(8, YELLOW, BLACK,
            "Don't worry, you can always try again with a new hero.");
        ctx.print_color_centered(9, GREEN, BLACK,
            "Press 1 to play again.");
❸
❹      if let Some(VirtualKeyCode::Key1) = ctx.key {
            self.ecs = World::default();
            self.resources = Resources::default();
            let mut rng = RandomNumberGenerator::new();
            let map_builder = MapBuilder::new(&mut rng);
            spawn_player(&mut self.ecs, map_builder.player_start);
            map_builder.rooms
                .iter()
                .skip(1)
                .map(|r| r.center())
                .for_each(|pos| spawn_monster(&mut self.ecs, &mut rng, pos));
            self.resources.insert(map_builder.map);
            self.resources.insert(Camera::new(map_builder.player_start));
❺          self.resources.insert(TurnState::AwaitingInput);
        }
    }
```

❶ Switch to the tooltips layer. You don't want to use the monster layer, because letters replaced with graphics will render as the sprite rather than the letter.

❷ Use a series of print_color_centered() calls to display some text informing the player of their untimely demise.

❸ Check if '1' is pressed. if let Some(_) matches every value other than None. Using a key that isn't pressed during game play avoids skipping the screen by accident.

❹ Create a new universe, world, map, and other resources—exactly as you did when starting the program. Store these in your game state.

❺ Setting the turn state back to AwaitingInput restarts the game. The next iteration of tick() will act as if the player had never died.

With the functionality to display a game over screen in place, you still need to call it. In your tick() function, add the following to the list of game states handled by your match statement:

WinningAndLosing/losing/src/main.rs
```
TurnState::GameOver => {
    self.game_over(ctx);
}
```

Run the program now and do your best to die. When a monster slays the player, you'll see a game over screen as shown in the image on page 177.

```
              Your quest has ended.
   Slain by a monster, your hero's journey has come to a premature end.
   The Amulet of Yala remains unclaimed, and your home town is not saved.

        Don't worry, you can always try again with a new hero.
                   Press 1 to play again.
```

Tarn "Toady" Adams of *Dwarf Fortress* fame coined the phrase "Losing is fun." Many find winning to be equally fun—so let's add that option.

Finding the Amulet of Yala

You win the game when you collect the *Amulet of Yala*. Yala is an acronym for "yet another lost amulet," a gentle poke at Nethack's—and its many derivatives—plot.

Spawning the Amulet

You'll use two new tag components to denote the amulet:

WinningAndLosing/winning/src/components.rs
```rust
#[derive(Clone, Copy, Debug, PartialEq)]
pub struct Item;

#[derive(Clone, Copy, Debug, PartialEq)]
pub struct AmuletOfYala;
```

The Item component denotes that an entity is an item. It doesn't move or have health, but it should still appear on the map. You'll add further support for items in Chapter 13, Inventory and Power-Ups, on page 241. The AmuletOfYala tag indicates that the tagged item is the item that wins the game.

The amulet also shares components with other entities. It needs a name, a rendered graphic, and a map position. Open spawner.rs and add a function to create the amulet:

WinningAndLosing/winning/src/spawner.rs
```rust
pub fn spawn_amulet_of_yala(ecs : &mut World, pos : Point) {
    ecs.push(
        (Item, AmuletOfYala,
            pos,
            Render{
                color: ColorPair::new(WHITE, BLACK),
                glyph : to_cp437('|')
            },
            Name("Amulet of Yala".to_string())
        )
    );
}
```

This is very similar to your other spawning functions. It creates an entity tagged as an Item and the AmuletOfYala. It creates components containing a position, render information, and a name. The amulet is defined in dungeon-font.png as the | glyph.

Now that you can spawn the amulet, you have to decide where to put it.

Placing the Amulet

You want the amulet to be difficult to reach; otherwise, the game may be too easy. This lends itself to another use for Dijkstra maps: determining the *most distant* tile on the map.

Open map_builder.rs, and add a second Point to the MapBuilder type, storing the amulet's destination:

WinningAndLosing/winning/src/map_builder.rs
```
pub struct MapBuilder {
    pub map : Map,
    pub rooms : Vec<Rect>,
    pub player_start : Point,
➤   pub amulet_start : Point
}
```

You also need to initialize the amulet_start variable in the constructor:

WinningAndLosing/winning/src/map_builder.rs
```
pub fn new(rng: &mut RandomNumberGenerator) -> Self {

    let mut mb = MapBuilder{
        map : Map::new(),
        rooms : Vec::new(),
        player_start : Point::zero(),
➤       amulet_start : Point::zero()
    };
```

Now that you have a variable in which to place the destination, let's figure out where the amulet should go.

Navigate to the end of the build function. Before you return mb, create a Dijkstra map using the player's starting point as the map's starting point:

WinningAndLosing/winning/src/map_builder.rs
```
let dijkstra_map = DijkstraMap::new(
    SCREEN_WIDTH,
    SCREEN_HEIGHT,
    &vec![mb.map.point2d_to_index(mb.player_start)],
    &mb.map,
    1024.0
);
```

This is the same as the Dijkstra map you created for chasing the player. Unlike the previous example, you'll access the map directly. Each entry in the map contains a number indicating how distant the tile is from the player. You want to find a tile far from the player, ensuring that the player has to navigate much of the dungeon in order to win. Distances are stored in the dijkstra_map.map vector, but the index of each tile is determined by the entry's position in the vector. Rust's iterators include a function called enumerate that can help with this:

WinningAndLosing/winning/src/map_builder.rs

```
❶ const UNREACHABLE : &f32 = &f32::MAX;
❷ mb.amulet_start = mb.map.index_to_point2d
   (
       dijkstra_map.map
           .iter()
❸          .enumerate()
❹          .filter(|(_,dist)| *dist < UNREACHABLE)
❺          .max_by(|a,b| a.1.partial_cmp(b.1).unwrap())
❻          .unwrap().0
   );
```

❶ The Dijkstra map indicates that a tile is unreachable by placing the maximum possible 32-bit floating-point number into it. You can access the maximum value of Rust types with std::typename::MAX, in this case 'f32'. Storing the value in a constant makes the intent of the code more obvious.

❷ Wrap the entire iterator in a point2d_to_index() call. This will transform the result into a map array index.

❸ Iterate the Dijkstra map's content contained in .map. Calling enumerate adds an index to each entry. The iterator is now returning a tuple containing (index, distance).

❹ filter keeps only tiles that can be reached by removing all tiles whose distance is equal to UNREACHABLE.

❺ You're looking for the most distant tile, so you want the *maximum* value tile. The regular max iterator function won't work because each entry contains both a tile index and a distance. max_by allows you to specify a closure that specifies how each comparison should work.

Floating-point numbers aren't *always* directly comparable. They can be "Infinity" and "Not a Number" (the result of dividing by zero). Rust requires that you use the function partial_cmp()—short for partial compare—to compare f32 values. This returns an optional value, so you call unwrap() to obtain the result. If you *were* dividing by zero or trying to count to infinity, this would crash.

❻ The max_by() function returns an option. There might not *be* a maximum number if the collection were empty. You know that isn't the case, so you call unwrap(). This yields a tuple containing both the tile index and the distance to the player. Since you don't need the distance, you return .0, the first tuple entry.

The iterator chain eventually gives you the tile index of the most distant—but still accessible to the player—tile on the map. When the game calls the map builder's new() function, the function returns a location for the amulet. Open main.rs. In both places where you spawn the player, follow up by spawning the amulet:

WinningAndLosing/winning/src/main.rs
```
spawn_player(&mut self.ecs, map_builder.player_start);
spawn_amulet_of_yala(&mut self.ecs, map_builder.amulet_start);
```

Note that the new function will refer to &mut ecs rather than &mut self.ecs.

Run the game now and you can find the amulet in the dungeon:

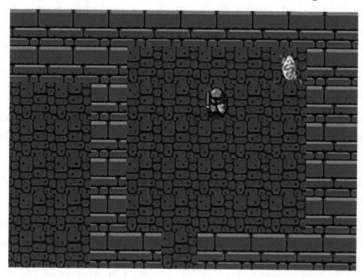

The last step is to detect when the player collects the amulet, and then congratulate them on winning the game.

Determining If the Player Won

You're already checking for *losing* conditions in the end_turn system, making it the logical place to also detect winning conditions.

Start by opening turn_state.rs and adding another game state:

WinningAndLosing/winning/src/turn_state.rs
```
#[derive(Copy, Clone, Debug, PartialEq)]
pub enum TurnState {
    AwaitingInput,
    PlayerTurn,
    MonsterTurn,
    GameOver,
    Victory
}
```

The Victory condition indicates that the player has won the game. You need to update systems/end_turn.rs to detect that the player has won the game. Amend the player query to also return the player's position, and add a second query to determine the location of the amulet:

WinningAndLosing/winning/src/systems/end_turn.rs
```
#[system]
#[read_component(Health)]
#[read_component(Point)]
#[read_component(Player)]
#[read_component(AmuletOfYala)]
pub fn end_turn(ecs: &SubWorld, #[resource] turn_state: &mut TurnState) {
    let mut player_hp = <(&Health, &Point)>::query()
        .filter(component::<Player>());
    let mut amulet = <&Point>::query()
        .filter(component::<AmuletOfYala>());
```

Before you query the player, you need to determine the amulet's position. You can do this with an iterator query using nth to return the first result (there should only ever be one amulet):

WinningAndLosing/winning/src/systems/end_turn.rs
```
let amulet_pos = amulet
    .iter(ecs)
    .nth(0)
    .unwrap();
```

Now that you know where the amulet is, you can update the player health query to also check the player's position relative to the amulet:

WinningAndLosing/winning/src/systems/end_turn.rs
```
player_hp.iter(ecs).for_each(|(hp, pos)| {
    if hp.current < 1 {
        new_state = TurnState::GameOver;
    }
    if pos == amulet_pos {
        new_state = TurnState::Victory;
    }
});
```

When the player's location matches that of the amulet, you set the turn state to Victory. That's sufficient to *detect* that the player has won. All that remains is to notify the player of their victory.

Congratulating the Player

Winning the game also resets the game state, just like losing does. It's a good idea to adhere to the "Do Not Repeat Yourself" (DRY) principle, so let's move the game state reset into a function. Create a new function, implemented as part of the State implementation:

Don't Repeat Yourself (DRY)

A common piece of advice to developers is "Do Not Repeat Yourself." This is the DRY principle. When you're repeating the same code, it's a great idea to wrap it into a function. When bugs appear, you only have to remember to fix it once.

Sometimes repeating yourself is okay. If you have what is essentially the same code that may operate slightly differently under different circumstances, it may be clearer to repeat the code—especially if wrapping it into a function that handles every possible combination will make it confusing. DRYUYNT ("Do Not Repeat Yourself Unless You Need To") is a much less catchy name.

WinningAndLosing/winning/src/main.rs
```
fn reset_game_state(&mut self) {
    self.ecs = World::default();
    self.resources = Resources::default();
    let mut rng = RandomNumberGenerator::new();
    let map_builder = MapBuilder::new(&mut rng);
    spawn_player(&mut self.ecs, map_builder.player_start);
    spawn_amulet_of_yala(&mut self.ecs, map_builder.amulet_start);
    map_builder.rooms
        .iter()
        .skip(1)
        .map(|r| r.center())
        .for_each(|pos| spawn_monster(&mut self.ecs, &mut rng, pos));
    self.resources.insert(map_builder.map);
    self.resources.insert(Camera::new(map_builder.player_start));
    self.resources.insert(TurnState::AwaitingInput);
}
```

This is the same functionality you implemented for game_over. Open the game_over() function, and replace the duplicate code with a call to your new function:

WinningAndLosing/winning/src/main.rs
```
fn game_over(&mut self, ctx: &mut BTerm) {
    ctx.set_active_console(2);
    ctx.print_color_centered(2, RED, BLACK, "Your quest has ended.");
    ctx.print_color_centered(4, WHITE, BLACK,
    "Slain by a monster, your hero's journey has come to a \
        premature end.");
    ctx.print_color_centered(5, WHITE, BLACK,
    "The Amulet of Yala remains unclaimed, and your home town \
        is not saved.");
    ctx.print_color_centered(8, YELLOW, BLACK,
        "Don't worry, you can always try again with a new hero.");
    ctx.print_color_centered(9, GREEN, BLACK, "Press 1 to play \
        again.");

    if let Some(VirtualKeyCode::Key1) = ctx.key {
        self.reset_game_state();
    }
}
```

Add another function to the State implementation in main.rs. It's very similar to the game_over() function you created earlier in this chapter:

WinningAndLosing/winning/src/main.rs
```
fn victory(&mut self, ctx: &mut BTerm) {
    ctx.set_active_console(2);
    ctx.print_color_centered(2, GREEN, BLACK, "You have won!");
    ctx.print_color_centered(4, WHITE, BLACK,
    "You put on the Amulet of Yala and feel its power course through \
        your veins.");
    ctx.print_color_centered(5, WHITE, BLACK,
        "Your town is saved, and you can return to your normal life.");
    ctx.print_color_centered(7, GREEN, BLACK, "Press 1 to \
        play again.");
    if let Some(VirtualKeyCode::Key1) = ctx.key {
        self.reset_game_state();
    }
}
```

Lastly, add a call to your new function into your tick function's state matcher:

WinningAndLosing/winning/src/main.rs
```
    TurnState::GameOver => self.game_over(ctx),
➤   TurnState::Victory => self.victory(ctx),
```

This function alerts the player of their victory and offers to let them play again. Run the game now, and once you find the amulet, you achieve a victory, as shown in the image on page 184.

You found the Amulet of Yala.   Congratulations, you have won the game.

Wrap-Up

In this chapter, you added some intelligence to your monsters—possibly too much intelligence as they now hunt down the player unerringly, with omniscient knowledge of the player's location. Don't worry, though. You'll limit their hunting capabilities in the next chapter.

You also gave the player a way to face the very real possibility of defeat. As such, you added a game over screen to notify them of their defeat, giving the player an option to try again. In contrast, you added the mythical *Amulet of Yala* to the game, carefully placing it as far from the player's starting position as possible. When the player reaches the amulet, they're rewarded with a victory screen and the ability to play again.

As you added these new features to your game, you learned some very important concepts like Dijkstra maps, pathfinding, and the implementation details of Rust traits.

CHAPTER 10

Fields of View

In the darkness ahead, the hero sees an orc. Hoping to sneak past, our hero skirts the room—but the orc turns to give chase. Sprinting down the hall with the orc hot on their heels, the hero turns into a side passage and hides. The hero was lucky this time—the orc broke off pursuit.

This scene requires that neither the hero nor the monsters know each other's position until they can see each other. Monsters still chase the player, but only when they can see their intended target. The player is able to maneuver to break line of sight and escape from the monster. In previous chapters, entities are effectively omniscient—able to see the entire map at once. The new features require that entities know what they can see—and query the map to interact only with targets they have spotted.

Restricting entities' view of the world adds several dimensions to the game:

- The player is no longer certain of their exact location on the map and has less warning about what may lie around the next corner.

- Restricted vision adds dramatic tension to the game—every corner *might* hide a terrible demise.

- The game is more tactical, with the player having the option to hide and avoid combat—and to engage at their own pace.

In this chapter, you'll give the player and monsters a *Field of View* component and system that lists tiles visible from their current location. You'll then limit map rendering to only show areas currently visible to the player. Next, you'll replace the "heat-seeking" monster chase AI with one that begins the chase when the player is visible—and breaks off the chase if the player escapes. Finally, you'll give the player a memory of the map they have discovered—and display the memorized map in grey. Along the way, you'll learn about a new Rust collection—the HashSet.

Defining an Entity's Field of View

You need to follow a few steps to determine which tiles are visible from any point on the map. First, you have to denote which tiles are see-through and which are opaque. Second, you need to prepare a component to store the visibility data. Finally, you need a system that runs a field-of-view algorithm and stores the results in the new component type.

Tile Opacity

The first step in implementing visibility is deciding which tiles are see-through and which are opaque. Bracket-lib defines a trait entry for this known as is_opaque. Your map is simple, with tiles being either solid walls or floors. That leads to walls being opaque and floors being transparent (or not opaque). To represent this, bracket-lib requires you to add one more function to your map's BaseMap implementation: is_opaque:

WhatCanISee/fov/src/map.rs
```
impl BaseMap for Map {
    fn is_opaque(&self, idx: usize) -> bool {
        self.tiles[idx as usize] != TileType::Floor
    }
```

Opaque and Blocked Are Not the Same

 is_blocked and is_opaque give similar results. In more complicated games, they aren't the same thing. A closed window is opaque—but blocks an entity from traveling through it. Likewise, an arrow slit prevents travel but is a great way to peek at the outside of your castle.

Once the trait function is implemented, you can request a field of view from bracket-lib with the field_of_view_set(START, radius, map reference) function. The function returns a HashSet, which merits a bit of explanation.

Collating Data with HashSets

So far, you've stored most of your game data in vectors. Rust provides several other collection types in the std::collections namespace. HashSet is well suited to storing field-of-view results. Unlike a vector, a HashSet:

- Only contains unique entries. Adding a duplicate replaces the existing entry.

- Searching for an entry is *very* fast. A vector would require you to search each entry in turn—a HashSet consults its index.

- Adding data is slower than for a vector, because a hash has to be computed and the index updated in addition to just storing the entry.

HashSet includes a lot of functionality—this chapter will focus on the most common operations.[1]

When you add an entry to a HashSet—with the insert function—the container first calculates a *hash* of the data to be stored. You can customize the *hash function* but the default functionality is adequate for most use cases—it's decently fast and quite accurate.

A hash function works by iterating the input data, performing mathematical operations on each element, and producing an output hash of a known size—often a lot smaller than the original data. A good hash function will ensure that a tiny variation in the input produces a different output. A hash function that produces a 64-bit hash will produce the same output size whether it's hashing a single integer or the entirety of *War and Peace*. If you changed a single letter in *War and Peace*, the hash would change—but the hash would remain 64-bits in length rather than the length of *War and Peace* (approximately 3 Mb). This makes for very efficient indexing; you can store a *lot* of data inside your HashSet, but indexing remains compact and fast.

When you add an item to a HashSet (using the insert function), the hash of your data is computed. If the set doesn't already contain an entry with that hash, your data is added to the set—and the index updated to include the new hash. If the set already includes the hash, the new entry replaces the old one. The internal process for adding to a HashSet may be visualized like this:

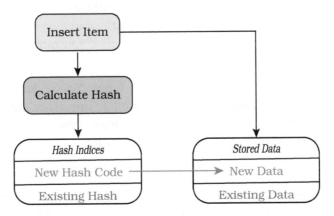

---

1. https://doc.rust-lang.org/std/collections/struct.HashSet.html

Now that you know what a HashSet is, let's add one to a component and use it to store tile visibility information.

Storing Visible Tile Sets in a Component

You should be familiar with this story by now—if you want to add functionality to entities, you add a component to store the data required by the system. Open components.rs. At the top, import the HashSet from std::collections:

WhatCanISee/fov/src/components.rs
```
use std::collections::HashSet;
```

Now that Rust knows where to find the definition of HashSet, you can use it in the rest of the module. Add a new component type named FieldOfView:

WhatCanISee/fov/src/components.rs
```
❶ #[derive(Clone, Debug, PartialEq)]
   pub struct FieldOfView{
❷     pub visible_tiles : HashSet<Point>,
❸     pub radius: i32,
❹     pub is_dirty: bool
   }
```

This component includes some new functionality and concepts, so let's go over them in turn.

❶ You aren't deriving Copy. HashSet doesn't implement copy, so you can't either. Inside a component, this makes very little difference—you are generally accessing it in place rather than moving it around. If you were to assign a new variable to the contents of an existing FieldOfView (e.g. let my_comp = old_comp;) the component data would be moved. The content of old_comp would become invalid, and the data would exist *only* in my_comp. Both the compiler and Clippy will warn you if you move something and then try to use the moved-from variable.

❷ Component types can include complex types. You've kept components simple so far, but component structs are like any other struct—you can put whatever you want in there. In this case, you are adding a HashSet containing the visible map points for the entity.

❸ The radius defines how many tiles in each direction an entity can see.

❹ Plotting visibility graphs can be time-consuming, so it's best to recalculate them only when you have to. A common way to do this is to mark data as "dirty" when it needs updating. You'll learn to implement this optimization pattern in this section.

Components are regular structs. You don't have "magic" to worry about. Components can implement or associate functions, and hold complicated data—including other structs. Once your structure reaches the point that you find yourself trying to remember, "How do I initialize this?"—it's time to add a constructor. You are also going to need to make quick clones of your field-of-view components. Let's add two functions to assist with this:

```
WhatCanISee/fov/src/components.rs
impl FieldOfView {
    pub fn new(radius: i32) -> Self {
        Self{
            visible_tiles: HashSet::new(),
            radius,
            is_dirty: true
        }
    }

    pub fn clone_dirty(&self) -> Self {
        Self {
            visible_tiles: HashSet::new(),
            radius: self.radius,
            is_dirty: true,
        }
    }
}
```

❶ Create an empty HashSet with new(), just like a vector.

❷ Mark the new field-of-view data as dirty—it will be updated the first time the associated system runs.

❸ Later in this chapter, you'll need to make perfect copies of the component —but with a dirty set. You won't need the contents of the now invalid field of view, so this function makes a new one—with dirty set to true.

You'll use clone_dirty in Updating Fields of View, on page 195. You could perform the cloning in place, but adding a function makes it easier to see what you are doing.

Dirty Data

It's very common to refer to data that needs updating as "dirty." You'll encounter this in cache systems, render systems, and many other places. Sometimes, it's fast enough to calculate whatever you need when you need it. If the calculation is slow, it's a good idea to only update it when the inputs change. You can find many dirty algorithms online, and despite the name, they are generally safe for work.

Now that the component is defined, open spawner.rs and add the component to the player's spawn function:

WhatCanISee/fov/src/spawner.rs
```
pub fn spawn_player(ecs : &mut World, pos : Point) {
    ecs.push(
        (Player,
            pos,
            Render{
                color: ColorPair::new(WHITE, BLACK),
                glyph : to_cp437('@')
            },
            Health{ current: 10, max: 10 },
➤           FieldOfView::new(8)
        )
    );
}
```

Now the player can store a set of visible tiles. You need the monsters to have a field of view, too, so add a FieldOfView component to their spawn function as well:

WhatCanISee/fov/src/spawner.rs
```
ecs.push(
    (Enemy,
        pos,
        Render{
            color: ColorPair::new(WHITE, BLACK),
            glyph,
        },
        ChasingPlayer{},
        Health{current: hp, max: hp},
        Name(name),
        FieldOfView::new(6)
    )
);
```

Now that you have a component to store fields of view, let's create a system to populate the component.

Plotting Fields of View

A *lot* of different implementations of field-of-view algorithms exist, often optimized to the needs of a specific game. Bracket-lib includes a relatively simple one, based on *path tracing*. It works by drawing an imaginary circle around the starting point, and then plotting a line to each of the points on the circle's exterior. Each tile encountered along the line is visible—and the line plot stops when it hits an opaque tile. The algorithm may be visualized like the image shown on page 191.

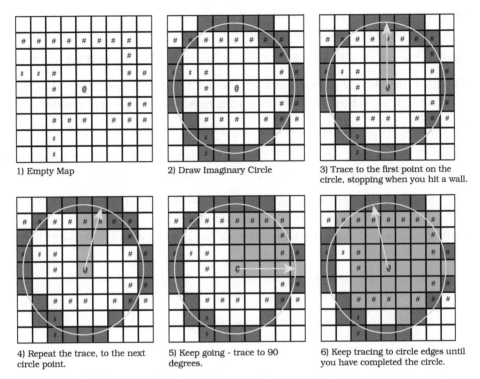

1) Empty Map

2) Draw Imaginary Circle

3) Trace to the first point on the circle, stopping when you hit a wall.

4) Repeat the trace, to the next circle point.

5) Keep going - trace to 90 degrees.

6) Keep tracing to circle edges until you have completed the circle.

As a counterpart to the FieldOfView component, a system needs to be created that implements the field-of-view algorithm. Create a new file named systems/fov.rs and add the following to the file:

```
WhatCanISee/fov/src/systems/fov.rs
use crate::prelude::*;

#[system]
#[read_component(Point)]
#[write_component(FieldOfView)]
pub fn fov(
    ecs: &mut SubWorld,
    #[resource] map: &Map,
) {
    let mut views = <(&Point, &mut FieldOfView)>::query();
    views
        .iter_mut(ecs)
        .filter(|(_, fov)| fov.is_dirty)
        .for_each(|(pos, mut fov)| {
            fov.visible_tiles = field_of_view_set(*pos, fov.radius, map);
            fov.is_dirty = false;
        }
    );
}
```

❶ `let mut views = <(&Point, &mut FieldOfView)>::query();`
❷ `.iter_mut(ecs)`
❸ `.filter(|(_, fov)| fov.is_dirty)`
❹ `fov.visible_tiles = field_of_view_set(*pos, fov.radius, map);`
❺ `fov.is_dirty = false;`

❶ Create a query that reads the Point component (the entity's position) and can write to the FieldOfView component.

❷ Run the query with iter_mut(), allowing you to change the FieldOfView entries.

❸ Filter the iterator with a check on the is_dirty field. This ensures that only dirty entries—those fields of view that need updating—are updated.

❹ Call the field_of_view_set() function, as described above.

❺ Mark the field of view as not dirty. The visibility set won't be processed again until it changes—and is marked as dirty once more.

Don't forget to register the system in systems/mod.rs—you need to add a mod fov; statement, and add the system to the schedule. You also need to include it in the input scheduler (to ensure that all fields of view are calculated when the game starts):

WhatCanISee/fov/src/systems/mod.rs
```
pub fn build_input_scheduler() -> Schedule {
    Schedule::builder()
        .add_system(player_input::player_input_system())
        .add_system(fov::fov_system())
        .flush()
```

The field-of-view system needs to be included in the player's schedule:

WhatCanISee/fov/src/systems/mod.rs
```
pub fn build_player_scheduler() -> Schedule {
    Schedule::builder()
        .add_system(combat::combat_system())
        .flush()
        .add_system(movement::movement_system())
        .flush()
        .add_system(fov::fov_system())
        .flush()
```

Finally, include the system in the monsters' schedule:

WhatCanISee/fov/src/systems/mod.rs
```
pub fn build_monster_scheduler() -> Schedule {
    Schedule::builder()
        .add_system(random_move::random_move_system())
        .add_system(chasing::chasing_system())
        .flush()
        .add_system(combat::combat_system())
        .flush()
        .add_system(movement::movement_system())
        .flush()
        .add_system(fov::fov_system())
        .flush()
```

That's sufficient to create a field of view for every entity that wants one. Now that you have the data, it's time to use it in your rendering code.

Rendering Fields of View

Limiting map rendering to only display the portions currently visible to the player requires a relatively small change to your map rendering code. Open systems/map_render.rs. Start by adjusting the system header to obtain access to the player's field of view:

```
WhatCanISee/fov/src/systems/map_render.rs
#[system]
#[read_component(FieldOfView)]
#[read_component(Player)]
pub fn map_render(
    ecs: &SubWorld,
    #[resource] map: &Map,
    #[resource] camera:&Camera
) {
    let mut fov = <&FieldOfView>::query().filter(component::<Player>());
```

❶

❶ Create a new query that reads FieldOfView, and filters the query to only include the player.

Before you begin iterating tiles to render, add a line of code that locates the player's field of view:

```
WhatCanISee/fov/src/systems/map_render.rs
let player_fov = fov.iter(ecs).nth(0).unwrap();
```

This uses the same nth and unwrap pattern that you used in Rendering the HUD, on page 144, to run a query filtered to only include the player and extract that entry's field of view.

Find the line that reads if map.in_bounds... and extend it to check if the tile is in the player's field of view:

```
WhatCanISee/fov/src/systems/map_render.rs
if map.in_bounds(pt) && player_fov.visible_tiles.contains(&pt) {
```

HashSet implements a function named contains. It quickly checks if a value is contained inside the set. By comparing the tile location with the visible tiles set, you can quickly see if the tile is visible to the player—and only render the tile when it is visible.

If you run the game now, you'll see a limited area around you—but the monsters are still visible. The visible area doesn't move with you, as shown in the image on page 194.

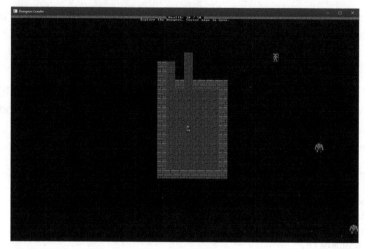

Now that the player's view of the map has been limited, let's also hide monsters that the player can't see.

Hiding Entities

Open systems/entity_render.rs. You're going to make changes that are very similar to your adjustments to the map renderer. Start by adding the same player visibility query to the system:

WhatCanISee/fov/src/systems/entity_render.rs
```
#[system]
#[read_component(Point)]
#[read_component(Render)]
#[read_component(FieldOfView)]
#[read_component(Player)]
pub fn entity_render(
    #[resource] camera: &Camera,
    ecs: &SubWorld,
) {
    let mut renderables = <(&Point, &Render)>::query();
➤   let mut fov = <&FieldOfView>::query().filter(component::<Player>());
```

You can then extract the player's field of view in the same way that you did before, and use it to filter the entity renderer to display only visible entities:

WhatCanISee/fov/src/systems/entity_render.rs
```
let player_fov = fov.iter(ecs).nth(0).unwrap();

renderables.
    iter(ecs)
➤   .filter(|(pos, _)| player_fov.visible_tiles.contains(&pos))
    .for_each(|(pos, render)| {
        draw_batch.set(
            *pos - offset,
```

```
            render.color,
            render.glyph
        );
    }
);
```

That small change was enough to hide entities from view if they're outside of the player's field of vision. If you play the game a bit, you'll notice that you can still ferret out hidden monsters with your mouse—holding the mouse over a location that contains a hidden monster still shows their name in a tooltip. You can use the same code to fix this. Open systems/tooltips.rs. Start by adding the same query to the system header:

WhatCanISee/fov/src/systems/tooltips.rs
```
#[system]
#[read_component(Point)]
#[read_component(Name)]
➤ #[read_component(FieldOfView)]
➤ #[read_component(Player)]
pub fn tooltips(
    ecs: &SubWorld,
    #[resource] mouse_pos: &Point,
    #[resource] camera: &Camera
) {
    let mut positions = <(Entity, &Point, &Name)>::query();
➤    let mut fov = <&FieldOfView>::query().filter(component::<Player>());
```

Then adjust the filter call to check for both the mouse position matching the entity position and the visibility of the tile:

WhatCanISee/fov/src/systems/tooltips.rs
```
let player_fov = fov.iter(ecs).nth(0).unwrap();
positions
    .iter(ecs)
➤    .filter(|(_, pos, _)|
➤        **pos == map_pos && player_fov.visible_tiles.contains(&pos)
➤    )
```

This filters the positions list down to only include entities that are at the currently rendered grid location *and* included in the player's visible tiles list.

Updating Fields of View

The visible area should update when the player moves. Likewise, areas visible to monsters should update when the monsters move. You also don't want to waste processor time by building visibility lists for entities that *haven't* moved. The good news is, the movement system already stores whether an entity moved with the dirty flag. Open systems/movement.rs, and add a query to the header:

WhatCanISee/fov/src/systems/movement.rs
```
#[system(for_each)]
#[read_component(Player)]
#[read_component(FieldOfView)]
pub fn movement(
```

❶ Create a new query that reads FieldOfView.

Add a check similar to the one you use to see if an entity is the player, but this time seeing if the entity has a FieldOfView:

WhatCanISee/fov/src/systems/movement.rs
```
if let Ok(entry) = ecs.entry_ref(want_move.entity) {
    if let Ok(fov) = entry.get_component::<FieldOfView>() {
        commands.add_component(want_move.entity, fov.clone_dirty());
    }

    if entry.get_component::<Player>().is_ok()
    {
        camera.on_player_move(want_move.destination);
    }
}
```

❶ Use if let to check that the target entity is available for use in an entry.

❷ If the entry is available, use another if let to see if a FieldOfView component is available for the entity. If available, use a command list to replace the visible set with an identical copy of the field of view—but with the *dirty* flag set to true.

Run the game now. Your view is restricted to the area around the player, you can't see hidden monsters, and your visible tile set updates as you move. But if you wait around, you still face a gauntlet of heat-seeking monsters. Let's fix that.

Limiting Monsters' Fields of View

You can significantly improve game play by making the monsters chase the player only when they can see them. Doing so introduces new tactics—if you can break line of sight to the monster, it won't follow you. It removes the certainty that if you "camp" long enough, you will defeat the level's denizens. It also adds some uncertainty—the player isn't given many clues as to what may reside beyond the next corner.

Fortunately, you've already done most of the hard work. Monsters have a FieldOfView component just like the player. By generically implementing the system, the game mechanic applies to *any* entity that has a FieldOfView component. You've also already learned how to use contains to see if a tile is visible for a given set.

Open systems/chasing.rs. The first query in systems/chasing.rs needs to be updated to include the entity's field of view:

```
WhatCanISee/eyesight/src/systems/chasing.rs
#[system]
#[read_component(Point)]
#[read_component(ChasingPlayer)]
➤ #[read_component(FieldOfView)]
#[read_component(Health)]
#[read_component(Player)]
pub fn chasing(
  #[resource] map: &Map,
  ecs: &SubWorld,
  commands: &mut CommandBuffer
) {
➤   let mut movers= <(Entity, &Point, &ChasingPlayer, &FieldOfView)>::query();
    let mut positions = <(Entity, &Point, &Health)>::query();
    let mut player = <(&Point, &Player)>::query();
```

You already determine the player's position. Combined with the monsters' FieldOfView, you have all the data you need to determine if a monster can see the player. Modify the query iterator as follows:

```
WhatCanISee/eyesight/src/systems/chasing.rs
movers.iter(ecs).for_each(| (entity, pos, _, fov) | {
  if !fov.visible_tiles.contains(&player_pos) {
    return;
  }
```

For each entity, the system checks to see if that entity's FieldOfView contains the player's position. If it doesn't, you call return. You've used return to return values from functions. You can *also* use return to escape from a function—when you call it inside a function, it immediately exits the function.

If a monster can't see the player, the monster will do nothing. If they *can* see the player, they'll operate exactly as before.

Run the game now, and notice that you aren't besieged by a wall of monsters. Instead, the monsters wait for you and chase you as you approach, as shown in the image on page 198.

You might have noticed that when spawning the monsters, you gave them a lower viewing radius than the player. This was deliberate—the player spots monsters one turn before the monsters spot them, enabling them to retreat.

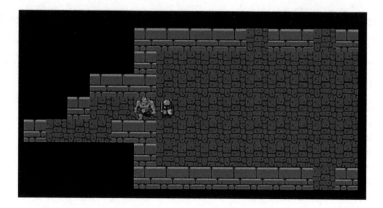

As you introduce more monster types, you'll have gained another tool in your toolbox—giving monsters better or worse eyesight.

Adding Spatial Memory

Whether the adventurer is unspooling thread as they work through a minotaur's labyrinth or scribbling a map as they explore, it's reasonable to expect the adventurer has some memory of where they have been. It also gives the player valuable clues about which parts of the dungeon they haven't explored yet—reducing player frustration. In this section, you'll give the player a memory of where they've been—and learn to render areas they remember but aren't currently visible.

Revealing the Map

Open map.rs. Add a new vector named revealed, containing the revealed status of each tile. If the player has seen the tile, the tile's entry in revealed will be set to true. If they haven't, it will be false. Create the new vector and set the entire revealed vector to false:

WhatCanISee/memory/src/map.rs
```
pub struct Map {
    pub tiles: Vec<TileType>,
    pub revealed_tiles: Vec<bool>
}

impl Map {
    pub fn new() -> Self {
        Self {
            tiles: vec![TileType::Floor; NUM_TILES],
            revealed_tiles: vec![false; NUM_TILES]
        }
    }
```

Arrays of Structs or Structs of Arrays

A common debate in game development communities is whether you should put all of the information you have about a tile into a struct, and store the map as a single array or vector of the combined type, or if you should have a separate container for different elements of data.

Good arguments exist for either approach. Grouping the data can be easier to think about—all the data is in one place. If you're using different parts of the data in different parts of your code—such as the revealed structure—it often makes more sense to separate them. Separating also has a small performance benefit. Your CPU cache can often hold the entirety of a vector of bool data. Accessing data from the cache is very fast, giving you an easy performance boost.

Now that you are storing the player's map memory, let's populate the revealed list with useful data.

Updating the Map

When the player moves, you need to update the revealed list. You can set every visible tile to true. You aren't clearing the list, so this is a cumulative process—as the player moves, more of the map is revealed. This can be accomplished relatively easily by modifying the movement system again. Open systems/movement.rs and apply the following changes to the movement function body:

```
WhatCanISee/memory/src/systems/movement.rs
if let Ok(entry) = ecs.entry_ref(want_move.entity) {
    if let Ok(fov) = entry.get_component::<FieldOfView>() {
        commands.add_component(want_move.entity, fov.clone_dirty());

        if entry.get_component::<Player>().is_ok()
        {
            camera.on_player_move(want_move.destination);
            fov.visible_tiles.iter().for_each(|pos| {
                map.revealed_tiles[map_idx(pos.x, pos.y)] = true;
            });
        }
    }
}
```

❶ This has been rearranged to check if the entity is the player and is contained within the if let section that retrieves the field of view.

❷ For every tile in the player's visible tile list, set the corresponding entry in revealed_tiles to true. Note that you aren't clearing the revealed list—the effect is cumulative, gradually revealing the map as the player explores.

You also need to make the map mutable in the function signature by adding a mut to its declaration: #[resource] map: &mut Map.

Now that you know where the player has been, let's adjust the map rendering to reflect the player's map memory.

Rendering Your Memory

Open systems/map_render.rs. With a little bit of rearranging, you can detect tiles that are revealed but not visible, and render them differently.

WhatCanISee/memory/src/systems/map_render.rs

```
let idx = map_idx(x, y);
if map.in_bounds(pt) && (player_fov.visible_tiles.contains(&pt)
❶    | map.revealed_tiles[idx]) {
❷    let tint = if player_fov.visible_tiles.contains(&pt) {
        WHITE
    } else {
        DARK_GRAY
    };
    match map.tiles[idx] {
        TileType::Floor => {
            draw_batch.set(
                pt - offset,
                ColorPair::new(
❸                   tint,
                    BLACK
                ),
                to_cp437('.')
            );
        }
        TileType::Wall => {
            draw_batch.set(
                pt - offset,
                ColorPair::new(
                    tint,
                    BLACK
                ),
                to_cp437('#')
            );
        }
    }
}
```

❶ If the tile is valid, and is either visible to the player or in the player's tile memory, proceed to render it. You can use parentheses to combine && and | (and/or) into complicated conditions.

❷ If the player can currently see the tile (because it's in the player's visible_tiles list), set tint to WHITE. Otherwise, set the tint to DARK_GREY.

❸ When bracket-lib renders a character, it multiplies the sprite/font color by the specified tint. Multiplying by WHITE doesn't change anything. Multiplying by DARK_GREY lowers the value of the color's red, green, and blue components—giving a darker tile.

Run the game now. Notice how the areas that you previously visited are darker:

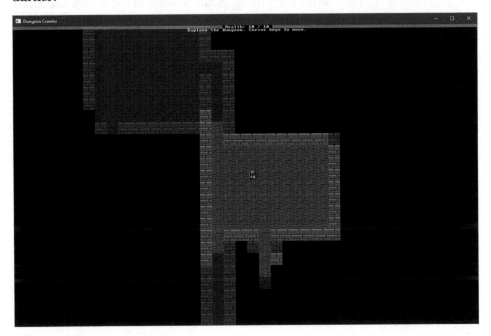

Other Uses for Fields of View

The field-of-view system has added a very powerful tool to your arsenal. You can use the same principles in several ways, helping you make your own unique game. Here are some ideas to ponder:

• You now know how to check line of sight between points. If you'd like to implement ranged combat, this solves one of the hardest problems—determining if the shooter can see their target.

- If you'd like a fog effect, you could calculate two fields of view with different ranges and vary the rendering effect on each.

- You could add items that vary the player's visibility range—maybe magical spectacles or night vision goggles.

- Using the render tinting system, you don't *have* to use grey for areas. A green tint provides a night-vision effect. Red tints could represent heat signatures in a suspenseful "bug hunt" game. The sky's the limit for your imagination.

- You could include items such as a Scroll of Magic Mapping that reveal the map as a reward.

- Explosions typically affect everything in line of sight of the boom. Calculate a visibility set for your explosion and you have a list of all of the targets.

Wrap-Up

In this chapter, you implemented fields of view for the player and the monsters. You restricted map rendering to what the player can see, and limited monsters to chasing the player only if they can see them. This has enabled more tactical play, and made running to hide a valid option for the player. You also gave the player a memory of where they've been, and learned how to *tint* rendered tiles with a color.

In the next chapter, you'll add difficulty to the game by further randomizing monster spawns. You'll combine this with new ways to generate maps to create a much more tactically varied game. You'll also learn how to *theme* your maps, varying the look and feel of your dungeons.

CHAPTER 11

More Interesting Dungeons

It's the hero's twentieth descent into yet another dungeon in search of the mythical Amulet of Yala—not surprisingly, both you and the hero are bored. Despairingly, the hero cries out, "Surely, not every dungeon is a bunch of rect-angular rooms with dog-leg corridors?"

So far, your dungeons have all used the same room-based generation system that you created in Chapter 5, Build a Dungeon Crawler, on page 75. This system works, but it makes for entirely predictable—maybe even bor-ing—maps. So, how do you generate a map where the player can explore a field of underground fungal trees, a sprawling city, or a dark forest? As it turns out, there's an entire field of game development known as *procedural generation* that's built around using algorithms to create exciting environments like these—and game developers have been using it since the 1980s.

Using different procedural generation algorithms allows you to inject variety into your game. Rooms and corridors look designed, implying a sentient builder. Other algorithms generate a more natural-looking map. Varying the map keeps the player interested.

In this chapter, you'll learn to use traits to easily substitute your room-based generator with other map builders. You'll learn two of the more popular map generation algorithms—*Cellular Automata* and *Drunkard's Walk*—as you learn how to place monsters in maps that don't feature explicit rooms. You'll also learn how to design parts (or all) of your map by hand, storing the data in your game and integrating your designs with the computer-generated maps.

Creating Traits

You've already used traits a lot in previous chapters. When you implemented BaseMap and Algorithm2D in Supporting Pathfinding with Traits, on page 163, you *consumed* the associated traits. It's time to learn about the inner workings of traits by making one of your own.

Traits provide an *interface* and describe the functions that a trait consumer *must* implement. Traits can also specify constraints to ensure that types that implement your trait are compatible with their intended use.

Traits are very powerful, especially when working with a team or shipping a library. By requiring that all consumers of a trait provide a known interface, you can seamlessly switch between traits without changing the code that calls it. You're going to turn map building into a trait, and use it to expose several algorithms for designing maps. This will give you substitutable map builders—allowing you to add more or change your map design.

The first step is to divide map_builder into a directory-based module that supports sub-modules. Rather than cram all of your builders into one map_builder.rs file, separate them into modules to make it easier to find the code for each builder.

Dividing the Map Builder

map_builder.rs is a single-file module. As you add map architects, it'll be easier to track them if each new architect resides in its own file. You used a similar strategy in the systems module. Converting a file-based module into a directory-based module requires three steps:

1. Create a new directory with the same name as the existing module, but do not include the file extension. Create a directory named src/map_builder.

2. In the new directory, create a file named mod.rs, and copy the contents of your existing module (map_builder.rs) into the new mod.rs file.

3. Delete the old map_builder.rs file.

Following the steps above, you transform your map_builder module from a single file into a directory as shown in the image on page 205.

The game will run as before, but you now have a directory into which you can insert sub-modules associated with the map_builder.

Let's start to divide the room-based map builder into a reusable trait.

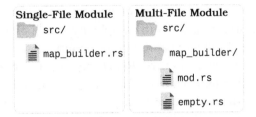

Offering Map Services with the MapBuilder

All implementations of MapArchitect provide a MapBuilder. This allows you to put some commonly used code into MapBuilder—simplifying the design of your architects.

MapBuilder already contains some room code which you can leave in place. However, you'll need to add two common functions: fill and find_most_distant. You've used the contents of these functions in your room builder. Open map_builder/mod.rs so that you can implement a generalized version of these functions:

MoreInterestingDungeons/traits/src/map_builder/mod.rs
```
fn fill(&mut self, tile : TileType) {
    self.map.tiles.iter_mut().for_each(|t| *t = tile);
}

fn find_most_distant(&self) -> Point {
    let dijkstra_map = DijkstraMap::new(
        SCREEN_WIDTH,
        SCREEN_HEIGHT,
        &vec![self.map.point2d_to_index(self.player_start)],
        &self.map,
        1024.0
    );

    const UNREACHABLE : &f32 = &f32::MAX;
    self.map.index_to_point2d
    (
        dijkstra_map.map
            .iter()
            .enumerate()
            .filter(|(_,dist)| *dist < UNREACHABLE)
            .max_by(|a,b| a.1.partial_cmp(b.1).unwrap())
            .unwrap().0
    )
}
```

You initially wrote fill in Fill the Map With Walls, on page 90. It fills the entire map with a given tile type. You created the body of find_most_distant in Placing the Amulet, on page 178. Moving useful code into functions is a great idea and is part of a process known as *refactoring*.

Refactoring

As your programs grow in complexity, you'll often realize that you may have duplicated some functionality, or you could improve your program's structure. Rearranging your code to assist with these problems is called refactoring. The idea behind refactoring is that your program will work exactly as it did before you made your changes—allowing for any syntax changes needed to use the new layout. It may seem like a lot of effort to refactor for no visible gain, but it's worth it if it makes it easier for you to come back to your program after a break and still understand how it all works.

Defining the Architect Trait

Toward the top of map_builder/mod.rs (underneath your use statements), define a new trait:

MoreInterestingDungeons/traits/src/map_builder/mod.rs
```
❶ trait MapArchitect {
❷     fn new(&mut self, rng: &mut RandomNumberGenerator) -> MapBuilder;
   }
```

❶ Trait definition is similar to struct definition. Start with the keyword trait, and append the trait's name. Rust encourages you to use CamelCase for trait names. If you need to export a trait to other parts of your program, you can prefix it with pub.

❷ Define only the function *signature* in the trait. You're listing functions that must be implemented by types that implement your trait.

Creating the trait doesn't build any actual function implementations. It simply creates an interface or contract. Traits offer a guarantee that any structure that implements the trait will offer the trait definition functions. You can then use traits interchangeably, with the same interface and function signatures.

The MapArchitect trait you created requires that implementors of this trait create a function named build that accepts a RandomNumberGenerator as a parameter and returns a MapBuilder ready for the game to use.

Default Implementations

You can include full functions in your trait definition. These serve as *default implementations*. The consumer doesn't have to define them, but can override them when needed. This can save a lot of typing. The BaseMap trait you consumed provides default implementations of several functions.

Test Your Trait with a Reference Implementation

It's a good idea to make a *reference implementation* to validate that the trait works. Reference implementations do the minimum required to use a trait and nothing else. Your trait needs to accept a random number generator as a parameter and return a working MapBuilder with sufficient data to start playing the game level.

Create a new file named map_builder/empty.rs, and add the following code to it:

MoreInterestingDungeons/traits/src/map_builder/empty.rs

```
use crate::prelude::*;
❶ use super::MapArchitect;

❷ pub struct EmptyArchitect {}

❸ impl MapArchitect for EmptyArchitect {
❹     fn new(&mut self, rng: &mut RandomNumberGenerator) -> MapBuilder {
❺         let mut mb = MapBuilder{
               map : Map::new(),
               rooms: Vec::new(),
               monster_spawns : Vec::new(),
               player_start : Point::zero(),
               amulet_start : Point::zero()
           };
           mb.fill(TileType::Floor);
           mb.player_start = Point::new(SCREEN_WIDTH/2, SCREEN_HEIGHT/2);
❻         mb.amulet_start = mb.find_most_distant();
❼         for _ in 0..50 {
               mb.monster_spawns.push(
                   Point::new(
                       rng.range(1, SCREEN_WIDTH),
                       rng.range(1, SCREEN_WIDTH)
                   )
               )
           }
           mb
       }
}
```

❶ You can import an item from its immediate parent with super. This imports the MapArchitect trait you defined.

❷ Define an empty struct as the EmptyArchitect type. You need to declare a new type, which can then implement your trait.

❸ Implement the MapArchitect trait. This tells Rust that EmptyArchitect supports the MapArchitect trait interface.

❹ The new() function signature must *exactly* match the signature you defined in the trait definition.

❺ The remainder of this function does the absolute minimum to create a working map: it creates the map, fills it with floor tiles, and adds the player and amulet starting positions.

❻ Use the find_most_distant() function you created earlier to place the Amulet of Yala.

❼ The architect also spawns 50 monsters in random positions. The _ tells Rust that you won't be using the range variable of your for loop—you want to run the loop 50 times.

You also need to open map_builder/mod.rs and add monster_spawns to the MapBuilder structure:

MoreInterestingDungeons/traits/src/map_builder/mod.rs
```
pub struct MapBuilder {
    pub map : Map,
    pub rooms : Vec<Rect>,
    pub monster_spawns : Vec<Point>,
    pub player_start : Point,
    pub amulet_start : Point
}
```

Sure, this isn't an incredibly exciting map generator—since it makes a giant, mostly empty open space map—but it does illustrate the use of your new trait. It also tests that the trait's definition is sufficient to make a game level.

Test Harnesses

When you're working on procedurally generated content, it's beneficial to make a *test harness*. A test harness is the relevant parts of the game, linked to some code to display the results of your generators. You can find the test harness I used for this chapter in the downloadable code, MoreInterestingDungeons/output_harness. It's mostly the same code as the regular game code in the book, but with some additional display code to help make the screenshots used in this chapter.

Calling the Empty-Map Architect

Now that you have a simple architect that creates an empty map, let's adjust MapBuilder to use it. Open map_builder/mod.rs. Don't forget to add mod empty and use empty::EmptyArchitect to the top of the file to include your new architect in the project. Replace the new() function as follows:

MoreInterestingDungeons/traits/src/map_builder/mod.rs
```
pub fn new(rng: &mut RandomNumberGenerator) -> Self {
    let mut architect = EmptyArchitect{};
    architect.new(rng)
}
```

The new() function is pretty straightforward: it creates an EmptyArchitect and calls the new() function it provides. Lastly, update main.rs to spawn monsters. Add the following to the State's constructor:

MoreInterestingDungeons/traits/src/main.rs
```
    spawn_amulet_of_yala(&mut ecs, map_builder.amulet_start);
➤   map_builder.monster_spawns
➤       .iter()
➤       .for_each(|pos| spawn_monster(&mut ecs, &mut rng, *pos));
    resources.insert(map_builder.map);
```

You also need to add monster spawning to reset_game_state:

MoreInterestingDungeons/traits/src/main.rs
```
    spawn_amulet_of_yala(&mut self.ecs, map_builder.amulet_start);
➤   map_builder.monster_spawns
➤       .iter()
➤       .for_each(|pos| spawn_monster(&mut self.ecs, &mut rng, *pos));
```

Run your game now, and you'll find yourself on an empty map, surrounded by monsters:

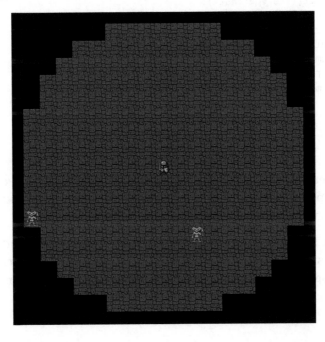

Converting the Room Builder

Let's make your first useful MapArchitect by converting the room builder to use the trait. You created the room system in Building a Dungeon, on page 88. This section won't go through the algorithm again; instead, it'll convert it to run inside of a MapArchitect trait.

You can make your first useful MapArchitect by converting the room builder to use the trait. Create a new file named map_builder/rooms.rs, and add the following code to the new file:

MoreInterestingDungeons/traits_rooms/src/map_builder/rooms.rs
```
use crate::prelude::*;
use super::MapArchitect;

pub struct RoomsArchitect {}

impl MapArchitect for RoomsArchitect {
❶    fn new(&mut self, rng: &mut RandomNumberGenerator) -> MapBuilder {
        let mut mb = MapBuilder{
            map : Map::new(),
            rooms: Vec::new(),
            monster_spawns : Vec::new(),
            player_start : Point::zero(),
            amulet_start : Point::zero()
        };

        mb.fill(TileType::Wall);
        mb.build_random_rooms(rng);
        mb.build_corridors(rng);
        mb.player_start = mb.rooms[0].center();
        mb.amulet_start = mb.find_most_distant();
        for room in mb.rooms.iter().skip(1) {
            mb.monster_spawns.push(room.center());
        }

        mb
    }
}
```

❶ Implement the MapArchitect trait using the same signature specified in your trait implementation. Notice that the actual room building code is the same as the room builder you created before.

Don't forget to activate your module: open map_builder/mod.rs, and insert code that imports and uses the module (mod rooms; use rooms::RoomsArchitect;). While you're in map_builder/mod.rs, adjust the new() function to call your room-based builder:

MoreInterestingDungeons/traits_rooms/src/map_builder/mod.rs
```
pub fn new(rng: &mut RandomNumberGenerator) -> Self {
    let mut architect = RoomsArchitect{};
    architect.new(rng)
}
```

Now that you've got an empty map builder and have ported your room-based builder to use traits, it's time to explore some more interesting dungeon generators.

Creating Cellular Automata Maps

Cellular automata is a fun algorithm. It starts with completely random chaos, and order gradually emerges as rules are applied repeatedly. This algorithm is great for producing organic-looking levels, such as a forest with clearings or an old cavern network. It was first popularized in *Conway's Game of Life.*[1]

Cellular Automata Theory

Cellular automata was originally designed to simulate organic life. Each map tile independently lives (becomes a wall) or dies (becomes open space) based on a count of its neighbors. You keep running iterations until you have a usable map. You can visualize the algorithm applied to each tile like this:

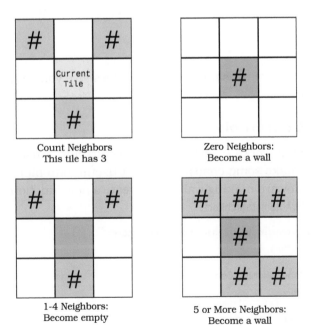

Count Neighbors
This tile has 3

Zero Neighbors:
Become a wall

1-4 Neighbors:
Become empty

5 or More Neighbors:
Become a wall

---

1.   https://en.wikipedia.org/wiki/Conway%27s_Game_of_Life

Now that you know the theory behind the map generation algorithm, you're ready to build a cellular automata map generator.

Implement Cellular Automata

Create a new file, map_builder/automata.rs. Add mod automata; to map_builder/mod.rs to include it in your project.

You need to start by implementing the minimum boilerplate code required to create a structure to hold your cellular automata algorithm. You also need to add the minimum boilerplate code required to implement the trait:

```
use crate::prelude::*;
use super::MapArchitect;

pub struct CellularAutomataArchitect {}

impl MapArchitect for CellularAutomataArchitect {
  fn new(&mut self, rng: &mut RandomNumberGenerator) -> MapBuilder {
    let mut mb = MapBuilder{
      map : Map::new(),
      rooms : Vec::new(),
      monster_spawns : Vec::new(),
      player_start : Point::zero(),
      amulet_start : Point::zero()
    };

    mb
  }
}
```

That code won't create a usable map, but it does give you a starting point on which to build.

Make Some Random Noise

Cellular automata works by evolving pure chaos into a useful map, so the first step is to make some chaos. You get a useful map more quickly if you *bias* the chaos toward making wall tiles. Create a new function, implemented as part of CellularAutomataArchitect:

MoreInterestingDungeons/cellular/src/map_builder/automata.rs
```
fn random_noise_map(
    &mut self,
    rng: &mut RandomNumberGenerator,
    map: &mut Map)
{
❶    map.tiles.iter_mut().for_each(|t| {
❷        let roll = rng.range(0, 100);
❸        if roll > 55 {
❹            *t = TileType::Floor;
```

```
        } else {
            *t = TileType::Wall;
        }
    });
}
```

❶ Mutably iterate all the tiles on the map.

❷ Generate a random number between 0 and 99.

❸ Check if the random number is greater than 55. This biases the random decision since it's more likely that the roll will be less than 55 than greater than 55.

❹ If you rolled above 55, make a floor; otherwise, make a wall.

This function makes a chaotic, random map—probably completely unplayable. Approximately 55% of the map tiles will be walls and the remaining 45% floors. Part of a random noise map looks like this:

As expected, it's beautifully chaotic, but also unplayable. Let's start to bring some order to the chaos, making it a fun and playable map.

Counting Neighbors

The cellular automata algorithm works by counting each tile's neighbors. You need to make a function—implemented as part of CellularAutomataArchitect—to do this for you:

MoreInterestingDungeons/cellular/src/map_builder/automata.rs
```
fn count_neighbors(&self, x: i32, y: i32, map: &Map) -> usize {
    let mut neighbors = 0;
    for iy in -1 ..= 1 {
        for ix in -1 ..= 1 {
```

❶
```
            if !(ix==0 && iy == 0) &&
                map.tiles[map_idx(x+ix, y+iy)] == TileType::Wall
            {
                neighbors += 1;
            }
        }
    }

    neighbors
}
```

❶ Don't count the current tile; only count its neighbors.

This function doesn't have any new concepts: it checks each adjacent tile, and if it's a wall, it adds 1 to the neighbor count. Note that it includes diagonally adjacent tiles in the count.

Iterating Away the Chaos

Now that you can count neighbors, you need to build a function to perform a cellular automata iteration on the map. Add another function to CellularAutomataArchitect:

MoreInterestingDungeons/cellular/src/map_builder/automata.rs
```
fn iteration(&mut self, map: &mut Map) {
    let mut new_tiles = map.tiles.clone();
    for y in 1 .. SCREEN_HEIGHT -1 {
        for x in 1 .. SCREEN_WIDTH -1 {
            let neighbors = self.count_neighbors(x, y, map);
            let idx = map_idx(x, y);
            if neighbors > 4 || neighbors == 0 {
                new_tiles[idx] = TileType::Wall;
            } else {
                new_tiles[idx] = TileType::Floor;
            }
        }
    }
    map.tiles = new_tiles;
}
```
❶
❷
❸
❹

❶ Create a copy of the map. You don't want to count neighbors on the map you're adjusting since your changes will bias the results on subsequent tiles, leading to odd results.

❷ Iterate all of the tiles on the map *except* for the edges. The neighbor count references tiles around a map entry. If you include the edge tiles, your program will crash with a range-check error as it tries to read outside of the map area. If it didn't crash, it would have invalid results because there can't be any tiles to count outside the map.

❸ Use the function you just created to count the neighbors adjacent to this tile.

❹ If there are 0 or more than 4 neighbors, turn the tile into a wall; otherwise, turn the tile into a floor.

This function applies the cellular automata tile algorithm described above. Its results can seem magical as a single iteration delivers a much more interesting map:

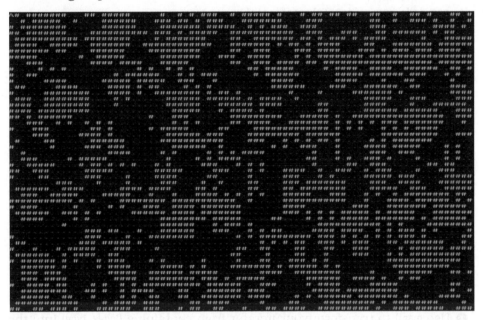

With one iteration, order starts to emerge from the chaos: open areas become more open, and walls begin to cluster together.

Place the Player

In the room-based architect, placing the player was easy—you put them in the first room. But now, there are no clearly defined rooms with this algorithm, so you have to use a different approach. In this case, you'll find all of the floor tiles and determine their distance to the center. You'll then start the player in the closest open tile to the center. Add another function to CellularAutomataAr-chitect:

MoreInterestingDungeons/cellular/src/map_builder/automata.rs
```
fn find_start(&self, map: &Map) -> Point {
❶    let center = Point::new(SCREEN_WIDTH/2, SCREEN_HEIGHT/2);
     let closest_point = map.tiles
❷        .iter()
❸        .enumerate()
```

```
④        .filter(|(_, t)| **t == TileType::Floor)
⑤        .map(|(idx, _)| (idx, DistanceAlg::Pythagoras.distance2d(
             center,
             map.index_to_point2d(idx)
         )))
         .min_by(|(_, distance), (_, distance2)|
⑥            distance.partial_cmp(&distance2).unwrap()
         )
⑦        .map(|(idx, _)| idx)
⑧        .unwrap();
⑨    map.index_to_point2d(closest_point)
}
```

❶ Start by storing the center of the map in a Point.

❷ Iterate all of the map tiles.

❸ Call enumerate() to append the tile's index in the tile vector to the result. Each iteration now contains a tuple of (index, tiletype).

❹ Use filter() to remove all of the tiles that aren't a floor. The tile indices are preserved. You now have a list of the index and type of all floors on the map.

❺ Calculate the Pythagorean distance from each remaining tile to the map's center.

❻ The function min_by() finds the lowest value in an iterator set, using a closure to determine how to calculate the minimum. You are comparing the distances to the center.

❼ Use map() to transform your iterator from containing (index, type) into the map indices.

❽ min_by() finds the lowest value in an iterator set and allows you to specify the comparison technique. Distance is a floating-point number, and cannot be perfectly compared with another floating-point number; NaN (Not a Number) and Infinity are both valid floating-point numbers—but their comparison with other numbers is undefined. Instead, you use partial_cmp() when comparing floats.

min_by() returns an Option. There's no guarantee of a lowest value in the iterator set. Pythagorean distance doesn't return infinity or an invalid number, so you can safely use unwrap() to extract the option's value.

❾ Convert the map index to an x,y point and return it.

Now that you know where to put the player, it's time to tie things together and complete the algorithm.

Spawning Monsters without Rooms

A major difference between cellular automata and your room-based builder is that there aren't any rooms, which makes spawning monsters in each room impossible. Other algorithms will also skip the concept of rooms—so let's make a helper in MapBuilder to spawn monsters into available open spaces that aren't too close to the player:

MoreInterestingDungeons/cellular/src/map_builder/mod.rs

```
fn spawn_monsters(
    &self,
    start: &Point,
    rng: &mut RandomNumberGenerator
) -> Vec<Point> {
    const NUM_MONSTERS : usize = 50;
    let mut spawnable_tiles : Vec<Point> = self.map.tiles
        .iter()
        .enumerate()
❶      .filter(|(idx, t)|
            **t == TileType::Floor &&
                DistanceAlg::Pythagoras.distance2d(
                    *start,
                    self.map.index_to_point2d(*idx)
                ) > 10.0
        )
        .map(|(idx, _)| self.map.index_to_point2d(idx))
        .collect();

    let mut spawns = Vec::new();
    for _ in 0 .. NUM_MONSTERS {
❷      let target_index = rng.random_slice_index(&spawnable_tiles)
            .unwrap();
        spawns.push(spawnable_tiles[target_index].clone());
❸      spawnable_tiles.remove(target_index);
    }
    spawns
}
```

❶ Build an iterator containing all tile indices (from enumerate) and tile types. Filter to only include tiles that are floors and more than 10 tiles distant from the player's start point.

❷ random_slice_index() returns a randomly selected entry from a slice. In this case, the vector of possible spawn points.

❸ Remove the target tile once it's been used; otherwise, you may find monsters standing on top of one another.

This function scans the map for possible places to add monsters and fills 50 of those places at random with monsters.

Build the Map

Go back to the build function. You need to integrate all of the steps you've created into the map builder:

MoreInterestingDungeons/cellular/src/map_builder/automata.rs
```
fn new(&mut self, rng: &mut RandomNumberGenerator) -> MapBuilder {
    let mut mb = MapBuilder{
        map : Map::new(),
        rooms: Vec::new(),
        monster_spawns : Vec::new(),
        player_start : Point::zero(),
        amulet_start : Point::zero()
    };
    self.random_noise_map(rng, &mut mb.map);
    for _ in 0..10 {
        self.iteration(&mut mb.map);
    }
    let start = self.find_start(&mb.map);
    mb.monster_spawns = mb.spawn_monsters(&start, rng);
    mb.player_start = start;
    mb.amulet_start = mb.find_most_distant();
    mb
}
```

Notice that you're using the services you created to add a boundary to the map, place the amulet, and spawn monsters.

Call the Cellular Automata Architect

One more step remains: you need to call the new map builder. Open map_builder/mod.rs, and adjust the new() function to call your new algorithm:

MoreInterestingDungeons/cellular/src/map_builder/mod.rs
```
impl MapBuilder {
    pub fn new(rng: &mut RandomNumberGenerator) -> Self {
        let mut architect = CellularAutomataArchitect{};
        architect.new(rng)
    }
}
```

Run the program now, and the player has an open cavern network to explore (the screenshot shown on page 219 is from the test harness to show you the complete map).

Let's build another map algorithm.

Creating Drunkard's Walk Maps

Drunkard's Walk produces very natural looking caverns—worn away by erosion. It works by randomly placing a drunken miner on a solid map. The

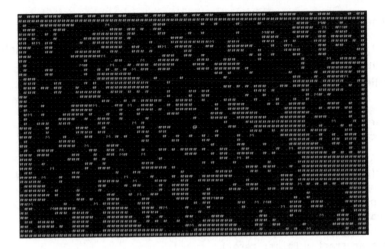

miner digs randomly, carving pathways into the map. Eventually, the miner either passes out—having exceeded their maximum number of turns—or exits the map. You then check if the map is ready by counting the number of open tiles. If it isn't ready, you spawn another drunken miner until the map is sufficiently open. The algorithm's name arises from the random nature of drunken movement. The algorithm may be visualized as follows:

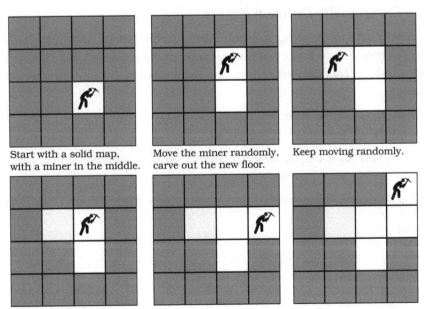

Start with a solid map, with a miner in the middle.

Move the miner randomly, carve out the new floor.

Keep moving randomly.

It's ok if the miner returns to a previously dug tile.

Let's start building a drunkard's walk map.

Implement the Boilerplate

Create a new file named map_builder/drunkard.rs. In map_builder/mod.rs include the file in your project with mod drunkard;. Once again, you need to create the minimal boilerplate code to implement your MapArchitect trait:

```
use crate::prelude::*;
use super::MapArchitect;
pub struct DrunkardsWalkArchitect {}

impl MapArchitect for DrunkardsWalkArchitect {
  fn new(&mut self, rng: &mut RandomNumberGenerator) -> MapBuilder {
    let mut mb = MapBuilder{
      map : Map::new(),
      rooms : Vec::new(),
      monster_spawns : Vec::new(),
      player_start : Point::zero(),
      amulet_start : Point::zero()
    };

    mb
  }
}
```

With the basic structure in place, let's add some drunken miners.

Carve Caverns with Drunken Miners

You need to decide how far a miner can stumble before passing out. Lower numbers tend to give less open maps; larger numbers tend toward more open spaces. Add a constant to the top of mod/drunkard.rs so you can tweak this number:

MoreInterestingDungeons/drunkard/src/map_builder/drunkard.rs
```
const STAGGER_DISTANCE: usize = 400;
```

Now that you have the tunable parameter in place, create a new function, implemented by DrunkardsWalkArchitect:

MoreInterestingDungeons/drunkard/src/map_builder/drunkard.rs
```
fn drunkard(
    &mut self,
    start: &Point,
    rng: &mut RandomNumberGenerator,
    map: &mut Map
) {
❶    let mut drunkard_pos = start.clone();
❷    let mut distance_staggered = 0;

❸    loop {
        let drunk_idx = map.point2d_to_index(drunkard_pos);
❹        map.tiles[drunk_idx] = TileType::Floor;
```

```
❺      match rng.range(0, 4) {
           0 => drunkard_pos.x -= 1,
           1 => drunkard_pos.x += 1,
           2 => drunkard_pos.y -= 1,
           _ => drunkard_pos.y += 1,
       }
❻      if !map.in_bounds(drunkard_pos) {
           break;
       }
❼      distance_staggered += 1;
       if distance_staggered > STAGGER_DISTANCE {
           break;
       }
   }
}
```

❶ Clone the start position. It will act as the miner's current location.

❷ Set the digger's distance traveled so far to zero.

❸ loop runs the code in its scope continually until a break statement is called.

❹ Set the map tile at the digger's current location to be a floor.

❺ Randomly pick a direction and adjust the digger's current position accordingly.

❻ If the digger has left the map, break out of the loop.

❼ Add 1 to the number of tiles traveled by the digger. If it exceeds the STAGGER_DISTANCE constant, break out of the loop.

This algorithm quickly carves a map out of a solid level. A single miner moving randomly might produce a map like this one:

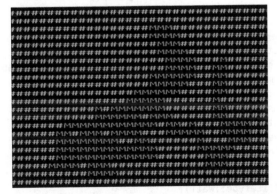

Let's implement the second half of the Drunkard's Walk algorithm: knowing when to stop.

Determining Map Completeness

Unlike the drunken dwarves, you probably have an end point in mind for their inebriated tunneling. One approach is to determine how many tiles you want to be open spaces. Unlike cellular automata, you can guarantee that all tiles will be accessible from the starting position since a drunken miner had to stagger there for it to be open. This allows you to count the number of open tiles and divide by the total number of tiles to determine how much of the map is open to play. You can set your desired map openness in a constant at the top of mod/drunkard.rs:

MoreInterestingDungeons/drunkard/src/map_builder/drunkard.rs
```
const NUM_TILES: usize = (SCREEN_WIDTH * SCREEN_HEIGHT) as usize;
const DESIRED_FLOOR : usize = NUM_TILES / 3;
```

This code calculates the number of tiles on the map and divides it by three to find the desired number of floor tiles. You can check if the map meets the openness criteria with a simple iterator that counts floor tiles:

```
self.map.tiles.iter().filter(|t| **t == TileType::Floor).count() < DESIRED_FLOOR
```

Keep Digging until It's Done

You want to keep adding diggers until your coverage requirement is met. Always starting a dwarf in the same location tends to give a very boring map—it eventually becomes a circle, as dwarves pass out at the edges of their stagger range. You can significantly improve the look of your map by having the dwarf start at a random location. However, this creates a problem: you lose the guarantee that the entire map is reachable from the starting point. Fortunately, you can use a Dijkstra map to trim out the inaccessible regions.

Let's finish DrunkardsWalkArchitect by completing the new() function and adding these features:

MoreInterestingDungeons/drunkard/src/map_builder/drunkard.rs
```
impl MapArchitect for DrunkardsWalkArchitect {
    fn new(&mut self, rng: &mut RandomNumberGenerator) -> MapBuilder {
        let mut mb = MapBuilder{
            map : Map::new(),
            rooms : Vec::new(),
            monster_spawns : Vec::new(),
            player_start : Point::zero(),
            amulet_start : Point::zero()
        };

        mb.fill(TileType::Wall);
        let center = Point::new(SCREEN_WIDTH /2, SCREEN_HEIGHT/2);
        self.drunkard(&center, rng, &mut mb.map);
```

```
                while mb.map.tiles.iter()
❶                    .filter(|t| **t == TileType::Floor).count() < DESIRED_FLOOR
                {
                    self.drunkard(
                        &Point::new(
                            rng.range(0, SCREEN_WIDTH),
                            rng.range(0, SCREEN_HEIGHT)
                        ),
                        rng,
                        &mut mb.map
❷                    );
❸                    let dijkstra_map = DijkstraMap::new(
                        SCREEN_WIDTH,
                        SCREEN_HEIGHT,
                        &vec![mb.map.point2d_to_index(center)],
                        &mb.map,
                        1024.0
                    );
❹                    dijkstra_map.map
                        .iter()
❺                        .enumerate()
❻                        .filter(|(_, distance)| *distance > &2000.0)
❼                        .for_each(|(idx, _)| mb.map.tiles[idx] = TileType::Wall);
                }
                mb.monster_spawns = mb.spawn_monsters(&center, rng);
                mb.player_start = center;
                mb.amulet_start = mb.find_most_distant();
                mb
            }
        }
```

❶ Use the map evaluation iterator to determine if you should keep digging.
While the map is incomplete, run more diggers.

❷ Start the digger at a random location on the map.

❸ Build a Dijkstra map, exactly as you did for determining where to place
the amulet.

❹ Iterate the Dijkstra map results.

❺ Use enumerate() to add a tile index to each entry in the iterator.

❻ Use filter() to retain values with a distance greater than 2,000 tiles from
the starting point. These tiles are inaccessible.

❼ For each remaining entry in the iterator, convert the tile to a wall.

The algorithm will now repeat until the map has enough floor tiles, and
dwarves will start at random places. The last step is to tell the architect to
use your new map type.

Activating the New Map Type

Open map_builder/mod.rs and change the new() function to call your new map architect:

MoreInterestingDungeons/drunkard/src/map_builder/mod.rs
```
impl MapBuilder {
    pub fn new(rng: &mut RandomNumberGenerator) -> Self {
        let mut architect = DrunkardsWalkArchitect{};
        architect.new(rng)
    }
}
```

Run the program now, and you'll find yourself on a very natural looking map, similar to this one:

Randomly Selecting an Architect

You now have room building, cellular automata, and Drunkard's Walk algorithms available to build maps—all implemented using traits, making them interchangeable at runtime. Let's add some variety to your game by randomly selecting which architect to use when a map is created.

Open map_builder/mod.rs, and replace the new() function with the following code:

```
pub fn new(rng: &mut RandomNumberGenerator) -> Self {
    let mut architect : Box<dyn MapArchitect> = match rng.range(0, 3) {
        0 => Box::new(DrunkardsWalkArchitect{}),
        1 => Box::new(RoomsArchitect{}),
        _ => Box::new(CellularAutomataArchitect{})
    };
    let mut mb = architect.new(rng);
    mb
}
```

There are two new concepts here: Box and dyn.

When you use just one type of architect, Rust knows exactly what type that architect is. However, when you're storing a type that might be anything that implements the MapArchitect trait, Rust has a harder time determining the type and size. So instead of just creating the type, you have to put it into a box. Box is a *smart pointer*; it creates the architect type you requested and holds a pointer to it. When the Box is destroyed, it takes care of deleting the contained object.

You can put (almost) anything into a box. While a box's content may vary, the type needs to be annotated with dyn. dyn is short for "dynamic dispatch." Rust will allow you to put any type that implements the named trait into the box, and you can call the trait's functions in the box as if it were a regular variable. Internally, Rust has added a table that looks up what type is actually in the box and runs the appropriate code.

With this in place, you can now work with a team to create map builders—and as long as the team obeys the trait's requirements, you can switch between them whenever you want.

Prefabricating Map Sections

Random dungeons are great, but sometimes you want to represent something specific. You might have a great idea for part—or even all—of a map. This has been used to great effect in many games. Games as varied as Diablo and Dungeon Crawl Stone Soup procedurally generate a large portion of their content—and intersperse pre-made sections called *vaults.*

Handmade Dungeons

Create a new file named map_builder/prefab.rs. Add the usual use crate::prelude::* and define your first prefabricated map section:

MoreInterestingDungeons/prefab/src/map_builder/prefab.rs

```
use crate::prelude::*;

const FORTRESS : (&str, i32, i32) = ("
------------
---#####---
---#----#---
---#-M--#---
-###----###-
--M------M--
-###----###-
---#----#---
---#----#---
---#####---
------------
", 12, 11);
```

The two variables represent the size of your map section. The real magic is in the FORTRESS string. You're representing your desired map as characters within the string constant. - represents an open space, and # represents a wall. M represents a monster spawning location. You can design any map section you want—but be sure to set the size appropriately.

Don't Use Spaces for Floors

 You can make your map look much prettier by using spaces in your map string. Unfortunately, this makes it very difficult to see which tiles are intentionally empty and which ones are whitespace. Because of this discrepancy, inadvertently breaking your vaults is possible.

Placing Your Vault

Unless you plan to draw the entire level as a pre-designed map (an excellent idea for boss levels), you'll need to be able to place your vault on an existing map. You'll want to place your prefab somewhere on the map that the player can reach. You may also want to abandon the effort—and not use the vault on this level—if placement proves intractable.

Start by creating a new function in map_builder/prefab.rs:

MoreInterestingDungeons/prefab/src/map_builder/prefab.rs

```
pub fn apply_prefab(mb: &mut MapBuilder, rng: &mut RandomNumberGenerator) {
```

You already know how to find the accessible parts of a map with a Dijkstra map. Start your function by setting a variable placement—representing the destination for the vault—to None and building a Dijkstra map:

MoreInterestingDungeons/prefab/src/map_builder/prefab.rs
```
let mut placement = None;

let dijkstra_map = DijkstraMap::new(
    SCREEN_WIDTH,
    SCREEN_HEIGHT,
    &vec![mb.map.point2d_to_index(mb.player_start)],
    &mb.map,
    1024.0
);
```

Next, repeatedly try to place your vault until it either fits or you give up trying. Add the following to your function:

MoreInterestingDungeons/prefab/src/map_builder/prefab.rs
```
❶ let mut attempts = 0;
❷ while placement.is_none() && attempts < 10 {
❸     let dimensions = Rect::with_size(
           rng.range(0, SCREEN_WIDTH - FORTRESS.1),
           rng.range(0, SCREEN_HEIGHT - FORTRESS.2),
           FORTRESS.1,
           FORTRESS.2
       );

❹     let mut can_place = false;
❺     dimensions.for_each(|pt| {
           let idx = mb.map.point2d_to_index(pt);
           let distance = dijkstra_map.map[idx];
❻         if distance < 2000.0 && distance > 20.0 && mb.amulet_start != pt {
               can_place = true;
           }
       });

❼     if can_place {
           placement = Some(Point::new(dimensions.x1, dimensions.y1));
           let points = dimensions.point_set();
❽         mb.monster_spawns.retain(|pt| !points.contains(pt) );
       }
       attempts += 1;
   }
```

❶ Create a mutable variable named attempts and set it to zero.

❷ While placement is empty, and attempts are less than 10, loop.

❸ Create a Rect type starting at a random map location, with the height and width of your vault.

❹ Create a variable named can_place and set it to false.

❺ Iterate every tile in the rectangle using Rect's for_each() function.

⑥ If the Dijkstra map distance for the tile is less than 2,000, the tile is reachable. You also want to check that the tile is more than 20 tiles away from the player's starting position. You do this so that the player doesn't start inside your creation. Finally, check that the tile doesn't contain the amulet. This ensures that you won't overwrite the player's chance to win the game. If all of these statements are true, set can_place to true.

⑦ can_place will be true if the rectangle is a valid position for the vault. Set placement to Some(position).

⑧ You don't want to spawn your vault on top of existing monsters. Obtain a set of points located in your placement rectangle with point_set(). Then erase any monster spawning positions that fall within the rectangle using the Vector function retain(). Retain takes a closure as a parameter. If the closure returns true, the element is kept (retained); otherwise, it's deleted.

This removes any monster spawns that fall within the vault boundaries. If you don't do this, your vault may have random monsters in it—or even monsters stuck in the walls.

Now that you know where to spawn your vault, let's add it to the level. Add the following code to finish your apply_prefab function:

MoreInterestingDungeons/prefab/src/map_builder/prefab.rs

```
❶ if let Some(placement) = placement {
       let string_vec : Vec<char> = FORTRESS.0
           .chars().filter(|a| *a != '\r' && *a !='\n')
❷          .collect();
❸      let mut i = 0;
❹      for ty in placement.y .. placement.y + FORTRESS.2 {
           for tx in placement.x .. placement.x + FORTRESS.1 {
               let idx = map_idx(tx, ty);
❺              let c = string_vec[i];
❻              match c {
❼                  'M' => {
                       mb.map.tiles[idx] = TileType::Floor;
                       mb.monster_spawns.push(Point::new(tx, ty));
                   }
❽                  '-' => mb.map.tiles[idx] = TileType::Floor,
                   '#' => mb.map.tiles[idx] = TileType::Wall,
❾                  _ => println!("No idea what to do with [{}]", c)
               }
               i += 1;
           }
       }
   }
```

❶ Use if let to unwrap placement if it contains a value.

❷ Your constant string will contain extra characters representing the enter key. It may contain \r and \n characters. You can use an iterator to remove these quickly. Use chars() to convert a string to a character iterator. You can then filter() the string to remove the special characters, and call collect() to turn it back into a string.

You may remember the trim() function from [xxx](#sec.firststeps.trimming). That would also remove the special characters, but it can be aggressive. If you decide to use special characters in your string, it's safer to remove the ones you *know* you don't want.

❸ Rather than subtract the vault's map position from each position, use a variable i to store the current location in the prefab string as you iterate through it.

❹ Iterate every tile that your prefab will cover.

❺ Retrieve the character at position i from the string, just as if it were an array or vector.

❻ Match the character from the vault definition.

❼ Monsters need a floor to stand on, so set the tile to be a floor. Add the current map location to the monster_spawns vector.

❽ Floors and walls set the map tile to the corresponding type.

❾ If the game doesn't know what to do with a character type, it should warn you. This helps you find typos in your map definitions.

Lastly, you need to add a call to apply_prefab() in the new() function in map_builder/mod.rs. Don't forget to add mod prefab; use prefab::apply_prefab; to activate the module and bring apply_prefab into scope:

MoreInterestingDungeons/prefab/src/map_builder/mod.rs
```
pub fn new(rng: &mut RandomNumberGenerator) -> Self {
    let mut architect : Box<dyn MapArchitect> = match rng.range(0, 3) {
        0 => Box::new(DrunkardsWalkArchitect{}),
        1 => Box::new(RoomsArchitect{}),
        _ => Box::new(CellularAutomataArchitect{})
    };
    let mut mb = architect.new(rng);
    apply_prefab(&mut mb, rng);
    mb
}
```

Run the game now and you will find your prefabricated map section. Here's a layout generated with the test harness:

Wrap-Up

In this chapter, you learned how to use a powerful Rust feature known as traits. You also extended your game to produce a variety of maps with cellular automata and Drunkard's Walk. The next chapter will continue to take advantage of traits—varying your map rendering with *themes*.

CHAPTER 12

Map Themes

You don't have to keep your adventurer indoors, endlessly exploring dungeons. If you'd rather your hero explore a forest or an abandoned city overrun by hordes of monsters instead, you can—thanks to *themes*. With themes, you can radically change the look and feel of your game.

Changing map themes is a great way to make a game design your own. By changing level appearance, you have an opportunity to make a bold visual statement about your game—whether it be sci-fi, fantasy, gothic horror, or something completely different.

In this chapter, you'll continue working with traits as you create a map theme trait to handle theming your map and randomly picking an appearance for levels when the player starts a new one.

Theming Your Dungeon

Now that you know how to use traits to make replaceable components, let's give the game a bit more visual flair by substituting different map themes at runtime. Your dungeon could become a forest—or anything else you can draw. Alongside varied map design, this also helps to keep players interested.

Open map_builder/mod.rs, and add a new trait defining a map theme:

MapTheming/themed/src/map_builder/mod.rs
```
pub trait MapTheme : Sync + Send {
    fn tile_to_render(&self, tile_type: TileType) -> FontCharType;
}
```

The required function signature should make sense: given a tile type, you return a character to render from the map font. Sync+Send is new.[1] Rust

---

1. https://doc.rust-lang.org/nomicon/send-and-sync.html

emphasizes "fearless concurrency," which means you can write multi-threaded code without fearing that it will do something terrible. A large part of how Rust enforces safe concurrency is with the Sync and Send traits. The traits are defined to mean:

- If an object implements Sync, you can safely access it from multiple threads.
- If an object implements Send, you can safely share it between threads.

Most of the time, you don't need to implement Sync and Send yourself. Rust can figure out that some types of code are safe to send between threads. For example, *pure functions* are always thread-safe—they operate only on their inputs and don't affect any long-term stored data.

Traits can be *constrained* to only work with certain types of data. You could specify a variable type, or specify the presence of other traits. Sync+Send are traits. Appending : Sync+Send to your trait definition *constrains* the trait to only work when implemented on types that themselves implement (or inherit) those traits. In other words, MapTheme can only be implemented by types that are Sync+Send—and therefore safe to use across threads.

You'll be using MapTheme inside Legion's resource system. Legion resources are accessible to systems that may be running on any thread, and may be running at the same time. Legion makes this safe—and satisfies Rust's safety requirements—by requiring that resources are Sync+Send safe.

Race Conditions

Rust protects you from *race conditions* with the Sync+Send system. A race condition can occur when two threads try to access the same data simultaneously. If neither is changing the data, all is well. However, if one thread changes the data while the other uses it, bad things can happen. For example, the other thread might receive incomplete, partially updated, or even invalid data.

Synchronization prevents this from happening. Threads *block* one another from concurrently modifying the stored data—making a race condition impossible. Rust requires that either your structures be safe to share, or that they be wrapped in a Mutex, RwLock, or similar synchronization primitive to prevent this type of bug from happening.

Your renderer currently uses a dungeon theme. Let's formalize the renderer as a reference implementation of the MapTheme trait.

Implement a Dungeon Theme

Create a new file named map_builder/themes.rs.

MapTheming/themed/src/map_builder/themes.rs

```
use crate::prelude::*;

pub struct DungeonTheme {}

impl DungeonTheme {
❶    pub fn new() -> Box<dyn MapTheme> {
❷        Box::new(Self{})
    }
}

impl MapTheme for DungeonTheme {
    fn tile_to_render(&self, tile_type: TileType) -> FontCharType {
        match tile_type {
            TileType::Floor => to_cp437('.'),
            TileType::Wall => to_cp437('#')
        }
    }
}
```

❶ Rather than wrapping the function call in a Box, you can return a ready-boxed variable. This makes for an easier to use API for your consumer functions.

❷ You can Box your result with Self.

This code is similar to the code you've been using in your render system from Map Rendering System, on page 118. It matches on a tile type and then returns the appropriate character to output for rendering the dungeon. Dungeons using this theme retain the look from the dungeons you've been using in previous chapters:

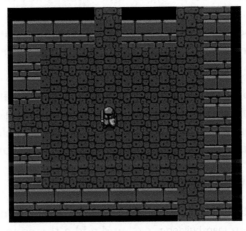

Let's give your brave adventurer a chance to get some vitamin D and implement an outdoor theme.

Build a Forest

Adding a second theme requires that you create another type that implements the MapTheme trait. Add the following to the bottom of your themes.rs file:

```
MapTheming/themed/src/map_builder/themes.rs
pub struct ForestTheme {}

impl MapTheme for ForestTheme {
    fn tile_to_render(&self, tile_type: TileType) -> FontCharType {
        match tile_type {
            TileType::Floor => to_cp437(';'),
            TileType::Wall => to_cp437('"')
        }
    }
}

impl ForestTheme {
    pub fn new() -> Box<dyn MapTheme> {
        Box::new(Self{})
    }
}
```

You'll notice that the code is almost the same as the dungeon theme code, but it returns different characters for tile types. You now have the code to calculate different tile types for each theme. It's time to adjust the rendering code to use it.

Pure Functions

tile_to_render() is a *pure function*. A pure function is a function that only operates on its inputs and doesn't store any state. Pure functions are *always* safe to use in a multi-threaded environment. Since there is no state, there is nothing to synchronize. Data races are impossible for pure functions because there are no external data for which they can compete.

If you do need to store state, you should investigate *synchronization primitives*.[2] In particular, *Mutex* and Rust's *Atomic* data types make synchronization easy. There are also various reference counted— and atomic reference counted—types to help you.

Rendering with Themes

The MapBuilder needs to know what theme you're associating with your newly designed map. Open map_builder/mod.rs, and add a theme to the MapBuilder:

---

2.   https://doc.rust-lang.org/std/sync/

MapTheming/themed/src/map_builder/mod.rs
```rust
const NUM_ROOMS: usize = 20;
pub struct MapBuilder {
    pub map : Map,
    pub rooms : Vec<Rect>,
    pub monster_spawns : Vec<Point>,
    pub player_start : Point,
    pub amulet_start : Point,
    pub theme : Box<dyn MapTheme>
}
```

If you're using an IDE, it probably just highlighted all of your map builders as compilation errors. These errors happen because you've extended MapBuilder to include a new field. Rust requires that you initialize every field in a struct on creation—uninitialized fields are a common source of bugs in other languages. So open each of your map builders (automata.rs, drunkard.rs, empty.rs, and rooms.rs), and add the following line to the initialization of each MapBuilder:

```rust
theme: super::themes::DungeonTheme::new()
```

Creating a new theme object is a little wasteful since you're creating a theme and never using it. You could wrap it in an Option and use None and Some(x) if you prefer. Map rendering happens so infrequently that it isn't worth worrying about a tiny bit of overhead when the map is generated.

Perfect Can Be the Enemy of Finished

It's common to make compromises in your code. When you're working toward getting a minimum viable product done, it's ok to cut a few corners. Make a note or code comment, and consider fixing the minor problems later. It's more important to finish your project than for your project to be perfect.

Now that your game supports multiple themes, let's randomly choose which one to display when the game begins.

Picking a Theme

Your code supports themes, but it will always return a dungeon theme: the default you added to the map builders. Open map_builder/mod.rs. Add mod themes; use themes::* to the top of the file to activate your themes module and bring it into scope. Modify the new() function to randomly select a theme:

MapTheming/themed/src/map_builder/mod.rs
```rust
pub fn new(rng: &mut RandomNumberGenerator) -> Self {
    let mut architect : Box<dyn MapArchitect> = match rng.range(0, 3) {
        0 => Box::new(DrunkardsWalkArchitect{}),
        1 => Box::new(RoomsArchitect{}),
```

```
            _ => Box::new(CellularAutomataArchitect{})
    };
    let mut mb = architect.new(rng);
    apply_prefab(&mut mb, rng);
➤   mb.theme = match rng.range(0, 2) {
➤       0 => DungeonTheme::new(),
➤       _ => ForestTheme::new()
➤   };

    mb
}
```

With this change, you generate a random number and match to create either
a DungeonTheme or a ForestTheme. Now that you have selected a theme to use,
you're ready to use it to render the map.

Use the Selected Theme

MapBuilder returns a MapTheme when you build your maps. You want to make
this available as a Legion resource, so your rendering systems can use it.
This is the other half of why Sync+Send is important: Legion resources are
shared between systems that may run in multiple threads.

Open main.rs and add your theme as a resource when you create the game's
state:

MapTheming/themed/src/main.rs
```
impl State {
    fn new() -> Self {
        let mut ecs = World::default();
        let mut resources = Resources::default();
        let mut rng = RandomNumberGenerator::new();
        let map_builder = MapBuilder::new(&mut rng);
        spawn_player(&mut ecs, map_builder.player_start);
        spawn_amulet_of_yala(&mut ecs, map_builder.amulet_start);
        map_builder.monster_spawns
            .iter()
            .for_each(|pos| spawn_monster(&mut ecs, &mut rng, *pos));
        resources.insert(map_builder.map);
        resources.insert(Camera::new(map_builder.player_start));
        resources.insert(TurnState::AwaitingInput);
        resources.insert(map_builder.theme);
```

The theme also needs to be added to your reset_game_state function:

MapTheming/themed/src/main.rs
```
fn reset_game_state(&mut self) {
    self.ecs = World::default();
    self.resources = Resources::default();
    let mut rng = RandomNumberGenerator::new();
```

```
let map_builder = MapBuilder::new(&mut rng);
spawn_player(&mut self.ecs, map_builder.player_start);
spawn_amulet_of_yala(&mut self.ecs, map_builder.amulet_start);
map_builder.monster_spawns
    .iter()
    .for_each(|pos| spawn_monster(&mut self.ecs, &mut rng, *pos));
self.resources.insert(map_builder.map);
self.resources.insert(Camera::new(map_builder.player_start));
self.resources.insert(TurnState::AwaitingInput);
self.resources.insert(map_builder.theme);
}
```

You're making great progress. You've built a theme structure and you inserted it into Legion's resource list.

All that remains is to use the new theme object to render your map.

Render the Map with Your Theme

The good news is that you don't need to completely rewrite your map rendering code. Most of it is the same—you need to use the MapTheme objects to pick which characters to render. Open systems/map_render.rs. The system needs access to the MapTheme resource you added to Legion's resource handler. You can grant the access to the MapTheme resource by adding it to the system header:

```
MapTheming/themed/src/systems/map_render.rs
#[system]
#[read_component(FieldOfView)]
#[read_component(Player)]
pub fn map_render(
    #[resource] map: &Map,
    #[resource] camera: &Camera,
    #[resource] theme: &Box<dyn MapTheme>,
    ecs: &SubWorld,
) {
```

As with other resources, adding #[resource] theme: &Box<dyn MapTheme> is enough to tell Legion that the system requires the map theme.

Next, find the portion that selects a tile graphic to render:

```
MoreInterestingDungeons/drunkard/src/systems/map_render.rs
match map.tiles[idx] {
    TileType::Floor => {
        draw_batch.set(
            pt - offset,
            ColorPair::new(
                tint,
                BLACK
            ),
```

```
                to_cp437('.')
        );
    }
    TileType::Wall => {
        draw_batch.set(
            pt - offset,
            ColorPair::new(
                tint,
                BLACK
            ),
            to_cp437('#')
        );
    }
}
```

Replace it with a call to the `MapTheme` resource:

MapTheming/themed/src/systems/map_render.rs
```
let glyph = theme.tile_to_render(map.tiles[idx]);
draw_batch.set(
    pt - offset,
    ColorPair::new(
        tint,
        BLACK
    ),
    glyph
);
```

Run your program now, and you'll have a 50% chance of finding your player deep in a forest-themed map, as shown in the image on page 239.

By adding themes to your game, you've opened a world of possibilities. By adding or changing themes and their associated graphics, you can create a huge range of environments.

Unleashing Your Imagination

Between this chapter and Chapter 11, More Interesting Dungeons, on page 203, you've covered a lot of important ground. Changing the layout of your maps can completely change the nature of a game. Battling monsters in the tight confines of a room and corridor-based dungeon requires care and offers regular breaks between battles in which the player can regain their strength. A more open map can easily leave the player surrounded. The additional room to maneuver can lead to less breathing room between fights. Whether you prefer to generate your maps or craft them by hand, this is your chance to shine.

Changing the theme of a map can completely change the feel of your game. A brightly lit dungeon implies a fun romp. The same dungeon with dark,

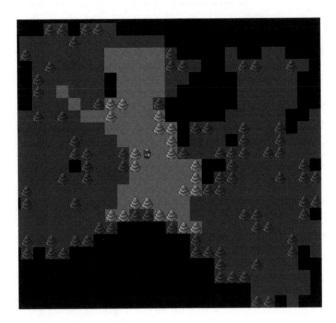

intimidating walls and cobwebs feels more like a horror setting. Replace walls with trees, and you have a forest. Replace walls with machinery and metal flooring, and you've created a steampunk labyrinth. Replace the theme with sci-fi effects, and you're now battling inside a spaceship.

Using different graphics for levels completely changes the feel of your game and what players expect. Find a tileset that works for you and unleash your creativity. A good place to find tilesets is at OpenGameArt.[3]

Wrap-Up

In this chapter, you used traits to build two alternatives for level theming. The dungeon you used in previous chapters is joined by a forest. You also learned an essential technique: trading in themes as needed. This technique gives you the creative freedom to make a vast array of game themes.

In the next chapter, you'll learn how to add items and power-ups to your game. Power-ups make the game more strategic—collecting and managing resources becomes a conscious decision. Making your player ponder, "Do I go for the potion, despite the goblin guards? Or can I make it to the amulet without it?" encourages them to keep playing—and makes their failures feel less arbitrary and frustrating. It also rewards clever play.

3. https://opengameart.org/

CHAPTER 13

Inventory and Power-Ups

Badly wounded by the goblin, the hero reaches into their backpack. Uncorking a terrible smelling potion and drinking it, their wounds close. Refreshed, the hero is ready to return to the good fight.

This scene is a staple of modern fantasy games: the adventurer finds an item on the map, stores it in their inventory, and then uses it later when needed. Substitute the smelly potion for a healing system controlled by sympathetic nanobots, and you have a similar game mechanic for a sci-fi game.

With items and inventory systems, you can add variety to your game. Players can now make tactical decisions based on item use—they'll need to consider whether it's worth the potential injuries to reach an item despite the number of monsters who might be guarding it.

However, before you can offer items for pickup, you first need to design and create them.

Designing Items

Item design is fun. You probably have some ideas for the items you want to include in your game. Taken alongside Chapter 15, Combat Systems and Loot, on page 269, this chapter will give you the experience you need to add items to your game and build a unique experience.

Here, you're going to add two items: *Healing Potions* and *Dungeon Maps*. Healing potions restore the player's hit points, and dungeon maps reveal the entire map, allowing the player to carefully plan a route to the Amulet of Yala. The graphics for these items are included in the dungeonfont.png file.

Let's start by giving the new items some component definitions.

Describing the Items with Components

You already have most of the components you need to describe the healing potion and dungeon map items—they need a name, appearance, and position on the map, which means you can re-use the following existing components:

- Item: Potion or Scroll
- Name: The name that appears in tooltips and the player's inventory list
- Point: The item's position on the map
- Render: The visual display component for the item

You also need new component types to describe what each item does.

The healing potion restores the drinker's hit points up to their maximum. You can describe this by creating a ProvidesHealing component. Open components.rs, and add a new component type:

InventoryAndPowerUps/potions_and_scrolls/src/components.rs
```
#[derive(Clone, Copy, Debug, PartialEq)]
pub struct ProvidesHealing{
    pub amount: i32
}
```

The amount field specifies how much health a given potion will restore. You could use this value to differentiate between types of healing potion, allowing you to make potions of varying strength.

The dungeon map reveals the entire level map when activated. You need to create a component indicating that this effect occurs:

InventoryAndPowerUps/potions_and_scrolls/src/components.rs
```
#[derive(Clone, Copy, Debug, PartialEq)]
pub struct ProvidesDungeonMap;
```

Why Not Use an Enum?

 Each item you're adding provides only one effect. It's tempting to create a generic UseEffect component containing an enumeration. Enums can only have one value—if you want to make an item with multiple effects, you'd be out of luck. It's a good idea to separate effects into their own components in case you decide to create an item that does more than one thing.

Now that you have described your items with components, it's time to spawn these items on the map.

Spawning Potions and Maps

Open spawner.rs, and add two item spawning functions, one for each item type:

InventoryAndPowerUps/potions_and_scrolls/src/spawner.rs
```
pub fn spawn_healing_potion(ecs: &mut World, pos: Point) {
    ecs.push(
        (Item,
            pos,
            Render{
                color: ColorPair::new(WHITE, BLACK),
                glyph : to_cp437('!')
            },
            Name("Healing Potion".to_string()),
            ProvidesHealing{amount: 6}
        )
    );
}

pub fn spawn_magic_mapper(ecs: &mut World, pos: Point) {
    ecs.push(
        (Item,
            pos,
            Render{
                color: ColorPair::new(WHITE, BLACK),
                glyph : to_cp437('{')
            },
            Name("Dungeon Map".to_string()),
            ProvidesDungeonMap{}
        )
    );
}
```

The item spawning code is similar to the code you used to spawn the Amulet of Yala in Spawning the Amulet, on page 177, but with a different set of components.

Calling spawn_healing_potion() adds a healing potion to the map at the specified location. Likewise, spawn_magic_mapper() adds a dungeon map to the game level.

Now that you can spawn items, you also need to add the items to the list of things that might spawn in a designated tile. The spawn_monster() function handles this for monsters. Make a new function named spawn_entity() that can spawn your new items as well as monsters:

InventoryAndPowerUps/potions_and_scrolls/src/spawner.rs
```
pub fn spawn_entity(
    ecs: &mut World,
    rng: &mut RandomNumberGenerator,
    pos: Point
) {
    let roll = rng.roll_dice(1, 6);
    match roll {
        1 => spawn_healing_potion(ecs, pos),
```

```
            2 => spawn_magic_mapper(ecs, pos),
            _ => spawn_monster(ecs, rng, pos)
    }
}
```

The function rolls a six-sided dice. If the dice roll results in a 1, a healing potion is spawned. A roll of 2 spawns a dungeon map. Otherwise, the spawn_monster() function is called.

Most items are liberally scattered throughout the game levels, but it's up to you how random you want to be versus how deliberate you are when placing these items. Managing the probabilities for spawns is a good way to tweak the balance of your game level. You might decide to make items less frequent or adjust the weighting of monster types. Probability tables for spawns are discussed in Chapter 15, Combat Systems and Loot, on page 269.

Open main.rs, and replace all calls to spawn_monster() with spawn_entity(). Use your editor's search and replace function to replace all instances of spawn_monster with spawn_entity.

Run your game now, and you'll find potions and dungeon maps scattered throughout the dungeon level:

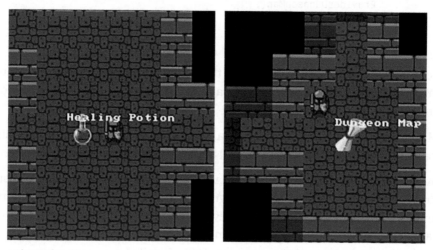

Now that the items are in the game, it's time to permit the player to pick them up.

Managing Inventory

Items don't always sit passively on the map, hoping someone will walk onto them. Unless you're making a Pac-Man style game, it also doesn't make sense to have items activate when the player walks into them. Instead, let's allow players to pick up items and carry them in their inventory until they're needed. This adds strategy to the game, letting players decide when they want to use their precious items.

Items are entities, and they exist on the map because they have a Point component indicating their location. The entity rendering system query requires a Point to draw an item or display its tooltip. You can take advantage of the render system's query structure by removing the Point component from an item when it's picked up. In other words, the item no longer has a location on the map.

Picking up an item requires that you *remove* the Point component, and *add* a Carried component, with the stored Entity pointing at the entity carrying the item. Open components.rs, and add a new component representing that another entity is carrying an item:

InventoryAndPowerUps/carrying_items/src/components.rs
```
#[derive(Clone, PartialEq)]
pub struct Carried(pub Entity);
```

Let's add some input code to let the player collect items.

Picking Up Items

You handle player input in systems/player_input.rs. You're going to assign G to "get" any item the player is standing on. Start by adding Item and Carried to the list of components the system can read:

InventoryAndPowerUps/carrying_items/src/systems/player_input.rs
```
#[system]
#[read_component(Point)]
#[read_component(Player)]
#[read_component(Enemy)]
#[write_component(Health)]
➤ #[read_component(Item)]
➤ #[read_component(Carried)]
pub fn player_input(
```

This code allows the system to access these data types. Navigate into the player_input()> function, and find the section that begins with let delta = match key {. Add another option to the match statement:

InventoryAndPowerUps/carrying_items/src/systems/player_input.rs
```
❶ VirtualKeyCode::G => {
❷     let (player, player_pos) = players
            .iter(ecs)
❸         .find_map(|(entity, pos)| Some((*entity, *pos)))
            .unwrap();
```

```
④      let mut items = <(Entity, &Item, &Point)>::query();
       items.iter(ecs)
⑤          .filter(|(_entity, _item, &item_pos)| item_pos == player_pos)
            .for_each(|(entity, _item, _item_pos)| {
⑥              commands.remove_component::<Point>(*entity);
⑦              commands.add_component(*entity, Carried(player));
           }
       );
       Point::new(0, 0)
   },
```

❶ Match when the user has pressed the `G` key.

❷ Construct a query/iterator chain that will return a tuple containing both the player Entity and the player's position.

❸ find_map returns the first entry in an iterator, mapping the results to the specified fields.

❹ Build a query that returns only entities with an Item tag and a Point. Also return the parent Entity.

❺ Use filter to keep only iterator entries whose positions are the same as the player's position.

❻ Remove the Point component from the item.

❼ Add a Carried component, pointing to the player as the carrier.

Run the game now, and find a potion or scroll. Stand on it and press G. The item vanishes from the map because the item is now being "carried" by the player. Let's add a way to see the item in the player's inventory.

Displaying Inventory

When an item is picked up, it no longer has a Point component describing its location on the map. This removes the item from the entity rendering system automatically—the render query looks for entities with a Point and a Render component. The player needs to know what they're carrying. The Heads-Up Display is a great place to do this.

Open systems/hud.rs. You need to expand the system declaration to include the Item, Carried, and Name components:

InventoryAndPowerUps/carrying_items/src/systems/hud.rs
```
#[system]
#[read_component(Health)]
#[read_component(Player)]
➤ #[read_component(Item)]
➤ #[read_component(Carried)]
```

➤ #[read_component(Name)]
  pub fn hud(ecs: &SubWorld) {

Now that the system can read the Carried and Name component types, you can extend the system to display items. You want to list carried items below the main HUD, with a number next to each item. That number will correspond to the keystroke used to activate the item. Insert the following code before the batch.submit call:

InventoryAndPowerUps/carrying_items/src/systems/hud.rs

```
let player = <(Entity, &Player)>::query()
                    .iter(ecs)
                    .find_map(|(entity, _player)| Some(*entity))
❶                  .unwrap();
❷ let mut item_query = <(&Item, &Name, &Carried)>::query();
❸ let mut y = 3;
  item_query
      .iter(ecs)
❹    .filter(|(_, _, carried)| carried.0 == player)
      .for_each(|(_, name, _)| {
❺        draw_batch.print(
             Point::new(3, y),
             format!("{} : {}", y-2, &name.0)
         );
         y += 1;
      }
  );
❻ if y > 3 {
      draw_batch.print_color(Point::new(3, 2), "Items carried",
          ColorPair::new(YELLOW, BLACK)
      );
  }
```

❶ Obtain the Player entity with the same code you previously used.

❷ Build a query to find carried items. Retrieve the Item tag, Name component, and Carried component.

❸ Create a variable named y and set it to 3. This is where you'll start rendering the item list.

❹ Filter the carried items to include only items carried by the player. Filtering now ensures that if you let monsters carry things later, those items won't appear on the player's HUD.

❺ Print the item's name at position (3, y) and increment y.

❻ If any items were rendered, add a heading explaining why item names just appeared on the screen.

Run the game now and find a potion or scroll. Use G to pick up the scroll, and the item will appear on the Heads-Up Display. Find another item and pick it up. Notice the new item will also appear in the player's inventory list:

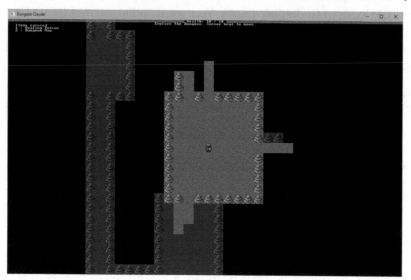

Collected items are displayed on the player's Heads-Up Display, alongside a number indicating the key that activates the associated item. Now you're ready to make them do something when used.

Sending an Item Activation Message

In Sending Messages of Intent, on page 135, you adopted a pattern in which systems indicate their *intent* to perform an action—and the actual action is handled in its own system. Using an item is no different. Decoupling intent and activation in this way allows your code to remain flexible. If you decide that a tough monster should be able to use magical items, you only need to send the message of intent rather than duplicating the effect code.

Open components.rs, and add a new component named ActivateItem:

InventoryAndPowerUps/carrying_items/src/components.rs
```
#[derive(Clone, Copy, Debug, PartialEq)]
pub struct ActivateItem {
    pub used_by : Entity,
    pub item : Entity
}
```

The player needs to send an ActivateItem message by pressing a number key that matches the numbers displayed next to items in the HUD. Open player_input.rs, and add a new function to the end of the file:

InventoryAndPowerUps/carrying_items/src/systems/player_input.rs
```
fn use_item(n: usize, ecs: &mut SubWorld, commands: &mut CommandBuffer)
❶ -> Point {
    let player_entity = <(Entity, &Player)>::query()
                        .iter(ecs)
                        .find_map(|(entity, _player)| Some(*entity))
❷                       .unwrap();

❸   let item_entity = <(Entity, &Item, &Carried)>::query()
        .iter(ecs)
        .filter(|(_, _, carried)| carried.0 == player_entity)
❹       .enumerate()
❺       .filter(|(item_count, (_, _, _))| *item_count == n)
❻       .find_map(|(_, (item_entity, _, _))| Some(*item_entity));

❼   if let Some(item_entity) = item_entity {
        commands
❽           .push(((), ActivateItem{
                used_by: player_entity,
                item: item_entity
            }));
    }

    Point::zero()
}
```

❶ The use_item() function needs access to the SubWorld and CommandBuffer from the parent system. Borrowing these variables allows you to pass the variables from the system and use them in a function.

❷ Use a query to find the Player entity, exactly as you did before.

❸ Using a similar query to the HUD item finder, iterate through carried items and filter out those not held by the player.

❹ Enumerate adds a number starting from zero to each result. It's a little confusing because you wind up with two tuples. The first contains (counter, other_tuple). The previous tuple is contained within the second tuple. The final structure is (counter, (Entity, Item, Carried)) The nested brackets destructure this into useful variable names.

❺ Filter out items whose enumerator doesn't match the n variable passed into the function. For example, if the user pressed 3, you're looking for an item with an enumerator of 2. Remember that the enumerator starts at zero. It's possible that there won't be any items left on the list.

❻ find_map() returns an Option. If there are any remaining items in the iterator, the first one will be returned as Some(entity). If no items match the keystroke, find_map() will return None.

❼ if let will extract the contents of the item_entity option if there is one and will run the enclosed code. If there are no matching items, if let won't do anything.

❽ Use the command buffer to create an ActivateItem entity, just like you did for WantsToMove.

In the player_input system, find the match statement once again. Add options to call the function you just created for each of the number keys on the user's keyboard:

```
VirtualKeyCode::Key1 => use_item(0, ecs, commands),
VirtualKeyCode::Key2 => use_item(1, ecs, commands),
VirtualKeyCode::Key3 => use_item(2, ecs, commands),
VirtualKeyCode::Key4 => use_item(3, ecs, commands),
VirtualKeyCode::Key5 => use_item(4, ecs, commands),
VirtualKeyCode::Key6 => use_item(5, ecs, commands),
VirtualKeyCode::Key7 => use_item(6, ecs, commands),
VirtualKeyCode::Key8 => use_item(7, ecs, commands),
VirtualKeyCode::Key9 => use_item(8, ecs, commands),
```

Now, when the player presses a numeric key, your system will look for an item associated with that key. If there is one, the system will send an ActivateItem message. It's time to write a system to consume these messages.

Activating Items

In a larger game, you might want to write one system per effect—along with a system to remove activation requests once all possible effects are processed. For this game, let's go with a simpler single system approach.

Create a new file, systems/use_item.rs. Add mod use_item to systems/mod.rs to include the system in your program build.

Start the new file by adding the boilerplate required to create a system and grant access to the map and components. The system requires read access to ActivateItem, ProvidesHealing, and ProvidesDungeonMap. It also needs write access to Health to implement healing. Add the following code to systems/use_item.rs:

```
use crate::prelude::*;

#[system]
#[read_component(ActivateItem)]
#[read_component(ProvidesHealing)]
#[write_component(Health)]
#[read_component(ProvidesDungeonMap)]
pub fn use_items(
```

```
    ecs: &mut SubWorld,
    commands: &mut CommandBuffer,
    #[resource] map: &mut Map
) {
```

The systems boilerplate should look familiar by now; there are no new concepts here, so let's continue to develop the system.

Applying Healing

Create a vector to store a list of healing effects to apply:

InventoryAndPowerUps/carrying_items/src/systems/use_items.rs
```
let mut healing_to_apply = Vec::<(Entity, i32)>::new();
```

As the system iterates item effects, it will add healing events to this list as a to-do list. Applying the effect inline would be more ergonomic, but it triggers a compiler error in Rust's *borrow checker*.

Rust has some hard-and-fast rules for borrowing:

- You may borrow something immutably as many times as you want.
- You may only borrow something *mutably* once.
- You can't simultaneously borrow something mutably and immutably.

If you apply healing in situ, you will run into borrow checker errors:

1. You would borrow the SubWorld to execute the query.
2. You borrow from within the SubWorld to access the item's entity and components.
3. You borrow again to find the healing properties of the potion.
4. You *mutably* borrow the Health component of the player. Unfortunately, you're also still borrowing the SubWorld. Rust will refuse to compile your program in case your changes make the SubWorld invalid.

To get around the borrow checker restrictions, you need to make sure that you're done with the world before you borrow it again. The easiest way to do this is to extract what you need from it, and then perform the healing operation.

The Borrow Checker

The borrow checker is both one of Rust's strongest benefits, and sometimes its most irritating feature. Particularly if you come from writing C++, you'll sometimes find yourself scratching your head and wondering why you have to rearrange your code to comply with the borrow checker.

The borrow checker is there for your own good. Microsoft reported that 70% of the security vulnerabilities reported in their software

---

The Borrow Checker

came from memory safety issues.[1] The borrow checker—and other Rust safety features—makes it very difficult to create a lot of these vulnerabilities.

Think of the borrow checker as a bossy librarian. They keep your memory borrowing under control and are adamant about returning things when you're done borrowing them. They may be irritating, but ultimately, they keep the entire library running.

Now that you have a place in which to store healing events, it's time to parse item activation effects.

Iterate Item Application

Every ActivateItem event contains an item Entity that was activated, and another Entity referencing who used it. You can make use of this by looking up the entity listed in the event component and checking to see what effect components (ProvidesHealing and ProvidesDungeonMap) the event has. Add the following code to your function:

InventoryAndPowerUps/carrying_items/src/systems/use_items.rs

```
<(Entity, &ActivateItem)>::query().iter(ecs)
❶ .for_each(|(entity, activate)| {

❷     let item = ecs.entry_ref(activate.item);
❸     if let Ok(item) = item {
❹         if let Ok(healing) = item.get_component::<ProvidesHealing>() {
❺             healing_to_apply.push((activate.used_by, healing.amount));
        }

❻         if let Ok(_mapper) = item.get_component::<ProvidesDungeonMap>() {
❼             map.revealed_tiles.iter_mut().for_each(|t| *t = true);
        }
    }

❽     commands.remove(activate.item);
❾     commands.remove(*entity);
});
```

❶ Create a query that returns ActivateItem components and their associated entities.

❷ entry_ref()> is Legion's way of accessing an entity that wasn't returned inside a query. It returns a reference to a single entity, which you can then query for components independently of a query.

---

1. https://visualstudiomagazine.com/articles/2019/07/18/microsoft-eyes-rust.aspx#:~:text=Memory%20Vulnera-
bilities%20(source%3A%20MSRC),to%20be%20memory%20safety%20issues.%22

❸ It's possible that you requested an entity that no longer exists. entry_ref() returns a Result to accommodate this. if let Ok(item) extracts the item entity from the result if there is one—and doesn't run any code if the entity was unavailable.

❹ Entity references provide a get_component() function to access components assigned to the entity. The entity might not have the specified component type, in which case the Result object returned by the function will be empty. Using if let to expand the result only runs the included code if the item entity has the requested component type.

❺ Add the healing information to the healing_to_apply vector you created.

❻ Use the same get_component() call to check if the entity has a ProvidesDungeon-Map component.

❼ If the item entity does have a ProvidesDungeonMap component, set all revealed_tiles entries in the level map to true, making the map layout visible.

❽ Delete the consumed item so it can't be used again.

❾ Delete the activation command so it doesn't fire again.

The use_item() function can now iterate activation events and reveal the map if a dungeon map was used. The system also cleans up after itself. The last task is to apply healing events.

Apply Healing Events

You're storing a list of healing targets and amounts in healing_to_apply. Iterate the vector and apply any required healing:

InventoryAndPowerUps/carrying_items/src/systems/use_items.rs

```
      for heal in healing_to_apply.iter() {
❶        if let Ok(mut target) = ecs.entry_mut(heal.0) {
❷            if let Ok(health) = target.get_component_mut::<Health>() {
                health.current = i32::min(
                    health.max,
                    health.current+heal.1
❸                );
            }
        }
      }
}
```

❶ Use entry_mut() to retrieve a mutable reference to an entity. Wrapping it with if let again ensures the code will only fire if the requested entity is valid.

❷ Check that the effect target has a Health component. get_component_mut() is just like get_component(), but it returns a mutable reference to the component, allowing you to change the component while it is borrowed.

❸ You don't want to heal entities beyond their maximum health. Set the current health to the minimum of their maximum health, and their current health plus the amount of healing to apply.

Your use_item() system is complete. Let's add the system to the scheduler to ensure that it runs.

Add to the Schedule

Open systems/mod.rs. This contains functions defining execution schedulers for each part of the turn. You need to add use_item to the player's schedule:

InventoryAndPowerUps/carrying_items/src/systems/mod.rs
```
pub fn build_player_scheduler() -> Schedule {
    Schedule::builder()
➤        .add_system(use_items::use_items_system())
        .add_system(combat::combat_system())
        .flush()
```

You may decide to let monsters use items, so let's add the use_item system to their schedule too:

InventoryAndPowerUps/carrying_items/src/systems/mod.rs
```
pub fn build_monster_scheduler() -> Schedule {
    Schedule::builder()
        .add_system(random_move::random_move_system())
        .add_system(chasing::chasing_system())
        .flush()
➤        .add_system(use_items::use_items_system())
        .add_system(combat::combat_system())
        .flush()
```

Run the program now and you can find potions and scrolls. Drinking a potion restores health, and reading the map reveals the entire level. A dungeon map in action is shown on page 255.

Remove Waiting to Heal

Now that the player has an item to provide healing, there's no need to make dungeon crawling easy by letting them pause to heal. It's still useful to skip a turn and wait for monsters to approach your preferred field of battle, but hit point maintenance is now a strategic decision. The tension of "Can I get to that potion I need?" adds a new level of drama to the gameplay.

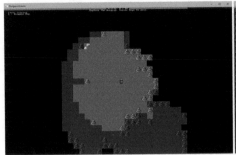

Unrevealed map with a Dungeon Map in the player's inventory.   Press 1 to use the Dungeon Map, and the level is revealed.

Open systems/player_input.rs. Find the following section of code, and delete it from your source file:

```
if !did_something {
    if let Ok(mut health) = ecs
        .entry_mut(player_entity)
        .unwrap()
        .get_component_mut::<Health>()
    {
        health.current = i32::min(health.max, health.current+1);
    }
}
```

You wrote this code in Waiting as a Strategy, on page 159. If the player didn't act, it restored some health to them as a reward for waiting. Now that the player can use potions to heal, having turn-skipping to restore health is overly generous.

Wrap-Up

In this chapter, you learned to craft items and power-ups. Items no longer just have a screen position—they can also reside in an entity's inventory. The player is notified of objects they're carrying, and they can activate those objects at a time of their choosing.

At this point, you've made great progress toward creating a traditional Dungeon Crawler game. In the next chapter, you'll add depth to the dungeon by adding more levels before the game ends.

CHAPTER 14

Deeper Dungeons

Very short games can be fun—there's an entire genre of "coffee-break rogue-likes" dedicated to making games you can play in under an hour. However, larger games tend to have better audience retention.

One way to increase the size of your game is to add additional levels. With more levels, you can step up the challenge of the game as the player progresses. You can also introduce more content—but be careful not to add too many levels. You don't want to have more levels than you have game content because players quickly notice when levels feel like filler.

In this chapter, you'll add a downward staircase to the first two levels of your game, leading the player deeper into the dungeon. When the player reaches the stairs, you'll generate the next level, which requires partially resetting the game state.

You'll also modify the code so that the Amulet of Yala spawns only on the final level. In doing so, you'll give the player a *reason* to explore beyond level 1. To help keep players motivated, you'll display their progress on the Heads-Up Display.

Let's start by adding some stairs to the game map.

Adding Stairs to the Map

Staircases provide a popular means of conveyance to deeper levels. Stairs can occupy a single tile, are relatively easy to render, and are intuitive. In this section, you'll define stairs as a new type of map tile. You'll add stairs to your map rendering and theming system, and update the navigation system to allow the player to enter the staircase. Rather than spawn the Amulet of Yala at the end of each level, you'll only add it to the *last* level—the other levels will feature an exit to the next dungeon layer.

Let's start by adding the staircase to the game map.

Making and Rendering Staircases

To render staircases within your dungeon, you'll need a new type of map tile. Open map.rs and find the TileType enumeration. Add a new Exit entry for the staircases:

```
DeeperDungeons/more_levels/src/map.rs
#[derive(Copy, Clone, PartialEq)]
pub enum TileType {
    Wall,
    Floor,
➤   Exit
}
```

If you're using a text editor with real-time error detection, you'll notice that it just marked every match on TileType as an error. This happens because Rust matches must include all possible options—and you just added a new option to TileType.

TileType is matched in map_builder/themes.rs, which makes sense since themes need to know how to render every tile type. Open map_builder/themes.rs, and add a match branch to draw the downward staircases (mapped to > in the font file):

```
DeeperDungeons/more_levels/src/map_builder/themes.rs
impl MapTheme for DungeonTheme {
    fn tile_to_render(&self, tile_type: TileType) -> FontCharType {
        match tile_type {
            TileType::Floor => to_cp437('.'),
            TileType::Wall => to_cp437('#'),
➤           TileType::Exit => to_cp437('>'),
        }
    }
}
```

The forest theme also needs to draw staircases, so make the same change in the forest renderer:

```
DeeperDungeons/more_levels/src/map_builder/themes.rs
impl MapTheme for ForestTheme {
    fn tile_to_render(&self, tile_type: TileType) -> FontCharType {
        match tile_type {
            TileType::Floor => to_cp437(';'),
            TileType::Wall => to_cp437('"'),
➤           TileType::Exit => to_cp437('>'),
        }
    }
}
```

Now that the game can render exit (staircase) tiles, it's time to make them accessible to the player—and maybe the monsters too.

Update Dungeon Navigation

This game uses the can_enter_tile() function in map.rs to determine if the player—or a monster—can enter a certain type of tile. Currently, only Floor tiles are accessible. Adjust can_enter_tile to also permit entry into Exit tiles:

DeeperDungeons/more_levels/src/map.rs
```
pub fn can_enter_tile(&self, point : Point) -> bool {
    self.in_bounds(point) && (
        self.tiles[map_idx(point.x, point.y)]==TileType::Floor ||
        self.tiles[map_idx(point.x, point.y)]==TileType::Exit
    )
}
```

The movement system and Dijkstra mapping system all make use of this function. Fixing it once fixes it for the rest of the game.

Now that you can render and navigate around stairs, it's time to add some to the game map.

Spawning Stairs Instead of the Amulet

The plan is to spawn the Amulet of Yala only on the final level of the game; however, you can reuse the amulet placement system to place a staircase on all of the other levels.

Open main.rs and locate the two calls to spawn_amulet_of_yala. Comment them out and add the following code:

DeeperDungeons/more_levels/src/main.rs
```
➤ let mut map_builder = MapBuilder::new(&mut rng);
  spawn_player(&mut self.ecs, map_builder.player_start);
➤ //spawn_amulet_of_yala(&mut self.ecs, map_builder.amulet_start);
➤ let exit_idx = map_builder.map.point2d_to_index(map_builder.amulet_start);
➤ map_builder.map.tiles[exit_idx] = TileType::Exit;
```

Notice that you broke the map update into two steps. The following line of code looks like it will accomplish the same thing:

```
map_builder.map.tiles
  [map_builder.map.point2d_to_index(map_builder.amulet_start)]
  = TileType::Exit;
```

Unfortunately, the single line version won't compile because of the borrow checker. Why? Because calling point2d_to_index borrows the map—and so does updating the tiles vector. Breaking the code into two lines solves the problem.

The first line retrieves the index and the second line updates the map. This is an example of some code that's probably safe despite the borrow checker's insistence, but you have to play by its rules.

Now that you can place the staircase instead of the amulet, it's time to fix an earlier assumption: that every level would feature an Amulet of Yala. This is no longer true, and the game will crash in the end_turn system when it searches for the amulet's location to see if you've won the game. It doesn't find a location, calls unwrap on an Option, and crashes. Let's fix that bug. Open systems/end_turn.rs, and fix the amulet location code as follows:

```
DeeperDungeons/more_levels/src/systems/end_turn.rs
let amulet_default = Point::new(-1, -1);
let amulet_pos = amulet
    .iter(ecs)
    .nth(0)
    .unwrap_or(&amulet_default);
```

This code has two new concepts:

- unwrap_or() is a very helpful function. Instead of crashing when it attempts to unwrap an Option, this function returns the value specified as its parameter if the option is None.

- Notice that you create a new variable—amulet_default—before you call the iterator. unwrap_or takes a borrowed reference to a value as a parameter. If you try to use unwrap_or(&Point::new(-1,-1)), the program won't compile. This happens because the temporary Point object is created inside the call to the unwrap_or function, and then it's borrowed. The temporary Point is destroyed before the remainder of the function finishes—leaving an invalid reference. In C++, your program would probably crash or behave oddly. Rust protects you from this error. Creating the amulet_default variable before the unwrap_or call, and then making a reference to it is safe. The amulet_default variable gets destroyed when the function finishes.

Lifetime Guarantees

Lifetimes are another important Rust safety feature. In other systems languages, referencing a variable that has been destroyed will compile—and crash your program. Rust won't let you do that.

Earlier versions of Rust required that you annotate most borrowed references with a lifetime indicator. The syntax for lifetime markers looks like this: &'lifetime variable. Fortunately, Rust can now infer lifetimes most of the time. If you aren't writing library code, you're unlikely to have to worry about it.

You now have a map system that understands and can render Exit tiles, as shown in the following image:

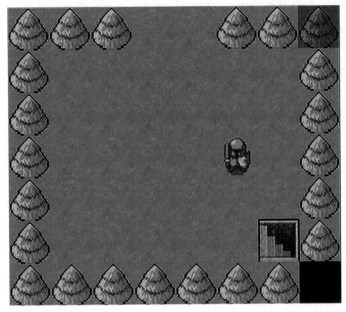

Now that players have a way to descend deeper into the dungeon, it's time to track their progress.

Tracking Game Level

Transitioning between levels is a great start—but it's helpful to know what level the player is on. You need this information to determine if you should spawn the Amulet of Yala or an exit. You'll use the current dungeon level to update the player with their progress through the dungeon. The current level will also be used in Chapter 15, Combat Systems and Loot, on page 269, to spawn increasingly more challenging monsters and nicer loot as the adventurer progresses.

Let's start by adding the current dungeon level to the Player component. The player is the only entity advancing through the dungeon, so the Player component is a good place to store the current map level. Open components.rs, and add a map_level field to the Player component:

DeeperDungeons/more_levels/src/components.rs
```
#[derive(Clone, Copy, Debug, PartialEq)]
pub struct Player{
    pub map_level: u32
}
```

Your text editor may have flagged spawner.rs as an error because you need to include every field when you create a structure. Open spawner.rs and update spawn_player to start the player on level zero:

```
DeeperDungeons/more_levels/src/spawner.rs
pub fn spawn_player(ecs : &mut World, pos : Point) {
    ecs.push(
        (Player{map_level: 0},
            pos,
            Render{
                color: ColorPair::new(WHITE, BLACK),
                glyph : to_cp437('@')
            },
            Health{ current: 10, max: 10 },
            FieldOfView::new(8)
        )
    );
}
```

With the current level safely stored in the Player component, you're ready to add transitions between levels when the player reaches an exit.

Level Transition State

Finishing the level is a major event, similar to a victory or defeat. Such an event requires that the main game loop do something drastic, outside of the ECS systems. Open turn_state.rs, and add a new condition to the TurnState enumeration:

```
DeeperDungeons/more_levels/src/turn_state.rs
#[derive(Copy, Clone, Debug, PartialEq)]
pub enum TurnState {
    AwaitingInput,
    PlayerTurn,
    MonsterTurn,
    GameOver,
    Victory,
    NextLevel
}
```

You match on TurnState in main.rs. Once again, adding to the enumeration will cause your development environment to flag an error. Open main.rs, and navigate to the match current_state block in the tick function. Add a new match clause:

```
DeeperDungeons/more_levels/src/main.rs
TurnState::NextLevel => {
    self.advance_level();
}
```

Inside the State implementation, add a stub function so that your program will compile:

```
impl GameState {
  ...
  fn advance_level(&mut self) {}
```

This is a stub function—it deliberately doesn't do anything other than provide enough of a placeholder to compile your game. You'll flesh out its details later when you get to Changing Level, on page 263. It's often useful to create a stub so you can continue implementing the details that *call* the stub—and then fill out the stub when you have finalized its inputs.

The end_turn system detects when the player reaches the amulet, and it sets the Victory condition when that happens. You can readily extend this system to set the NextLevel state when the player reaches an exit. Open systems/end_turn.rs, and add Map to the system's resource requests:

DeeperDungeons/more_levels/src/systems/end_turn.rs
```
pub fn end_turn(
    ecs: &SubWorld,
    #[resource] turn_state: &mut TurnState,
    #[resource] map: &Map
) {
```

You can then add a check for the end of turn to determine if the player walked onto an exit tile:

DeeperDungeons/more_levels/src/systems/end_turn.rs
```
player_hp.iter(ecs).for_each(|(hp, pos)| {
    if hp.current < 1 {
        new_state = TurnState::GameOver;
    }
    if pos == amulet_pos {
        new_state = TurnState::Victory;
    }
➤    let idx = map.point2d_to_index(*pos);
➤    if map.tiles[idx] == TileType::Exit {
➤        new_state = TurnState::NextLevel;
➤    }
});
```

Now that you're indicating to the main loop that a level transition needs to occur, it's time to add code to let the player advance to the next level.

Changing Level

Let's flesh out the advance_level function for which you created a stub. Advancing to the next level requires five steps:

1. Remove all entities from the ECS World that aren't either the player or items carried by the player.

2. Set the is_dirty flag on the player's FieldOfView to ensure that the map renders correctly on the next turn.

3. Generate a new level as you did before.

4. Check the current level number: if it's 0 or 1, spawn an exit staircase; if it's 2, spawn the Amulet of Yala.

5. Finish setting up spawned monsters and resources as you did before.

That's a lot to process, so let's tackle it in chunks. Note that the next few sections contain code that you'll add to main.rs in the advance_level() function.

Find the Player

The first thing to do is to obtain a copy of the player's Entity. You've done this before:

```
DeeperDungeons/more_levels/src/main.rs
let player_entity = *<Entity>::query()
    .filter(component::<Player>())
    .iter(&mut self.ecs)
    .nth(0)
    .unwrap();
```

You need the player entity so that you can detect which entities to keep. The plan is to keep the player around and any items they're carrying.

Mark Entities to Keep

Create a HashSet to store the entities you want to remain, and then add the player to it:

```
DeeperDungeons/more_levels/src/main.rs
use std::collections::HashSet;
let mut entities_to_keep = HashSet::new();
entities_to_keep.insert(player_entity);
```

Next, you need to know what items the player is carrying. You can accomplish this by querying for Carried items. If the player is holding an item, add its entity to the entities_to_keep set:

```
DeeperDungeons/more_levels/src/main.rs
<(Entity, &Carried)>::query()
    .iter(&self.ecs)
    .filter(|(_e, carry)| carry.0 == player_entity)
    .map(|(e, _carry)| *e)
    .for_each(|e| { entities_to_keep.insert(e); });
```

entities_to_keep now contains a complete list of the entities you want to retain.

Remove the Other Entities

Now you need to create a `CommandBuffer` to store ECS commands. It's much more efficient to batch your updates, which also avoids borrow-checker issues. Iterate all of the entities in the `World`, and add a `remove` command to the buffer for the entities you *don't* want to keep:

DeeperDungeons/more_levels/src/main.rs

```
❶ let mut cb = CommandBuffer::new(&mut self.ecs);
❷ for e in Entity::query().iter(&self.ecs) {
❸     if !entities_to_keep.contains(e) {
           cb.remove(*e);
       }
   }
❹ cb.flush(&mut self.ecs);
```

❶ You can create a `CommandBuffer` outside of a system by calling `new()` with a mutable reference to the parent ECS `World`.

❷ Legion allows you to query all entities with the associated function `Entities::query()`. You can use it like other queries.

❸ Check if the entity is in `entities_to_keep`. If it is not—the `!` is "not"—then remove the entity from the ECS world.

❹ When you use a `CommandBuffer` outside of a system, you have to apply it to the world by calling `flush()`.

This code iterates all entities and removes any that *aren't* the player or an item carried by the player. Using a command buffer is fast and ensures that you aren't modifying your entity data while you iterate it. The remaining steps are housekeeping, similar to the steps you need to perform when you reset the game state.

Set the Field of View to Dirty

Next, set the `is_dirty` flag on the player's `FieldOfView`. If you don't set this flag, the field of view will incorrectly retain the previous level's visibility until the player moves:

DeeperDungeons/more_levels/src/main.rs

```
<&mut FieldOfView>::query()
    .iter_mut(&mut self.ecs)
    .for_each(|fov| fov.is_dirty = true);
```

Create a New Map

Next up, you want to create a map—exactly as you did before:

DeeperDungeons/more_levels/src/main.rs
```
let mut rng = RandomNumberGenerator::new();
let mut map_builder = MapBuilder::new(&mut rng);
```

Place the Player in the New Map

The MapBuilder gives you the player's starting point. Rather than recreate the player, update the player's position to the new level. This is also a good time to update and store the player's map_level because you'll need it later. Add the following code:

DeeperDungeons/more_levels/src/main.rs
```
let mut map_level = 0;
<(&mut Player, &mut Point)>::query()
    .iter_mut(&mut self.ecs)
    .for_each(|(player, pos)| {
        player.map_level += 1;
        map_level = player.map_level;
        pos.x = map_builder.player_start.x;
        pos.y = map_builder.player_start.y;
    }
);
```

Spawn the Amulet of Yala or a Staircase

The next step is to either spawn the Amulet of Yala—if the player is on the final level—or spawn an exit:

DeeperDungeons/more_levels/src/main.rs
```
if map_level == 2 {
    spawn_amulet_of_yala(&mut self.ecs, map_builder.amulet_start);
} else {
    let exit_idx = map_builder.map.point2d_to_index(map_builder.amulet_start);
    map_builder.map.tiles[exit_idx] = TileType::Exit;
}
```

Finally, update the resources in the same way you did in the reset_game_state function:

DeeperDungeons/more_levels/src/main.rs
```
map_builder.monster_spawns
    .iter()
    .for_each(|pos| spawn_entity(&mut self.ecs, &mut rng, *pos));
self.resources.insert(map_builder.map);
self.resources.insert(Camera::new(map_builder.player_start));
self.resources.insert(TurnState::AwaitingInput);
self.resources.insert(map_builder.theme);
```

Run the game now, and you can transition between levels. If you survive to the final level, you can win the game.

Let's give the player a sense of progress by displaying the dungeon level on the Heads-Up Display.

Displaying the Current Level on the HUD

Currently, the Heads-Up Display shows the player's health and current inventory, but it doesn't indicate the player's current level. Adding the current level to the HUD can help players feel a sense of achievement when they see the number go up, so let's add it.

The hud_system handles Heads-Up Display rendering. Open systems/hud.rs, and add the following code (just before you start displaying the player's inventory):

DeeperDungeons/more_levels/src/systems/hud.rs
```
❶ let (player, map_level) = <(Entity, &Player)>::query()
       .iter(ecs)
       .find_map(|(entity, player)| Some((*entity, player.map_level)))
       .unwrap();

❷ draw_batch.print_color_right(
       Point::new(SCREEN_WIDTH*2, 1),
❸     format!("Dungeon Level: {}", map_level+1),
       ColorPair::new(YELLOW, BLACK)
   );
```

❶ Locate the Player component and entity.

❷ print_color_right() right justifies text output. All of the text will appear to the left of the specified coordinates.

❸ format!() provides a convenient macro to include the current level in the displayed string. Note that you're adding +1 to the map level. (Rust programmers tend to start counting at zero, but most people prefer to start counting at one.)

This code obtains the Player component and reads the current dungeon level stored inside. It then displays this level on the player's HUD. Run the game now, and you'll see a level progress indicator on the screen as shown in the image on page 268.

Wrap-Up

In this chapter, you added staircases to the dungeon map, providing a clever way for players to advance to the next level. In doing so, you learned how to make new map tile types, and how to detect when the player steps on an Exit tile.

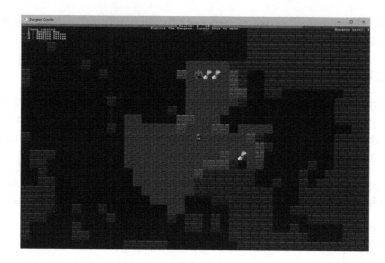

Now that you know how to add new tile types, consider the world full of new design possibilites: you could vary your floor tiles, add "fluff" decorative tiles that act as scenery, or introduce all new tile types that act as death-traps—heroes like that sort of thing, right?

In the next chapter, you'll add more items to the game, using them to extend the combat system. By extending the combat system, you give players something new to enjoy: equipment choice. You'll also use the player's progress through the dungeon to increase the level of difficulty the player encounters as they progress deeper into the belly of the beast.

CHAPTER 15

Combat Systems and Loot

Writing spawn functions for every item, monster, or other entity you think up can take time, and waiting for your game to recompile so that you can test those new ideas is not fun. But don't worry, there's something that can help: *data-driven design.*

With data-driven design, instead of hard-coding entities into your game's source code, you specify these entities in a data file, which gets read when the game generates a new level. This type of setup allows you to rapidly test new ideas.

Terminology Time

A *data-driven design* loads as much data as possible from data files, and then it uses that data to populate the game entities. This is useful if you're working with a team of designers and developers, because team members can change the game without having to learn Rust.

An ECS is *data-oriented* since it focuses on storing data in memory and providing efficient access to it.

In this chapter, you'll move your spawning functionality into a generic function that will read your entity definitions from a file and create components using that data. You'll also add varying damage levels to monsters and weapons, and you'll extend the combat system to use the new values—providing a much more varied game, with more tactical choices for the player to make.

The first step toward data-driven design is to create the data describing your dungeon's denizens.

Designing Data-Driven Dungeons

Your game's entities have a lot in common. For example, they all have a name, starting position, render information, and game stats. Rather than use a custom spawn function for every entity in the game—which is what you're doing now—you'll create a common spawn function that reads the game's data file and adds components using the values found in that file. But first, you need a data file and an appropriate format.

This book will use RON (*Rusty Object Notation*) files to store your game definition.[1] RON is similar to JSON and other structured data formats, but it's designed to look like Rust.

Create a new file named resources/template.ron and paste the following game definition into it:

```
Templates(
    entities : [
        Template(
            entity_type: Item,
            name : "Healing Potion", glyph : '!', levels : [ 0, 1, 2 ],
            provides: Some([ ("Healing", 6) ]),
            frequency: 2
        ),
        Template(
            entity_type: Item,
            name : "Dungeon Map", glyph : '{', levels : [ 0, 1, 2 ],
            provides: Some([ ("MagicMap", 0) ]),
            frequency: 1
        ),
        Template(
            entity_type: Enemy,
            name : "Goblin", glyph : 'g', levels : [ 0, 1, 2 ],
            hp : Some(1),
            frequency: 3
        ),
        Template(
            entity_type: Enemy,
            name : "Orc", glyph : 'o', levels : [ 0, 1, 2 ],
            hp : Some(2),
            frequency: 2
        ),
    ],
)
```

---

1.   https://github.com/ron-rs/ron

The contents of this template file should look familiar since it's the same list of monsters and items you've been using; however, there's now some new information that includes varying health levels. The format should also look familiar since the RON format is similar to Rust.

Entries follow a name : value format, or a name : [..] format for collections of data. The data file contains definitions of entity templates, collected in an array named entities. Each entry is of the Template type, and the contents are listed like a Rust structure. Each entity has the following properties:

- entity_type is either Item or Enemy.

- name is the entity's display name.

- glyph defines the character used to render the entity.

- provides is either not present or wrapped in an Option. This property is a list of effects the item provides, such as *Healing* or *MagicMap*. A second number, if provided in the tuple, indicates how much of the listed effect the item or enemy applies, if applicable (for example, healing potions heal for 6 hit points).

- hp is also an Option because not every item or enemy has hit points.

We also have two new fields:

- levels is a list of the levels on which the entity can spawn, starting at zero.
- frequency is an indicator for how often the item spawns; the higher the number, the more often it spawns.

The template.ron file describes all of the monsters and items in the game—except for the player and the Amulet of Yala. Those two entities are handled differently, so they're kept out of the spawn list. You don't want multiple players or victory conditions spawning as that would be confusing—and probably break the game.

Data or Structure First

 It might be difficult to decide what to do first: create the data format or the data. Do you write the data format, then fit the game data into it, or create the data first, and write a format that fits that data? Both approaches are correct, so use whichever one works for you. Either way, when you create a new format, you'll likely rearrange it until your intended data fits like a glove.

You've defined the game's entity data, now it's time to read that data into your program. Rust provides excellent facilities for reading and decoding files.

Reading Dungeon Data

Rust's crate library includes a crate named *Serde*[2] to assist with the process of *serializing* and *deserializing* data. (Writing structures to a file is known as serializing, and reading that data back is known as deserializing.)

To use Serde, you need to add it as a dependency. You also need to add the ron crate to provide Serde with an understanding of the RON data format since Serde supports *many* different data formats. Open your project's Cargo.toml file, and add two more dependencies:

```
[dependencies]
bracket-lib = "~0.8.1"
legion = "=0.3.1"
➤ serde = { version = "=1.0.115" }
➤ ron = "=0.6.1"
```

Now that you're including the crates required to load RON files into structures, you need to define the types to match the data file you created earlier. You also need to create a function to load the template file from disk and alert you to any errors.

Extending the Spawner Module

Since you're dealing with spawning entities, the spawner module is the natural place to find the code. Let's start by turning spawner into a multi-file module—as you did in Multi-File Modules, on page 111, and Dividing the Map Builder, on page 204. Follow the same steps you used before:

1. Create a new folder named spawner.
2. Move spawner.rs into the new directory.
3. Rename spawner.rs to mod.rs.

With the module in place, you're ready to add some deserialization code.

Mapping and Loading the Template

In the new spawnerfolder, create a file named template.rs. Don't forget to add it to your Rust project by adding mod template at the top of spawner/mod.rs.

Start the new template.rs file with some use statements to import the functionality you need:

Loot/loot_tables/src/spawner/template.rs
```
use crate::prelude::*;
❶ use serde::Deserialize;
```

2.   https://serde.rs/

```
❷ use ron::de::from_reader;
❸ use std::fs::File;
  use std::collections::HashSet;
  use legion::systems::CommandBuffer;
```

❶ serde::Deserialize imports the Deserialize procedural macro into your module. This allows you to add #[derive(Deserialize)] to your structs and enums, allowing them to be loaded from a file.

❷ ron::de::from_reader is a function that reads a RON file and returns a deserialized structure.

❸ std::fs::File is a type that represents a file on disk. It's similar to std::io, but it works with your file system instead of the console.

Next, define structs that match the format you used in the template.ron file:

Loot/loot_tables/src/spawner/template.rs
```
❶ #[derive(Clone, Deserialize, Debug)]
❷ pub struct Template {
❸     pub entity_type : EntityType,
❹     pub levels : HashSet<usize>,
       pub frequency : i32,
       pub name : String,
       pub glyph : char,
❺     pub provides : Option<Vec<(String, i32)>>,
       pub hp : Option<i32>
   }
❻ #[derive(Clone, Deserialize, Debug, PartialEq)]
   pub enum EntityType {
       Enemy, Item
   }

   #[derive(Clone, Deserialize, Debug)]
❼ pub struct Templates {
       pub entities : Vec<Template>,
   }
```

❶ The Deserialize derive directive allows a type to be read from a file. *Every* type in your struct or enum needs to support deserializing for this to work. Serde automatically supports most built-in Rust types.

❷ This structure matches the Template type you used in your game's RON data file.

❸ EntityType is an enum. Serde lets you serialize/deserialize enums just like any other type of data.

❹ levels is a HashSet containing the level numbers where an entity may spawn. In RON, you specify set elements just like an array.

❺ Note that provides is an Option, so you can omit it entirely from the RON file if you don't have any data for this field. If you do have data, wrap it in Some()—just like a Rust option.

❻ You can provide serialization support for enums in the same way as you do for structs.

❼ This is the top-level collection representing the file; it contains a vector of Template objects.

Now that you have the data types defined, it's time to load them from disk. Create a new constructor named load, implemented for the Templates structure:

Loot/loot_tables/src/spawner/template.rs
```
impl Templates {
    pub fn load() -> Self {
❶      let file = File::open("resources/template.ron")
            .expect("Failed opening file");
❷      from_reader(file).expect("Unable to load templates")
    }
}
```

❶ File::open returns a Result. Since the file may not exist, or you may not have access to it, you need to handle the error. Failing to load the game data is a game-ending error, so use expect() to unwrap the file handle and crash with an error if file opening fails.

❷ from_reader calls Serde to open your file. If Serde cannot read the contents of your file, the function will return an error—so once again, use expect to unwrap the returned option.

Your template type can now load all of the game data, so it's time to make use of the data to spawn some entities.

Data-Driven Spawning

Spawning data-driven entities is the process of reading the game definition data, and outputting an in-game object—a health potion begins life as a data template and awaits discovery on the map:

```
Template(
    entity_type: Item,
    name : "Healing Potion", glyph : '!', levels : [ 0, 1, 2 ],
    provides: Some([ ("Healing", 6) ]),
    frequency: 2
),
```

Data Definition   In-Game Potion

Let's create a new function, implemented as part of the Template. First, start with the function signature:

```
impl Template {
  ..
  pub fn spawn_entities(
      &self,
      ecs: &mut World,
      rng: &mut RandomNumberGenerator,
      level: usize,
      spawn_points: &[Point]
  ) {
```

The parameters for this function align closely with the spawning functions you already have in mod.rs. You take a borrowed reference to the ECS World and the RandomNumberGenerator. You note what game level you're creating, and you store a list of locations in which you can spawn entities.

The next section builds a spawn table for the current level. Add the following code to your new function:

Loot/loot_tables/src/spawner/template.rs
```
❶  let mut available_entities = Vec::new();
   self.entities
❷      .iter()
❸      .filter(|e| e.levels.contains(&level))
        .for_each(|t| {
❹          for _ in 0 .. t.frequency {
                available_entities.push(t);
            }
        }
   );
```

❶ Create a mutable vector in which you'll store a list of entities that may be spawned on this level.

❷ Iterate the list of entity templates you loaded in the constructor.

❸ Use filter to include only entities whose levels list includes the current level.

❹ Add each available entity many times equal to the entry's frequency.

The available_entities list contains *references* to members of the entities collection. Rather than duplicating each entry, you store a pointer to the original—saving a lot of memory. Each possible entity appears a number of times in the available_entities list equal to its frequency. This makes weighting their selection easier—you can generate a random number between 0 and the size of the available_entities list to pick a result—and the weighting is baked into the list. This operation may be visualized as shown in the image on page 276.

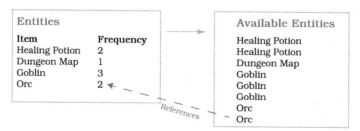

Now that you know what entities you can spawn, you have to decide where to spawn those entities. Add the following code to the function:

Loot/loot_tables/src/spawner/template.rs
```
let mut commands = CommandBuffer::new(ecs);
spawn_points.iter().for_each(|pt| {
    if let Some(entity) = rng.random_slice_entry(&available_entities) {
        self.spawn_entity(pt, entity, &mut commands);
    }
});
commands.flush(ecs);
}
```

❶ Create a single CommandBuffer, into which you'll push all of your spawn commands. This is more efficient than running every command separately, and it avoids borrow-checker issues.

❷ Iterate the list of spawn points passed into the function.

❸ random_slice_entry() is a helper function that randomly selects an entry from a collection.

❹ You'll be creating this function in a moment.

This code iterates all of the spawn points and randomly picks an entity to spawn in each location.

Next, you want to define the spawn_entity function. Add the function signature as part of the Template implementation:

```
impl Template {
    ..
    fn spawn_entity(
        &self,
        pt: &Point,
        template: &Template,
        commands: &mut legion::systems::CommandBuffer
    ) {
```

You call into this function from the spawn_entity function you just created. Because you're iterating each point in turn and calling the new function, it takes a single Point. It also takes a mutable reference to the CommandBuffer you created in the parent function. Combining all of your entity/component creations into a single command buffer is faster than performing them one at a time.

If you look at your orc, spawn_healing_potion, and other entity factory functions, you'll see a lot of repeated code. They all have names, locations (Point), and render information. You can create these components for all of the template entities that you're creating:

Loot/loot_tables/src/spawner/template.rs

```
let entity = commands.push((
    pt.clone(),
    Render{
        color: ColorPair::new(WHITE, BLACK),
        glyph: to_cp437(template.glyph)
    },
    Name(template.name.clone())
));
```

❶ Create a new entity with the push() function. You have to push a tuple of components that define the entity, hence the double brackets. push() returns the newly created entity, which you can use to adjust the entity after creation.

❷ Clone the position from pt to use it as a new component.

❸ Use the glyph value from the template.

❹ Clone the name from the template. If you don't clone it, Rust will try to move it out of the template and into your component, which will fail to compile.

Now that your entity has the common functionality found in all of your entities, it's time to add the optional components.

Monsters need an Enemy, FieldOfView, ChasingPlayer, and Health component. Items need only an Item tag. You can determine which entities need these components by calling match on the entity_type field and adding the appropriate components:

Loot/loot_tables/src/spawner/template.rs

```
match template.entity_type {
    EntityType::Item => commands.add_component(entity, Item{}),
    EntityType::Enemy => {
        commands.add_component(entity, Enemy{});
        commands.add_component(entity, FieldOfView::new(6));
        commands.add_component(entity, ChasingPlayer{});
        commands.add_component(entity, Health{
            current: template.hp.unwrap(),
```

```
                max: template.hp.unwrap()
            });
        }
    }
```

The component details are the same as your existing spawn functions, but it uses values derived from your data file. You're adding commands to the CommandBuffer rather than deriving an entry_ref and adding components for each. Using a single command buffer keeps your code short and efficient.

The Effects field in your data file is optional because not everything has an effect. Read the effects list with an if let and match pattern:

Loot/loot_tables/src/spawner/template.rs
```
    if let Some(effects) = &template.provides {
        effects.iter().for_each(|(provides, n)| {
            match provides.as_str() {
                "Healing" => commands.add_component(entity,
                    ProvidesHealing{ amount: *n}),
                "MagicMap" => commands.add_component(entity,
                    ProvidesDungeonMap{}),
                _ => {
                    println!("Warning: we don't know how to provide {}"
                        , provides);
                }
            }
        });
    }
}
```

If effects exist, iterate the list of effects and create components as needed. Healing and MagicMap are the same as they were in your spawn_healing_potion and spawn_magic_mapper functions from Chapter 13, Inventory and Power-Ups, on page 241.

You might be wondering why effects are stored using a list. With a list, you have more flexibility. For example, you might have an item that heals you and gives you knowledge of the map—or you might have a potion that heals you and makes you confused. Using an effects list saves you from having to write a new effect type for each combination.

Now that you have created a generic spawn_entity function, it's time to clean up the functions it replaces.

Spring Cleaning

You replaced a lot of functionality in spawner/mod.rs. Delete the following functions since you don't need them anymore:

- spawn_entity
- spawn_monster
- goblin
- orc
- spawn_healing_potion
- spawn_magic_mapper

Next, you need to provide an interface for the main function to call your spawning code. Open spawner/mod.rs and add use template::Template; to your import list at the top. Create a new function named spawn_level to act as an interface to your new spawning code:

Loot/loot_tables/src/spawner/mod.rs
```
pub fn spawn_level(
    ecs: &mut World,
    rng: &mut RandomNumberGenerator,
    level: usize,
    spawn_points: &[Point]
) {
    let template = Templates::load();
    template.spawn_entities(ecs, rng, level, spawn_points);
}
```

This code loads the template from disk and passes the spawn command to the new template. With the interface in place, you're ready to use it.

Open main.rs. There are three places you're calling spawn_entity. The old spawn code reads as follows:

```
map_builder.monster_spawns
  .iter()
  .for_each(|pos| spawn_entity(&mut ecs, &mut rng, *pos));
```

Find your new() function, and replace the above code with the following:

```
spawn_level(
  &mut self.ecs,
  &mut rng,
  0,
  &map_builder.monster_spawns
);
```

You can apply the same change to reset_game_level(). When starting a new game, you know that the player starts on map level 0.

A slightly different change is required in advance_level() because you need to include the current map level:

```
spawn_level(&mut self.ecs, &mut rng, map_level as usize,
  &map_builder.monster_spawns);
```

Run your game, and you'll see a familiar array of monsters and items— this time without redundancy in your spawning code. You now have a data-driven dungeon. Hooray!

You can also add new monsters and change the levels on which they appear, all from the data file, with no programming required. Try it now. Open resources/template.ron and add another type of healing potion:

```
Template(
    entity_type: Item,
    name : "Weak Healing Potion", glyph : '!', levels : [ 0, 1, 2 ],
    provides: Some([ ("Healing", 2) ]),
    frequency: 2
),
```

Run the game, and you'll see that some potions are now "weak healing potions." That's the power of data-driven design—it's easy to make changes to your game.

Extending the Combat System

The current combat system is simple. An entity attacks another entity—and *always* inflicts one point of damage. This type of combat system doesn't provide much of a difficulty curve as the adventurer progresses through the dungeon.

Let's fix this problem by allowing different entities to inflict varying amounts of damage. Specifically, you'll adjust the game so that the player can inflict more damage as they find better weapons, and *some* monsters cause more damage to the player thanks to bigger claws.

Damage from Weapons and Claws

Open spawner/template.rs, and add a base_damage field to the Template structure:

Loot/better_combat/src/spawner/template.rs
```
#[derive(Clone, Deserialize, Debug)]
pub struct Template {
    pub entity_type : EntityType,
    pub levels : HashSet<usize>,
    pub frequency : i32,
    pub name : String,
    pub glyph : char,
    pub provides : Option<Vec<(String, i32)>>,
    pub hp : Option<i32>,
    pub base_damage : Option<i32>
}
```

Now that you updated the data format, open resources/template.ron, so that you can add damage statistics to the monsters.

To begin, add more monsters and adjust the monsters' level distribution so that more dangerous monsters only appear later in the game:

Loot/better_combat/resources/template.ron
```
Template(
    entity_type: Enemy,
    name : "Goblin", glyph : 'g', levels : [ 0 ],
    hp : Some(1),
    frequency: 3,
    base_damage: Some(1)
),
Template(
    entity_type: Enemy,
    name : "Orc", glyph : 'o', levels : [ 0, 1, 2 ],
    hp : Some(2),
    frequency: 2,
    base_damage: Some(1)
),
Template(
    entity_type: Enemy,
    name : "Ogre", glyph : 'O', levels : [ 1, 2 ],
    hp : Some(5),
    frequency: 1,
    base_damage: Some(2)
),
Template(
    entity_type: Enemy,
    name : "Ettin", glyph : 'E', levels : [ 2 ],
    hp : Some(10),
    frequency: 1,
    base_damage: Some(3)
),
```

You've now implemented a difficulty curve. Monsters become progressively more dangerous as the adventurer explores dungeon levels:

Level Progression

Level 0	Level 1	Level 2
Goblin (1)	Orc (2)	Orc (2)
Orc (2)	Ogre (2)	Ogre (2)
		Ettin (3)

Base damage is in parentheses

Then, add a weapon to the entity list. Weapons are items that can inflict damage, so you can add them like other items but include the new base_damage field:

```
Template(
    entity_type: Item,
    name : "Rusty Sword", glyph: '/', levels: [ 0, 1, 2 ],
    frequency: 1,
    base_damage: Some(1)
),
```

Next, you need a new component type in which to store the amount of damage an entity inflicts.

Damage Components

Open components.rs and add a new component type:

Loot/better_combat/src/components.rs
```
#[derive(Clone, Copy, Debug, PartialEq)]
pub struct Damage(pub i32);
```

Items can inflict damage, but they aren't monsters, so you need a way to identify that an item is a weapon. Add another component to the components.rs file:

Loot/better_combat/src/components.rs
```
#[derive(Clone, Copy, Debug, PartialEq)]
pub struct Weapon;
```

You also want the player to be able to inflict damage. Open spawner/mod.rs and add a Damage component to the player when the spawn_player function creates them:

Loot/better_combat/src/spawner/mod.rs
```
pub fn spawn_player(ecs : &mut World, pos : Point) {
    ecs.push(
        (Player{map_level: 0},
            pos,
            Render{
                color: ColorPair::new(WHITE, BLACK),
                glyph : to_cp437('@')
            },
            Health{ current: 10, max: 10 },
            FieldOfView::new(8),
            Damage(1)
        )
    );
}
```

You need to extend your spawn_entity function to handle the additional damage information. Open spawner/template.rs and find the spawn_entity function. Insert the following code immediately after your effects-spawning code:

Loot/better_combat/src/spawner/template.rs
```
if let Some(damage) = &template.base_damage {
    commands.add_component(entity, Damage(*damage));
    if template.entity_type == EntityType::Item {
        commands.add_component(entity, Weapon{});
    }
}
```

This function uses if let to determine if there's a damage value. If there is, the function adds it to the component. It then checks to see if the entity is an item. If it is, the function adds the newly created Weapon component.

Now that you know how much damage a weapon or item inflicts, it's time to use that data in the combat system.

Doing Some Damage

Open systems/combat.rs. The combat system needs access to the Damage and Carried components:

Loot/better_combat/src/systems/combat.rs
```
#[system]
#[read_component(WantsToAttack)]
#[read_component(Player)]
#[write_component(Health)]
➤ #[read_component(Damage)]
➤ #[read_component(Carried)]
```

Since the attacker's data is now required to calculate their damage output, you need to extend the victims' list calculator to also return the attacker's Entity:

Loot/better_combat/src/systems/combat.rs
```
➤ let victims : Vec<(Entity, Entity, Entity)> = attackers
      .iter(ecs)
➤     .map(|(entity, attack)| (*entity, attack.attacker, attack.victim) )
      .collect();
➤ victims.iter().for_each(|(message, attacker, victim)| {
```

The changed lines are highlighted. Here, you're adding the attacker to the tuples stored in attackers, and including it in the victims loop.

Previously, you decremented the victim's health by 1. Instead, examine the attacker and calculate how much damage they inflict:

Loot/better_combat/src/systems/combat.rs

```
let base_damage = if let Ok(v) = ecs.entry_ref(*attacker) {
    if let Ok(dmg) = v.get_component::<Damage>() {
        dmg.0
    } else {
        0
    }
} else {
    0
❶ };

let weapon_damage : i32 = <(&Carried, &Damage)>::query().iter(ecs)
    .filter(|(carried, _)| carried.0 == *attacker)
    .map(|(_, dmg)| dmg.0)
❷    .sum();

let final_damage = base_damage + weapon_damage;

if let Ok(mut health) = ecs
    .entry_mut(*victim)
    .unwrap()
    .get_component_mut::<Health>()
{
    health.current -= final_damage;
```

❶ This function chain calculates the base damage associated with the attacker. It first acquires an entry_ref to access the entity's components directly. It then checks to see if a Damage component exists. If it does, the function returns the damage rating of the weapon. If access to the entity fails or a damage component isn't present, the function returns 0.

❷ Using an iterator chain, query all entities that are both Carried and have a Damage component. Filter to only include items held by the attacker. Then, use the iterator sum() function to total the damage of all carried weaponry.

Run the game now, and find one of the rusty swords in the dungeon. Pick it up, and you'll inflict 2 points of damage instead of 1. Also notice that monsters now do varying damage to the player, making for a much more engaging battle with the dungeon's occupants.

The Adventurer Isn't an Octopus

When the adventurer picks up a rusty sword, they use it. When the adventurer picks up a second rusty sword, they use that one too. You could justify this scenario as representing a sword in each hand, but what happens when the player picks up a third sword? As it turns out, the adventurer turns into a wild, octopus-like creature, wielding way more swords than hands available to hold them. Yeah, that's a problem.

Let's adjust the item collection system to keep only one weapon equipped at a time. Open systems/player_input.rs. You need to add #[read_component(Weapon)] to the system's component specifications, and adjust the item collection code as follows:

Loot/better_combat/src/systems/player_input.rs
```
let mut items = <(Entity, &Item, &Point)>::query();
items.iter(ecs)
    .filter(|(_entity, _item, &item_pos)| item_pos == player_pos)
    .for_each(|(entity, _item, _item_pos)| {
        commands.remove_component::<Point>(*entity);
        commands.add_component(*entity, Carried(player));

        if let Ok(e) = ecs.entry_ref(*entity) {
            if e.get_component::<Weapon>().is_ok() {
                <(Entity, &Carried, &Weapon)>::query()
                .iter(ecs)
                .filter(|(_, c, _)| c.0 == player)
                .for_each(|(e, c, w)| {
                    commands.remove(*e);
                })
            }
        }
    }
);
```

❶ Check the selected item to see if it's a weapon.

❷ If the item is a weapon, delete it from the game world—the player can only have one weapon at a time.

Now that the game supports multiple weapon types, you need to add some graphics to represent them on the map.

Adding More Swords

Rusty swords are handy. Shiny swords look nice. But an impractically enormous sword that slices and dices your foes—well, that's the stuff of legends.

Fortunately, you now have all of the tools you need to add more weapons to the game.

Open resources/template.ron and add some more sword types:

Loot/better_combat/resources/template.ron
```
Template(
    entity_type: Item,
    name : "Rusty Sword", glyph: 's', levels: [ 0, 1, 2 ],
    frequency: 1,
    base_damage: Some(1)
),
```

```
Template(
    entity_type: Item,
    name : "Shiny Sword", glyph: 'S', levels: [ 0, 1, 2 ],
    frequency: 1,
    base_damage: Some(2)
),
Template(
    entity_type: Item,
    name : "Huge Sword", glyph: '/', levels: [ 1, 2 ],
    frequency: 1,
    base_damage: Some(3)
),
```

The game now includes three sword types, one of which appears only on the last two levels. Run the game now, and you'll find an assortment of weaponry around the map:

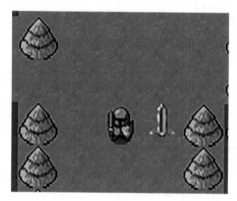

Wrap-Up

In this chapter, you learned to define your game's entities and components using a data file. Data files are great because you can use them to not only reduce the time it takes to test new entities, but you can also add new entries without having to alter the underlying code needed to load those entities.

Here, you used a data file to implement three new weapons and differentiate the dungeon denizens. You're getting close to the end of the book, so in the next chapter, you'll put some finishing touches to your game, and you'll learn how to distribute it.

CHAPTER 16

Final Steps and Finishing Touches

A lot of game projects start amidst great excitement. Sadly, many projects never reach a state where the developer can release a playable game. However, by focusing on the *Minimum Viable Product* and following the design guidelines in this book, you're one step closer to finishing and releasing your Rust game.

This chapter will help you put the cherry atop your cake, walking you through packaging your game for distribution, presenting ideas for expansion, and wrapping up this book.

Packaging Your Game for Distribution

In previous chapters, you compiled and ran your game in debug mode. Debug mode adds extra information to your executable (or .pdb file on Windows), mapping machine code to Rust code, allowing you to run the program inside a debugger and watch program state changes. Debug mode also disables many compiler optimizations that can make your game run faster; these optimizations might combine or remove parts of your code, making it confusing to debug. Since you aren't expecting your players to debug the game, you can take advantage of these optimizations in a Release build.

Why Not Always Run Release Mode?

 Release mode disables some safety checks, particularly bounds-checking on collections and overflow errors on numeric calcula-tions. It's possible to create code that works in Release mode, but will crash in Debug mode. It's a good idea to develop in debug mode and periodically test it as a release build.

Enabling Release Mode and Link-Time Optimization

You can run your game in Release mode with the command cargo run --release. Try it now, and you'll see that the game is *much* faster and more responsive. Play through the game to make sure that it still works. It should—but occasionally optimizations produce unexpected results.

You can further optimize your game with *Link Time Optimization (LTO)*. Normal compilation only optimizes the contents of each module. LTO analyzes the entire program, including all of your crate dependencies (and their dependencies). To enable LTO, open Cargo.toml, and add the following section to the end:

```
[profile.release]
lto = "thin"
```

Now, whenever you compile or run your game in release mode, LTO will optimize the complete binary. Compilation and linking are a *lot* slower, but the performance benefits of using LTO are sometimes dramatic. With LTO enabled, try running the game with cargo run --release. You'll see a further performance improvement, but not as much as you did from enabling release mode.

Now that you can compile your game in release mode, you're ready to package it up for distribution.

Distributing Your Game

It's a good idea to start with a clean slate, so begin by running cargo clean. This command removes all currently compiled code, which is helpful since Rust supports *incremental compilation*. Sometimes, it adds to your executable instead of completely rebuilding it. After the project is cleaned up, type cargo build --release to compile the entire game in release mode.

Next, create a new directory—somewhere else on your computer—to store the packaged game. You'll need to copy some files and directories from your project's directory into the new directory:

- The game *executable*, located in the target/release directory, is named the same as your project's name in Cargo.toml. If you've been working in the dungeoncrawl project you created in Chapter 5, Build a Dungeon Crawler, on page 75, look for dungeoncrawl (on UNIX-like systems) or dungeoncrawl.exe (on Windows).

- Copy the resources folder into your new directory as a complete directory.

You do *not* need any of the compiled dependencies. Rust *statically links* all of the dependencies into your executable file, so they're already included. No additional files or runtime is needed.

You'll end up with the following structure:

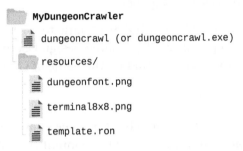

```
MyDungeonCrawler
    dungeoncrawl (or dungeoncrawl.exe)
    resources/
        dungeonfont.png
        terminal8x8.png
        template.ron
```

Run the game from the new directory. Everything should run normally. If not, verify that you copied all of the necessary files and folders.

The final step is compressing the game directory and sharing the zip file with your friends. You can also share your game on sites like Itch.[1]

On my system, the final game requires 2.3 Mb of disk space. Before LTO and optimization, my target directory was nearly 300 Mb—that's a significant difference.

You probably have some ideas to make the dungeon crawler better. Maybe there's something you want to add or remove. Or perhaps there's some design element you want to change. But where do you start?

Making the Dungeon Crawler Your Own

Tweaking games and making them your own is an important step for a game developer. You have the knowledge you need to add features to the game and make it your own. Try some of the following project ideas:

- Add different monsters and items, or change the existing ones.

- Change the theme to "re-skin" the game. You can radically alter the feel of the game with different tilesets.

- Add a score mechanism.

- Maybe you don't like turn-based games. Most of the systems can work in a real-time game, with a bit of tweaking and some timing code similar to what you used in *Flappy Dragon*.

- Review the *Flappy Dragon* bonus content and see if you can add some animation to your game.

- Look into the Amethyst Engine[2] and Bevy[3] to provide frameworks for more advanced games. Both are ECS-based engines and can be used to make very impressive 2D and 3D games.

Most importantly, think about what *you* want to write. Follow the design advice presented in Appendix 2, Short Game Design Documents, on page 297. Start simple and work towards building the game of your dreams.

Additional Content

Finishing a book is a lot like finishing a game. You feel a great sense of achievement, but also an awareness of the content that didn't make the cut. For additional content, you can visit my website.[4]

In particular, I'm planning to release the following content:

- *Web Assembly (WASM)*—publish your game to the web, playable in a browser.

- *Particle Effects*—add some more interactive graphics to your game.

- *Saving the Game*—learn how to serialize your ECS for easy game saving and resumption.

Wrap-Up

Congratulations! You've reached the end of the book. You started your journey learning to make "Hello, World" in Rust, and now you've made *Flappy Dragon* and a Dungeon Crawler (or Roguelike) featuring procedurally generated maps, health, melee combat, items, loot, and data-driven design. You've come a long way. Hopefully, the end of the book does not mark the end of your journey in game development or Rust. You now have the skills to create fun games and share your creativity with the world.

---

2. https://amethyst.rs/
3. https://bevyengine.org/
4. https://hands-on-rust.com/

Herbert says:

I'd love to hear from you

I love it when someone contacts me and says, "I made this with the help of your library or book." If this book inspires you to make something, please let me know. You can find me on Twitter as herberticus or on the Devtalk website.[a]

---

a.   https://forum.devtalk.com/t/hands-on-rust-effective-learning-through-2d-game-development-and-play/
     3919

Part III

Additional Resources

In this part of the book, you'll find the following extra resources: an ASCII/Codepage 437 chart that helps you use terminal-based rendering for prototyping. a short design document guide that you can use to assist with the planning of your game, and a Rust cheat sheet that summarizes much of the language syntax.

ASCII/Codepage 437 Chart

	☺	●	♥	♦	♣	♠	•	◘	○	◙	♂	♀	♪	♫	☼
0	1	2	3	4	5	6	7	8	9	10	11	12	13	14	15
►	◄	↕	‼	¶	§	▬	↨	↑	↓	→	←	∟	↔	▲	▼
16	17	18	19	20	21	22	23	24	25	26	27	28	29	30	31
32	!	"	#	$	%	&	'	(	)	*	+	,	-	.	/
	33	34	35	36	37	38	39	40	41	42	43	44	45	46	47
0	1	2	3	4	5	6	7	8	9	:	;	<	=	>	?
48	49	50	51	52	53	54	55	56	57	58	59	60	61	62	63
@	A	B	C	D	E	F	G	H	I	J	K	L	M	N	O
64	65	66	67	68	69	70	71	72	73	74	75	76	77	78	79
P	Q	R	S	T	U	V	W	X	Y	Z	[	\	]	^	_
80	81	82	83	84	85	86	87	88	89	90	91	92	93	94	95
`	a	b	c	d	e	f	g	h	i	j	k	l	m	n	o
96	97	98	99	100	101	102	103	104	105	106	107	108	109	110	111
p	q	r	s	t	u	v	w	x	y	z	{	|	}	~	⌂
112	113	114	115	116	117	118	119	120	121	122	123	124	125	126	127
Ç	ü	é	â	ä	à	å	ç	ê	ë	è	ï	î	ì	Ä	Å
128	129	130	131	132	133	134	135	136	137	138	139	140	141	142	143
É	æ	Æ	ô	ö	ò	û	ù	ÿ	Ö	Ü	¢	£	¥	₧	ƒ
144	145	146	147	148	149	150	151	152	153	154	155	156	157	158	159
á	í	ó	ú	ñ	Ñ	ª	º	¿	⌐	¬	½	¼	¡	«	»
160	161	162	163	164	165	166	167	168	169	170	171	172	173	174	175
░	▒	▓	│	┤	╡	╢	╖	╕	╣	║	╗	╝	╜	╛	┐
176	177	178	179	180	181	182	183	184	185	186	187	188	189	190	191
└	┴	┬	├	─	┼	╞	╟	╚	╔	╩	╦	╠	═	╬	╧
192	193	194	195	196	197	198	199	200	201	202	203	204	205	206	207
╨	╤	╥	╙	╘	╒	╓	╫	╪	┘	┌	█	▄	▌	▐	▀
208	209	210	211	212	213	214	215	216	217	218	219	220	221	222	223
α	ß	Γ	π	Σ	σ	µ	τ	Φ	Θ	Ω	δ	∞	φ	ε	∩
224	225	226	227	228	229	230	231	232	233	234	235	236	237	238	239
≡	±	≥	≤	⌠	⌡	÷	≈	°	∙	·	√	ⁿ	²	■	
240	241	242	243	244	245	246	247	248	249	250	251	252	253	254	255

Short Game Design Documents

A *short* game design document can help you focus on your core game idea—and not spend hours on peripheral features that sound awesome but won't work until you've built the game's foundations. It will also help you overcome writer's block, and a well-structured short design document can help you finish your game. The design document for the Dungeon Crawler example in this game is in Chapter 4, Design a Dungeon Crawler, on page 71.

Let's start with something that can help defeat writer's block: making notes.

Make a Note of Every Idea

As you play and create games, you'll find yourself brimming with ideas. Inspiration often hits at the least convenient moment—in the shower, at work, or while you're trying to sleep. So keep a notepad—physical or virtual—handy. When ideas pop into your brain, jot them down. You need just enough to remember what you were thinking about. "Pong, but with lasers" is a memorable note. "Metaphysical Monsters" is a great title but probably needs a little more commentary to remember what it means when you look back on your notes.

Use whatever note-taking system you like. From EMACS *Org Mode*[1] to Evernote,[2] *Google Keep*[3] to *Microsoft OneNote*,[4] there are plenty of note-taking systems to try. It doesn't matter what platform you use. Even a trusty old pad of paper and beat-up pen is fine.

It's a good idea to keep your notes organized by game idea. Write a top-level note with the basic game idea, and notes underneath for when you think of

---

1. https://orgmode.org//
2. https://evernote.com/
3. https://keep.google.com/
4. https://www.onenote.com/

features. Consider how important they are to the basic game idea. For example, is your idea a core concept of the game or a fun visual effect to accompany another idea?

When you feel the urge to create something and aren't sure what, you can open up your corpus of notes and find something that sounds like fun to write.

Game idea notes aren't a design document or plan. You'll often find that you can combine ideas from different sets of notes—many of the more interesting game ideas start by pondering the combination of a few genres/ideas. Before turning your notes into a design plan, let's consider what your plan should accomplish.

Why You Need a Design Document

A design document serves several purposes:

- It distills the essence of the game you want to make into an easy-to-describe target.

- Compiling your notes into a more formalized document makes your brain begin pondering how the game actually works rather than just a concept of the end product.

- Creating a design document helps you determine which features are essential and which are niceties.

- A well-structured design document breaks tasks into bite-sized chunks so when you find yourself with time to program, you know what to work on and can feel like you accomplished something in the available time.

Many gallons of digital ink have been devoted to the need for a design document and what it should look like. What you *need* depends on the scale of your project:

Working Alone	Small Team	Working for a Studio
A Short Game Design Document	Keep Everyone Moving in the Same Direction	Very Detailed
Keep It Simple	Track Sprint Progress	Producers Make It for You

This book targets beginners, so most likely you're working alone or with a friend. This gives you a lot of freedom. Your design document can be very informal, containing just enough information to remind you of what goes where.

Design Documents Are Alive

Game Design Documents aren't typically carved into stone as unchanging monuments. Instead, these documents are known as a *living document*—constantly edited to match reality.

Let's go over what goes into a minimal, focused design document.

Design Document Headings

Keep your design document short. You need a few basic headings and some rough estimates of the tasks required to realize your idea. This section will walk you through creating a focused design document, intended to help keep you on track as you make a game.

Naming Your Game

Names are difficult, and it's pretty unlikely that the first name you pick will be the name of your game. It's OK to start with something generic and come up with a fun name later. Start your design document with your working title on the first line.

Short Description

You should start your design document with a short description of the game. *Flappy Dragon* could be described as "a Flappy Bird Clone." A generic Roguelike might describe itself as "a Dungeon Crawler with procedurally generated levels, monsters of increasing difficulty, and turn-based movement."

The key is to keep it short. It's similar to an elevator pitch in marketing—this is how you'd describe the game in passing to a friend who wants to know what you're working on.

Story

Not every game *has* a story. Nobody knows why Flappy Bird desperately needs to fly to the East, and for a fun little game, it doesn't matter. If your game has a story, include a summary of the story. Otherwise, you can skip this heading altogether.

Basic Game Loops

Games tend to feature a "design loop." This describes the actions the protagonist takes, and the impact they have on the world. Flappy Dragon's loop is very simple: the dragon flies to the East, avoiding obstacles. A turn-based Dungeon Crawler loop looks like this:

1. Arrive in a randomly generated dungeon level.
2. Explore the dungeon.
3. Encounter monsters and either fight them or run away.
4. Pick up any items along the way.
5. Find the level exit, and repeat from step 1.

Your design may feature more than one loop. That's OK, but it can be a warning sign that you're making a large or convoluted game. A Real Time Strategy game features a few loops:

1. Locate resources and task workers with gathering them.

2. Construct your base, considering both resource use, unit creation, and defense.

3. Construct your armies.

4. Locate the enemy strongpoints and task your armies with their destruction.

Minimum Viable Product

It's very easy to think of ideas for your game but whittling them down to the essentials can be hard. The smallest program you can make that fulfills your basic design goals is the Minimum Viable Product—or MVP.

The MVP is your initial target. Build the chunks of your MVP and once it's together, you have a playable game. It may not be a *finished* game, but it's something you can be proud of. It's also something you can share with friends for feedback. You often don't know whether an idea is good until you try it. Focusing on the MVP saves you from wasting many hours polishing what turned out to be a fun-sounding idea that doesn't quite work in reality.

Stretch Goals

Once you've finalized your MVP, list all of the other features you'd like as stretch goals. Try and rank them by importance; you may not get to all of them. Ideally, you want to pick goals that fit your overall design and can be added in bite-sized chunks. Sitting down and adding a feature in one or two sessions is much more motivating than realizing "in 6 weeks, I may have this working."

Skip through the Forest, Don't March to Mordor

 If you've worked in the software industry, you've probably suffered through a death march project. Everyone's exhausted, and the more hours you put in, the further away you feel from a working product. That's not fun, so try not to inflict it upon yourself. If a goal is causing you stress, cut it from your design. This is especially true if you're working as a lone hobbyist. If you hated making the game, your players will probably notice and hate playing it.

You Aren't Gonna Need It

If you want to finish your game, be brutal. Move *everything* that isn't in the minimum viable product into a stretch goal. Once you start enjoying game development, you'll find yourself coming up with many ideas. Some of the ideas are good ideas—and some aren't. Note them down, but before adding them as another task on your game development document, ask yourself, "Do I really need this?" The sad truth is that beyond your core mechanics, you probably don't need it—it's a nicety. If it looks like a nicety you can make, add it to your stretch goals. Otherwise, keep it in your notebook—maybe you can incorporate it into version 2.0 or another game entirely.

Sprints and Motivation

Now that you have your top-level design document, it's time to turn it into a plan. Divide your ideas into bite-sized chunks. Does your game involve the player wandering around a dungeon? That's a good-sized chunk—make a basic map and move around it. Is your game turn-based? Setting up the turn structure is a good sprint. The chapters in this book are designed to represent realistic sprints.

As you come up with sprints, consider dependencies. You can't implement combat until you have a map, a player, and something for them to fight. Health potions aren't useful until the player has a health statistic. Enormous thermonuclear explosions are cool, but they require a target, a reason to use them, and a way to represent the massive damage they inflict.

Keeping your sprints short is also a very important motivator. A short sprint—preferably one you can finish in one or two sessions—gives you a solid feeling of progress. You can play your new feature and say, "I made this." This is *really* important. Avoid the old "waterfall" pattern of writing everything and then integrating it—and not seeing any meaningful progress for months. You'll have a high risk of becoming disheartened and losing interest in your project.

Don't be afraid to say "this isn't working" and throw some code away—but keep it somewhere, even if it's tucked away in a GitHub branch. You may think of a use for it later.

Long-Term Benefits of Design

Keeping your notes gives you a ready pool of ideas when you feel like writing some code. This can help avoid writer's block—nothing is worse than staring at an empty text editor wondering what you should try and create. Take an idea, hack up a quick design, and throw together a prototype. It doesn't matter if it's terrible. Everyone started by making terrible games. The important part is that you tried to make something and learned along the way.

As you become a better developer, both your thrown-away and completed projects add up. You develop experience and a much better feel for what will and won't work. You also begin to develop a body of code to draw on. If your game idea requires something from an old project, you can borrow from it.

Assess Yourself Realistically

If you visit game development forums or Discord servers, you'll quickly learn that everyone has some big ideas. Every new developer proposing their Massively-Multiplayer Online Game, huge Role-Playing Game, or pitching an idea the size of Assassin's Creed is greeted by a chorus of "Why don't you start with Pong?" Despite appearances, the experienced forum dwellers aren't mean. You do need to start small and gradually build up your experience. That's why this book starts with Flappy Dragon—you can complete it in a single chapter, and garner a lot of foundational knowledge along the way. One day, you—and a large team—may be ready to make the next World of Warcraft. Starting with a project of this scale will almost certainly follow an all-too-familiar cycle: initial enthusiasm, despair when you discover how hard it is to write good netcode for thousands of players, and a decision to either write something smaller or quit game development altogether.

Keep the notes you make describing your dream game. Just be aware that it remains a dream until you're ready for it.

Fail Fast

When you design a novel game, there's a chance that it will be missing one vital element: it isn't *fun*. The problem is, you won't know that until you've tried it (although experience helps). Create an ugly prototype that exposes the basic game loop of your idea. Show it to some trusted friends. If the core game is a good idea, it'll quickly become evident when they enjoy themselves.

If the core idea turns out to be a dud, that's OK too. File it away in your notes as "that was a nice idea" and move on. You may find a use for it as a mini-game inside something else in the future. Worst case, you've learned not to try that idea again.

Don't Stress about Deadlines

> *I love deadlines. I like the whooshing sound they make as they fly by.*

— Douglas Adams

If you're making games as a hobby, don't get hung up on deadlines. Nothing is worse than a "fun" project making you miserable because you feel you are late on a task. If you use a project management app, give yourself plenty of time—and if you miss a deadline, reschedule.

Wrap-Up

Between making notes and the *Short Design Document* template, you have everything you need to plan smaller game projects. You don't need to spend hours writing a massive design tome—but a quick outline at the beginning can help keep you on track to finish your project.

Rust Cheat Sheet

Variable Assignment

```
let n = 5;
```
Assign the value 5 to n. n's type is deduced.

```
let n : i32 = 5;
```
Assign the value 5 to n. n is an i32.

```
let n;
```
Create a placeholder variable named n. You may assign to it (once) later.

```
let mut n = 5;
```
Assign the value 5 to n. n is mutable and may be changed later.

```
let n = i == 5;
```
*Assign the result of the expression i==5 (true or false) to n.
n's type is deduced.*

```
x = y;
```
Move y's value into x (you can no longer use y), unless y is a copyable type. If its type implements `[derive(Copy)]` *a copy is made and y remains usable.*

Structures

```
struct S { x:i32 }
```
Create a structure containing a field named x of type i32. Access as `S.x`.

```
struct S (i32);
```
Create a tuple-structure containing an i32. Access as `S.0`.

```
struct S;
```
Create a unit structure that will be optimized out of your code.

Enumerations

```
enum E { A, B }
```
Define an enumeration type with the options A and B.

```
enum E { A(i32), B }
```
Define an enumeration type with A and B. A contains an i32.

Control Flow

```
while x { ... }
```
Run the enclosed code while x evaluates to true.

```
loop { break; }
```
Run the enclosed code until break; *is called.*

```
for i in 0..4 {...}
```
Run the enclosed code with x equal to 0, 1, 2, 3. Ranges are "exclusive".

```
for i in 0..=4 {...}
```
Run the enclosed code with x equal to 0, 1, 2, 3, 4. "Inclusive" range.

```
for i in iter {...}
```
Run code for each member of an iterator.

```
iter.for_each(|n|...)
```
The same as for i in iter(), *runs a closure on each element.*

```
if x {...} else {...}
```
If x is true, run the first code block. Otherwise, run the second.

Functions

```
fn my_func() {...}
```
Declare my_func with no parameters or return type.

```
fn my_func(i:i32) {..}
```
Declare my_func with i, an i32 parameter.

```
fn n2(n:i32) -> i32 { n*2 }
```
*Declare n2, taking an i32 parameter and returning n*2.*

```
|| { ... }
```
Create a closure with no parameters.

```
|| 3
```
Create a closure with no parameters that returns 3.

```
|a| a*3
```
*Create a closure that accepts a parameter named a and returns a*3.*

Member/Associated Functions

```
impl MyStruct {
```
Functions in this block will be associated with MyStruct.

```
  fn assoc() {...}
```
Associated function. Call as MyStruct::assoc()

```
  fn member(&self) {...}
```
Member function. Call as my_instance.member()

```
  fn mem_mut(&mut self) {...}
```
Mutable member function. Call as my_instance.member_mut(). It can change the structure instances values.

```
}
impl Trait for MyStruct {...}
```
Define trait member functions for MyStruct.

Matching Enumerations (including Result and Option types)

```
match e {
```
Match on the value of e

```
MyEnum::A => do_it(),
```
For entry A, call do_it()

```
MyEnum::B(n) => do_it(n),
```
Extract member variable called n.

```
_ => do_something_else()
```
_ represents the default if nothing else matched.

```
}
```

Optional Variables

`option.unwrap()`	*Unwrap an optional variable. Panic/crash if the option is empty.*
`option.expect("Fail")`	*Unwrap an optional variable, crash with a message if it is empty.*
`option.unwrap_or(3)`	*Unwrap an optional variable, substitute 3 if the option is empty.*
`if let Some(option) = option { ... }`	*Use `if let` to extract an option content and make it available as `option` if the option has a value.*

Result Variables

`result.unwrap()`	*Unwrap a result variable. Panic/crash if the result is an error.*
`result.expect("Fail")`	*Unwrap a result variable, crash with a message if it is an error.*
`result.unwrap_or(3)`	*Unwrap a result or substitute 3 if an error occurred.*
`if let Ok(result) = result { ... }`	*Use if let to extract a result.*
`function_that_might_fail()?`	*Functions that return a Result can use the ? short-hand to unwrap.*

Tuples & Destructuring

`let i = (1, 2);`	*Assign 1 and 2 to members 0 and 1 of tuple i.*
`let (i, j) = (1, 2);`	*Destructure i and j from the tuple (1, 2).*
`i.0`	*Access tuple i's first member.*

Modules and Imports

`mod m;`	*Reference the module m. Looks for m.rs or m/mod.rs file.*
`mod m { ... }`	*Declare a module inline. Available as m::x in scope.*
`use m::*;`	*Import all members of module m for use in current scope.*
`use m::a;`	*Import a from module m for use in current scope.*

Iterator Chains

`iter`	*An iterator. iter() from collections, any function that returns an iterator*
`.for_each(|n| ... )`	*Run the enclosed closure on all members of the iterator.*
`.collect::<T>()`	*Collect the iterator into a new collection of type T.*
`.count()`	*Count the members of the iterator.*
`.filter(|n| ...)`	*Filter the iterator, retaining only entries for whom the closure returns true.*
`.filter_map(|n| ...)`	*Filter the iterator, returning the first entry for whom the closure returns Some(x). Return None to ignore the entry.*
`.find(|n| ...)`	*Find an entry in the iterator. Returns None if no match.*
`.fold(|acc, x| ...)`	*Accumulate into acc for all entries in an iterator.*
`.map(|n| ...)`	*Transform members of an iterator into the closure result.*
`.max()`	*Find the highest value in an iterator (numeric entries only)*
`.max_by(|n| ...)`	*Find the highest value in an iterator, determined by the closure.*
`.min()`	*Find the lowest value in an iterator (numeric entries only)*
`.min_by(|n| ...)`	*Find the lowest value in an iterator, determined by the closure.*
`.nth(n)`	*Return the iterator entry at position n.*
`.product()`	*Multiply all elements (numeric entries only) of the iterator.*
`.rev()`	*Reverse the order of the iterator.*
`.skip(n)`	*Skip the next n entries in the iterator.*
`.sum()`	*Add all of the iterator entries together (numeric entries only)*
`.zip(other_it)`	*Merge with another iterator, placing merged entries together in an A, B, A, B pattern.*

Bibliography

[HT00]   Andrew Hunt and David Thomas. *The Pragmatic Programmer: From Jour-
           neyman to Master*. Addison-Wesley, Boston, MA, 2000.

[KN19]   Steve Klabnik and Carol Nichols. *The Rust Programming Language (Covers
           Rust 2018)*. No Starch Press, San Francisco, CA, 2019.

[McC04]   Steve McConnell. *Code Complete: A Practical Handbook of Software Con-
           struction, Second Edition*. Microsoft Press, Redmond, WA, 2004.

Index

Thank you!

How did you enjoy this book? Please let us know. Take a moment and email us at support@pragprog.com with your feedback. Tell us your story and you could win free ebooks. Please use the subject line "Book Feedback."

Ready for your next great Pragmatic Bookshelf book? Come on over to https://pragprog.com and use the coupon code BUYANOTHER2020 to save 30% on your next ebook.

Void where prohibited, restricted, or otherwise unwelcome. Do not use ebooks near water. If rash persists, see a doctor. Doesn't apply to *The Pragmatic Programmer* ebook because it's older than the Pragmatic Bookshelf itself. Side effects may include increased knowledge and skill, increased marketability, and deep satisfaction. Increase dosage regularly.

And thank you for your continued support,

Andy Hunt, Publisher

 SAVE 30%!
Use coupon code
BUYANOTHER2021

Kotlin and Android Development featuring Jetpack

Start building native Android apps the modern way in Kotlin with Jetpack's expansive set of tools, libraries, and best practices. Learn how to create efficient, resilient views with Fragments and share data between the views with ViewModels. Use Room to persist valuable data quickly, and avoid NullPointerExceptions and Java's verbose expressions with Kotlin. You can even handle asynchronous web service calls elegantly with Kotlin coroutines. Achieve all of this and much more while building two full-featured apps, following detailed, step-by-step instructions.

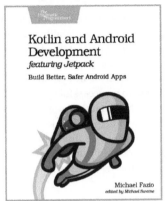

Michael Fazio
(444 pages) ISBN: 9781680508154. $49.95
https://pragprog.com/book/mfjetpack

Learn to Program, Third Edition

It's easier to learn how to program a computer than it has ever been before. Now everyone can learn to write programs for themselves—no previous experience is necessary. Chris Pine takes a thorough, but lighthearted approach that teaches you the fundamentals of computer programming, with a minimum of fuss or bother. Whether you are interested in a new hobby or a new career, this book is your doorway into the world of programming.

Chris Pine
(230 pages) ISBN: 9781680508178. $45.95
https://pragprog.com/book/ltp3

Intuitive Python

Developers power their projects with Python because it emphasizes readability, ease of use, and access to a meticulously maintained set of packages and tools. The language itself continues to improve with every release: writing in Python is full of possibility. But to maintain a successful Python project, you need to know more than just the language. You need tooling and instincts to help you make the most out of what's available to you. Use this book as your guide to help you hone your skills and sculpt a Python project that can stand the test of time.

David Muller
(140 pages) ISBN: 9781680508239. $26.95
https://pragprog.com/book/dmpython

Modern CSS with Tailwind

Tailwind CSS is an exciting new CSS framework that allows you to design your site by composing simple utility classes to create complex effects. With Tailwind, you can style your text, move your items on the page, design complex page layouts, and adapt your design for devices from a phone to a wide-screen monitor. With this book, you'll learn how to use the Tailwind for its flexibility and its consistency, from the smallest detail of your typography to the entire design of your site.

Noel Rappin
(90 pages) ISBN: 9781680508185. $26.95
https://pragprog.com/book/tailwind

Essential 555 IC

Learn how to create functional gadgets using simple but clever circuits based on the venerable "555." These projects will give you hands-on experience with useful, basic circuits that will aid you across other projects. These inspiring designs might even lead you to develop the next big thing. The 555 Timer Oscillator Integrated Circuit chip is one of the most popular chips in the world. Through clever projects, you will gain permanent knowledge of how to use the 555 timer will carry with you for life.

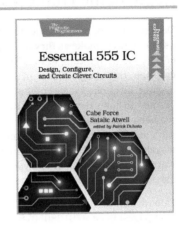

Cabe Force Satalic Atwell
(104 pages) ISBN: 9781680507836. $19.95
https://pragprog.com/book/catimers

Resourceful Code Reuse

Reusing well-written, well-debugged, and well-tested code improves productivity, code quality, and software configurability and relieves pressure on software developers. When you organize your code into self-contained modular units, you can use them as building blocks for your future projects and share them with other programmers, if needed. Understand the benefits and downsides of seven code reuse models so you can confidently reuse code at any development stage. Create static and dynamic libraries in C and Python, two of the most popular modern programming languages. Adapt your code for the real world: deploy shared functions remotely and build software that accesses them using remote procedure calls.

Dmitry Zinoviev
(64 pages) ISBN: 9781680508208. $14.99
https://pragprog.com/book/dzreuse

Apple Game Frameworks and Technologies

Design and develop sophisticated 2D games that are as much fun to make as they are to play. From particle effects and pathfinding to social integration and monetization, this complete tour of Apple's powerful suite of game technologies covers it all. Familiar with Swift but new to game development? No problem. Start with the basics and then layer in the complexity as you work your way through three exciting—and fully playable—games. In the end, you'll know everything you need to go off and create your own video game masterpiece for any Apple platform.

Tammy Coron
(504 pages) ISBN: 9781680507843. $51.95
https://pragprog.com/book/tcswift

Design and Build Great Web APIs

APIs are transforming the business world at an increasing pace. Gain the essential skills needed to quickly design, build, and deploy quality web APIs that are robust, reliable, and resilient. Go from initial design through prototyping and implementation to deployment of mission-critical APIs for your organization. Test, secure, and deploy your API with confidence and avoid the "release into production" panic. Tackle just about any API challenge with more than a dozen open-source utilities and common programming patterns you can apply right away.

Mike Amundsen
(330 pages) ISBN: 9781680506808. $45.95
https://pragprog.com/book/maapis

Distributed Services with Go

This is the book for Gophers who want to learn how to build distributed systems. You know the basics of Go and are eager to put your knowledge to work. Build distributed services that are highly available, resilient, and scalable. This book is just what you need to apply Go to real-world situations. Level up your engineering skills today.

Travis Jeffery
(258 pages) ISBN: 9781680507607. $45.95
https://pragprog.com/book/tjgo

Genetic Algorithms in Elixir

From finance to artificial intelligence, genetic algorithms are a powerful tool with a wide array of applications. But you don't need an exotic new language or framework to get started; you can learn about genetic algorithms in a language you're already familiar with. Join us for an in-depth look at the algorithms, techniques, and methods that go into writing a genetic algorithm. From introductory problems to real-world applications, you'll learn the underlying principles of problem solving using genetic algorithms.

Sean Moriarity
(242 pages) ISBN: 9781680507942. $39.95
https://pragprog.com/book/smgaelixir

Agile Web Development with Rails 6

Learn Rails the way the Rails core team recommends it, along with the tens of thousands of developers who have used this broad, far-reaching tutorial and reference. If you're new to Rails, you'll get step-by-step guidance. If you're an experienced developer, get the comprehensive, insider information you need for the latest version of Ruby on Rails. The new edition of this award-winning classic is completely updated for Rails 6 and Ruby 2.6, with information on processing email with Action Mailbox and managing rich text with Action Text.

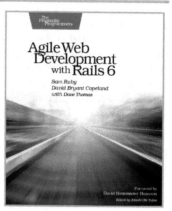

Sam Ruby and David Bryant Copeland
(494 pages) ISBN: 9781680506709. $57.95
https://pragprog.com/book/rails6

Modern Systems Programming with Scala Native

Access the power of bare-metal systems programming with Scala Native, an ahead-of-time Scala compiler. Without the baggage of legacy frameworks and virtual machines, Scala Native lets you re-imagine how your programs interact with your operating system. Compile Scala code down to native machine instructions; seamlessly invoke operating system APIs for low-level networking and IO; control pointers, arrays, and other memory management techniques for extreme performance; and enjoy instant start-up times. Skip the JVM and improve your code performance by getting close to the metal.

Richard Whaling
(260 pages) ISBN: 9781680506228. $45.95
https://pragprog.com/book/rwscala

Fixing Your Scrum

Broken Scrum practices limit your organization's ability to take full advantage of the agility Scrum should bring: The development team isn't cross-functional or self-organizing, the product owner doesn't get value for their investment, and stakeholders and customers are left wondering when something—anything—will get delivered. Learn how experienced Scrum masters balance the demands of these three levels of servant leadership, while removing organizational impediments and helping Scrum teams deliver real-world value. Discover how to visualize your work, resolve impediments, and empower your teams to self-organize and deliver using advanced coaching and facilitation techniques that honor and support the Scrum values and agile principles.

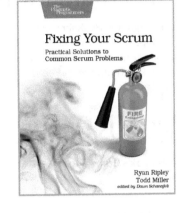

Ryan Ripley and Todd Miller
(240 pages) ISBN: 9781680506976. $45.95
https://pragprog.com/book/rrscrum

Software Estimation Without Guessing

Developers hate estimation, and most managers fear disappointment with the results, but there is hope for both. You'll have to give up some widely held misconceptions: let go of the notion that "an estimate is an estimate," and estimate for your particular need. Realize that estimates have a limited shelf-life, and re-estimate frequently as needed. When reality differs from your estimate, don't lament; mine that disappointment for the gold that can be the longer-term jackpot. We'll show you how.

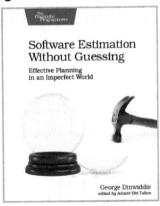

George Dinwiddie
(246 pages) ISBN: 9781680506983. $29.95
https://pragprog.com/book/gdestimate

The Pragmatic Bookshelf

The Pragmatic Bookshelf features books written by professional developers for professional developers. The titles continue the well-known Pragmatic Programmer style and continue to garner awards and rave reviews. As development gets more and more difficult, the Pragmatic Programmers will be there with more titles and products to help you stay on top of your game.

Visit Us Online

This Book's Home Page
https://pragprog.com/book/hwrust
Source code from this book, errata, and other resources. Come give us feedback, too!

Keep Up to Date
https://pragprog.com
Join our announcement mailing list (low volume) or follow us on twitter @pragprog for new titles, sales, coupons, hot tips, and more.

New and Noteworthy
https://pragprog.com/news
Check out the latest pragmatic developments, new titles and other offerings.

Save on the ebook

Save on the ebook versions of this title. Owning the paper version of this book entitles you to purchase the electronic versions at a terrific discount.

PDFs are great for carrying around on your laptop—they are hyperlinked, have color, and are fully searchable. Most titles are also available for the iPhone and iPod touch, Amazon Kindle, and other popular e-book readers.

Send a copy of your receipt to support@pragprog.com and we'll provide you with a discount coupon.

Contact Us

Online Orders:	*https://pragprog.com/catalog*
Customer Service:	*support@pragprog.com*
International Rights:	*translations@pragprog.com*
Academic Use:	*academic@pragprog.com*
Write for Us:	*http://write-for-us.pragprog.com*
Or Call:	+1 800-699-7764

Milton Keynes UK
Ingram Content Group UK Ltd.
UKHW051719010924
447702UK00004B/7